Autodesk Inve...
Intermediate Level:
Mastering the Rubicon

Elise Moss

autodesk
authorized author

SDC
PUBLICATIONS

Schroff Development Corporation
www.schroff.com

Schroff Development Corporation

P.O. Box 1334
Mission, KS 66222
(913) 262-2664
www.schroff.com

Trademarks

The following are registered trademarks of Autodesk, Inc.: AutoCAD, AutoCAD Mechanical Desktop, Inventor, RedSpark, pointA, Autodesk, AutoLISP, AutoCAD Design Center, Autodesk Device Interface, and HEIDI. Microsoft, Windows, Word, Visual Basic and Excel are either registered trademarks or trademarks of Microsoft Corporation.
All other trademarks are trademarks of their respective holders.

Moss, Elise
      Autodesk Inventor R5 Intermediate: Mastering the Rubicon/
Elise Moss

     ISBN 1-58503-043-0

The author and publisher of this book have used their best efforts in preparing this book. These efforts include the development, research, and testing of material presented. The author and publisher shall not be held liable in any event for incidental or consequential damages with, or arising out of, the furnishing, performance, or use of the material herein.

Printed and bound in the United States of America.

Preface

Even though Inventor is relatively new software, it has a treasure trove of features that many users are eager to try. This text takes the user up to the next level, exploring parameters, iParts, Engineer's Notebook, collaboration, and more advanced modeling.

I do listen to reader feedback. So, based on reader questions and comments, I have added additional exercises and corrected mistakes. The bicycle model has been replaced with a scooter model.

The files used in this text are available to download for free from www.schroff1.com/inventor.

We value your input. Please contact me with any comments, questions, or concerns about this text. I am keeping a list of readers who are interested in any updates; so if you wish to be notified by email when the next Inventor text is available, please let me know.

Elise Moss
Moss Designs
21951 Bear Creek Way
Los Gatos, CA 95033
www.mossdesigns.com
elise_moss@mossdesigns.com

Acknowledgements

This book would not have been possible without the support of some key Autodesk employees. A special thanks to Derrick Smith, Rebecca Bell, Lynn Allen, Melrose Ross, Denis Cadu, Bob Henry, Gary Smith, Ishwar Nagwani, Carolyn Gavriloff, and David Koel.

Additional thanks to the board and members of the Silicon Valley AutoCAD Power Users, a dedicated group of Autodesk users, for educating me about the needs and wants of CAD users.

A grateful nod to Brad Adams, Ole Germer, Drew Fulford, Charles Bliss, Kerwin Kassulker and Lay Fox, who provided input on this text.

My appreciation to Gabrielle Conway and Matt Brown, who spent an afternoon with me, brainstorming ideas on models I could use for this book until Gabrielle suggested I use a scooter instead of a bicycle. The scooter model used in this book was purchased at my local Target department store on sale for thirty-five dollars. Both Gabrielle and Matt are fellow engineers who work in Silicon Valley.

The effort and support of the editorial and production staff of Schroff Development Corporation is gratefully acknowledged. I especially thank Stephen Schroff for his helpful suggestions regarding the format of this text.

Finally, truly infinite thanks to Ari for his encouragement and his faith.

Elise Moss
Los Gatos, CA

Table of Contents

Notes:

Lesson 1
Lofting

Loft features are created by blending the shapes of two or more profiles on work planes or planar faces.

You can include the following in a loft feature:
- Sketches created on work planes offset from one another by a distance. The planes are usually parallel to one another, but any planes that are not perpendicular can be used.
- An existing planar face, as the beginning or end of a loft.
  To use an existing face as the beginning or end of a loft, create a sketch on that face (inserts a sketch icon in the browser). You do not need to draw anything in the sketch, but creating the sketch makes the edges of the face selectable for the loft.

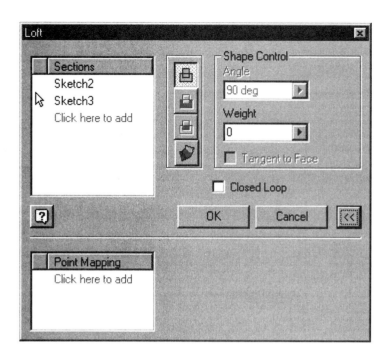

Sections	Specifies the profiles to include in the loft. Click in the row then click two or more profiles. Your selection is identified in the dialog box by sketch number, and a new row is added. To remove a section, highlight and press the 'Delete' key on the keyboard.
Shape Control	Specifies the profiles to include in the loft. Click in the row then click two or more profiles. Your selection is identified in the dialog box by sketch number, and a new row is added. To remove a section, highlight and press the 'Delete' key on the keyboard.
	Angle Represents the angle between the sketch plane and the faces created by the loft at the sketch plane. The default value is 90 degrees. Weight A unitless value that controls how the angle affects appearance of the loft. A large number creates a gradual transition, while a small number creates an abrupt transition. Large and small values are relative to the size of your model Tangent to Face Constrains profiles created on a planar face to be tangent to the face. (Angle is not selectable if Tangent to Face is selected.)
Point Mapping	Selects a point on a sketch to use as the starting point for the loft surface. Selecting mapping points aligns profiles linearly along the points to minimize twisting of the loft feature
Closed Loop	Joins the first and last sections of the loft to form a closed loop

Exercise 1-1
Bicycle Seat

Drawing Name: Open a new part using Metric template (MM)
Estimated time: 30 minutes

This exercise reinforces the following skills:

- Project Geometry
- Offset Work Planes
- Loft
- Sweep
- Spline

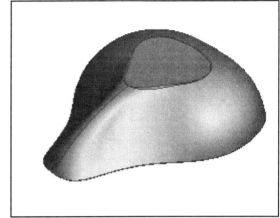

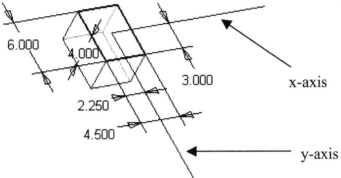

6.000   4.000   3.000   x-axis

2.250   4.500   y-axis

Create the following sketch on the XY plane.
Draw a rectangle 6 x 4.5 and center it on the origin.
Extrude it 4 mm. X & Y   endpoint

Select the YZ work plane for a new sketch.

XY

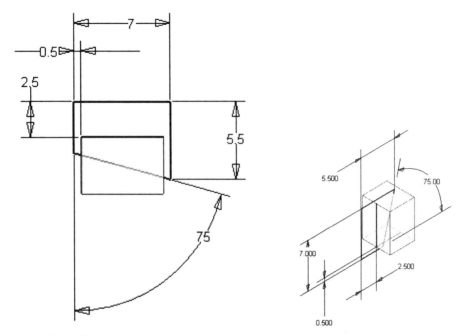

Create the following sketch.

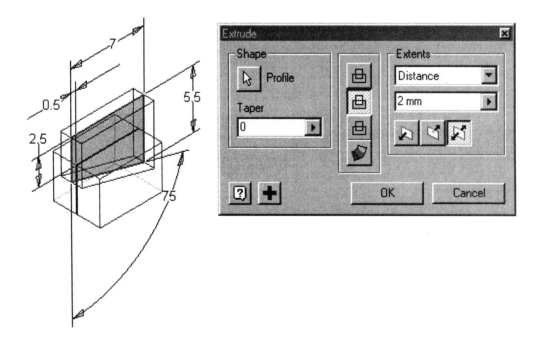

Extrude the sketch as a Cut mid-plane 2 mm.

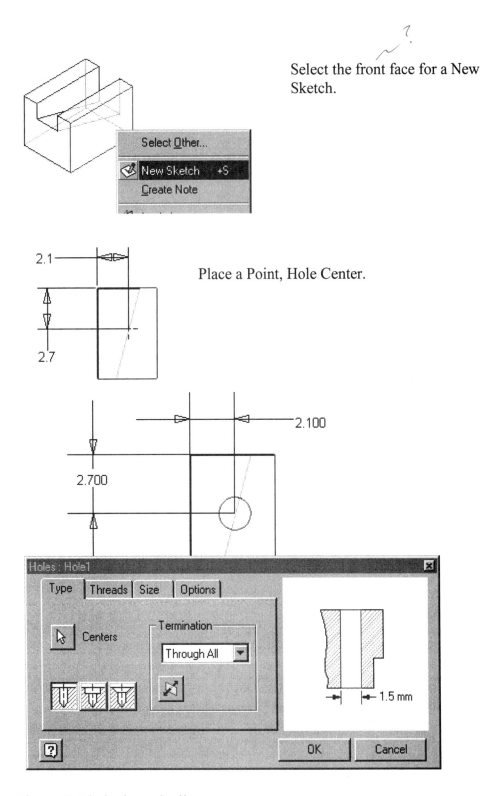

Select the front face for a New Sketch.

Place a Point, Hole Center.

Place a 1.5 hole through all.

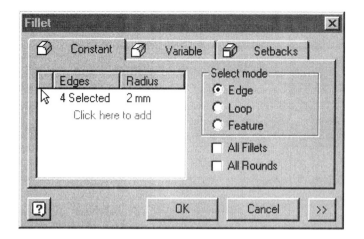
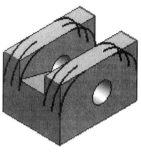

Add a 2 mm fillet to the edges as shown.

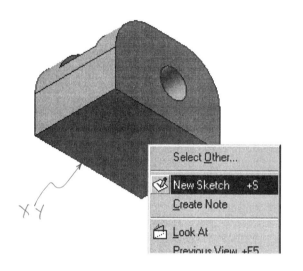

Select the XY planar face for a new sketch.

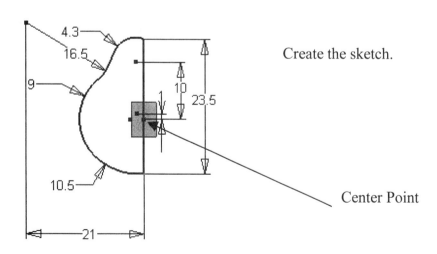

Create the sketch.

Center Point

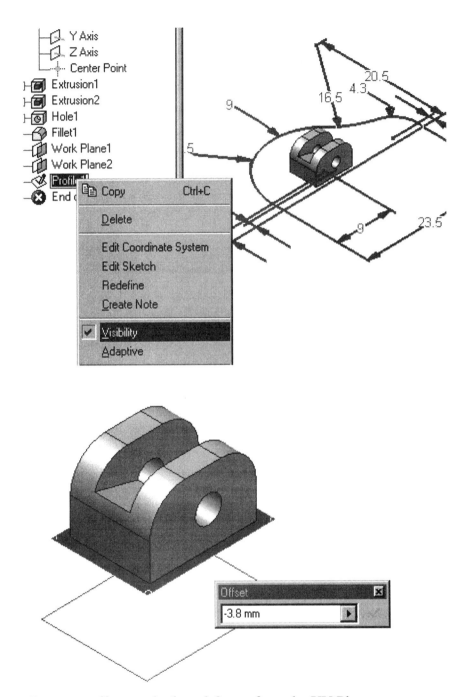

Rename the sketch
'Profile1'.
Turn off the
Visibility for now.

Create an offset work plane 3.8 mm from the XY Plane.

Select the Offset Work Plane for our second profile sketch.

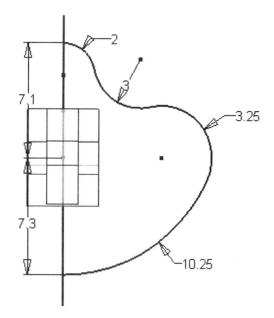

Create the sketch. Project the Y axis. Align the center points of the 10.25 radius and the 2.0 radius arc with the Y axis.

Rename the sketch Profile2 and turn it's visibility OFF.

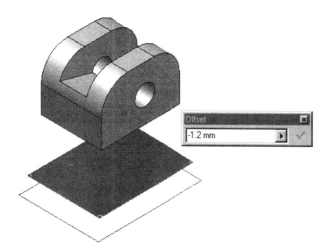

Create a second offset work plane 1.2 mm from the offset work plane you just made.

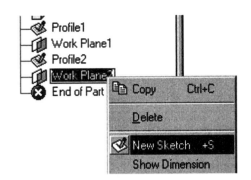

Select the second work plane for a New Sketch.

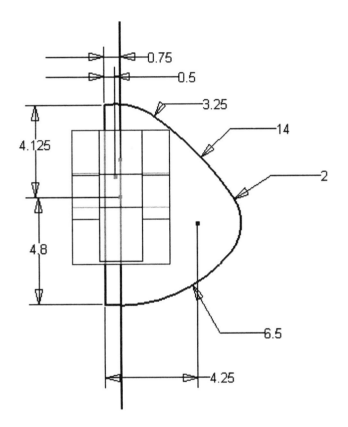

Create this third sketch. Rename it Profile3.

Turn the visibility ON for all the sketches.

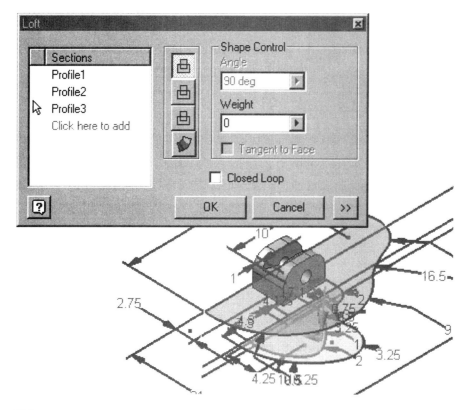

Select the LOFT tool from the Features toolbar.
Select the Profiles from the browser or the graphics window in order.

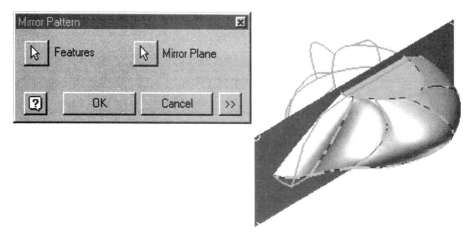

Select the Mirror Feature tool.
Press the Features button, then select the Loft in the browser.
Press the Mirror Plane button, then select the YZ plane in the browser.
Press 'OK'.

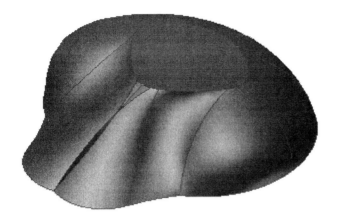

Our bicycle seat so far.

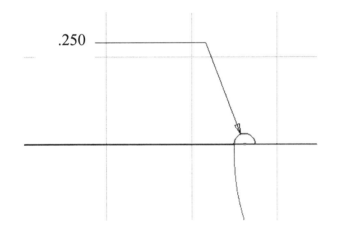

.250

Select the YZ plane and create the sketch shown.
This will be used as the sweep profile. Set the arc's center point coincident to the edge of the bicycle seat.
Rename the sketch 'Profile'.

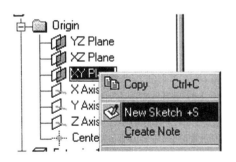

Select the XY Plane for a New Sketch.

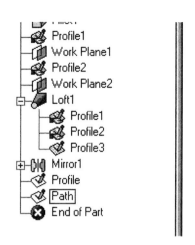

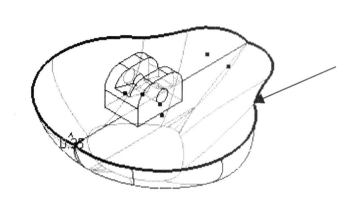

Project the edge. This will be used as the sweep path. You will need to select each section to create a closed path.

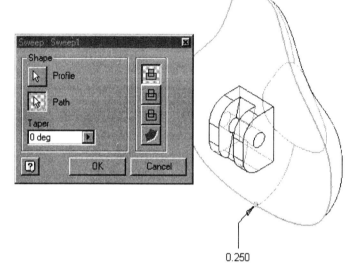

0.250

Select the Sweep tool from the Features toolbar.
Press the Profile button and select the Profile from the Browser.
Press the Path button and select the Path from the Browser.
Enable the Join button.
Press 'OK'.

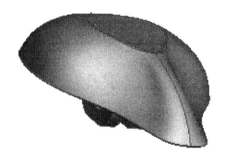

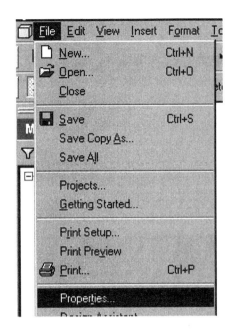

Go to File->Properties.

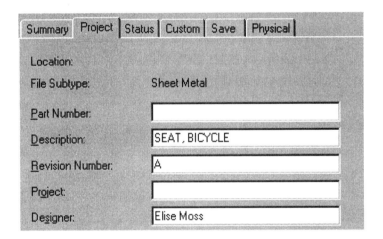

Select the Project tab.
Fill in a Description and
Revision Number.

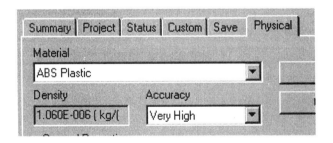

Select the Physical tab.
Select ABS Plastic for the Material.

Save the file as EX1-1.ipt.

Additional Tips:

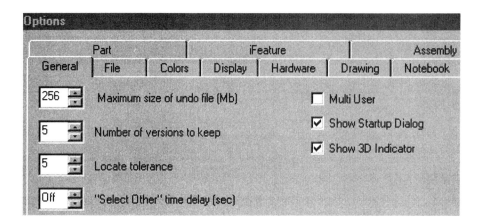

If you don't want the 'Select Other' option to appear, go to Tools->Application Options. Select the General Tab.
Under "Select Other" time delay, hit the down button until you see the OFF value.

By default, the Undo stream is limited to 10 Undo operations.

To change the number of Undo operations:

1. Open the Registry Editor and locate the following key:

   HKEY_CURRENT_USER\Software\Autodesk\Inventor\RegistryVersionX.X\System\Preferences\Transactions
2. Modify the value data for the UndoLevels from Hexadecimal to Decimal and then change the value from 10 to the desired value.

   Note: You may need to increase the dedicated size of the Undo File (default 64MB) listed in the Application Options.
3. Exit the Registry Editor.

Lesson 2
3D Sketches

Learning Objectives:

- Use of 3D Sketch
- Creating an Angled Work Plane
- Creating an Offset Work Plane
- Creating a Sweep
- Creating a Shell

The 3D Sketch environment can be accessed from the command toolbar or by right clicking in the graphics window and selecting 'New 3D Sketch' from the context menu.

This is only available when no sketch is currently active.

TIP: 3D sketches are useful for creating paths for wiring or piping.

TIP: Another use for 3D Sketch can be to create a sweep through a data set of free points.

You can see the difference between the two sketch environments can be studied in the table below.

	2D sketch environment	3D sketch environment
Sketching	• Sketch geometry on a planar face or work plane • Click anywhere on sketch plane to place sketch points	• Sketch geometry in 3D space (no sketch plane) • Click to connect point-to-point in space
Constraints	Sketch geometry can be manually constrained.	Geometry is automatically constrained to adaptive work features.
Geometry from other features	Project tool.	Include Geometry tool.
Edit sketch	Create new geometry, add dimensions, constraints, or delete.	Create new geometry or delete. Redefine point location.
Work features	Not available.	Used to locate points relative to geometry on other features.

3D Sketches cannot be extruded or revolved. They are primarily used for sweeps.
To define 3D Sketches, we create construction geometry and then define work points to snap to when creating the sketch.

Exercise 2-1:
Bent Tube

Drawing Name: Start a new part file using Standard (inches)
Estimated Time: 30 minutes

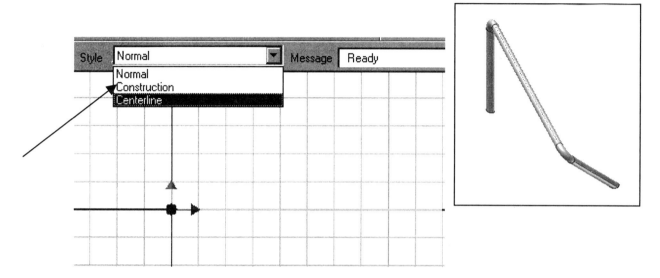

Create a 2D sketch on the Top Plane and draw a horizontal construction line from the origin point. This will be used to create an angled plane.

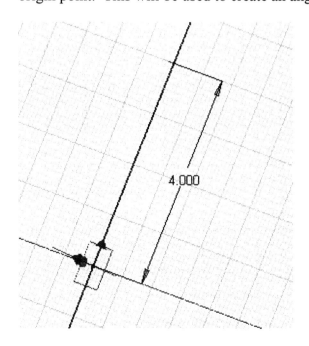

Add a 4.0 dimension to the construction line.

Add a point to the end of the line.

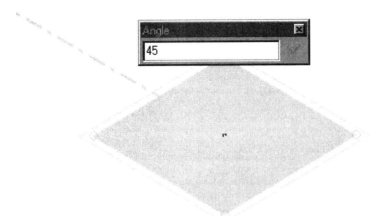

To create the angled plane, select the top plane and then the construction line we just drew.
Enter in an angle value of 45.
Press the green check mark.

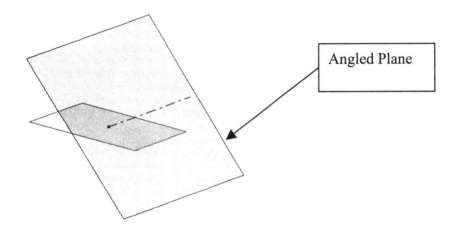

Angled Plane

Select the angled plane and start a New Sketch.

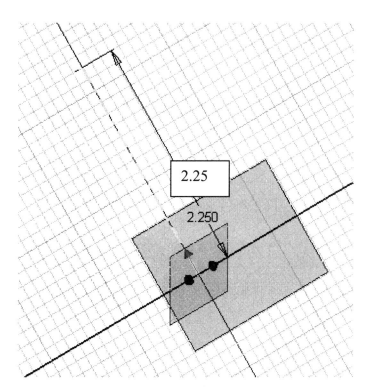

Create another construction line.
Project the center point.
Draw a vertical line with one end coincident to the center point.
Dimension with a length of 2.25.
Select the line and set the style to construction.
Add a point to the end of the line.

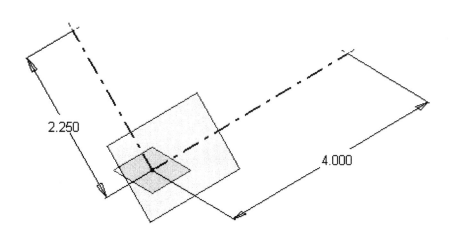

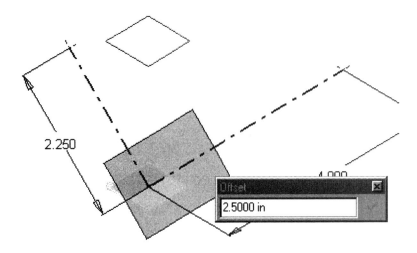

Create an Offset Work Plane 2.5 from the top plane.

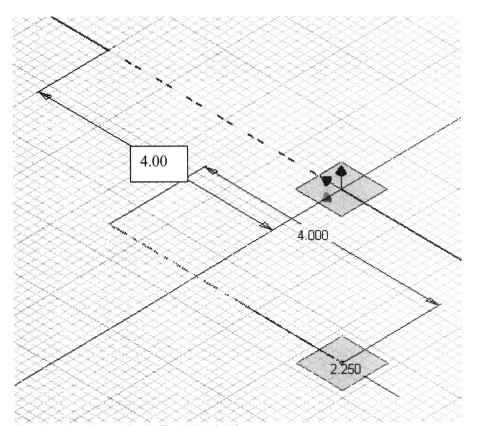

Start a sketch on the Offset Work Plane.
Create another line.
Project the center point.
Draw a vertical line with one end coincident to the center point.
Dimension with a length of 4.00.
Select the line and set the style to construction.
Add a point to the end of the line.

Select 3D Sketch mode

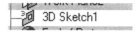

A 3D Sketch will appear in the browser as active.

Add Work Points at the end of all the centerlines coincident to the sketch points .
Add a Work Point at the Center Point.

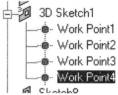

If you expand on the 3D Sketch in the browser, you should see the Work Points we
created.

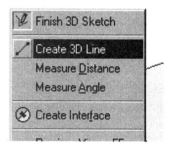

Right click and select Create 3D Line.

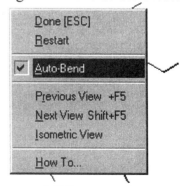

If you right click, you will see that Auto-Bend is enabled.
This will automatically add a fillet to the corners of the sketch.

Draw a line connecting the work points.

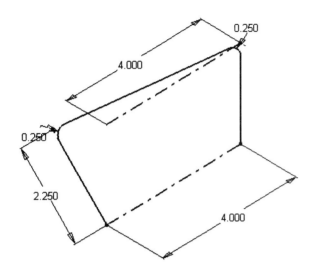

To change the value of the Auto-Bend, just double click on it and edit like any dimension.

We will keep the dimension as the default value of .250.

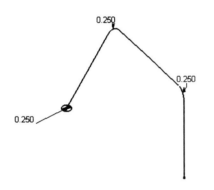

Create a circle on the top plane at the origin with a diameter of .25.

Exit the sketch.

Sweep the circle profile along the 3D Sketch.

Add a .01 shell to the tube.
Save as Ex2-1.ipt.

Exercise 2-2:
Handle Bar

Drawing Name: Start a new part
file using
Standard
(Inches)

Estimated Time: 30 minutes

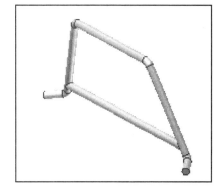

Learning Objectives:

Review the following tools:

- Mirror Feature
- 3D Sketch
- Sweep

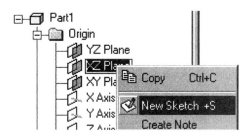

Select the XZ Plane in the browser for a New Sketch.

Project the Center Point.
Place a Point, Hole Center so that it is a distance of 2.75 units from the Point.

Call this Sketch Point A.

Create an offset work plane 10
inches above the XZ Plane.

Select the Offset Work Plane for a New Sketch.

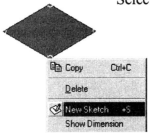

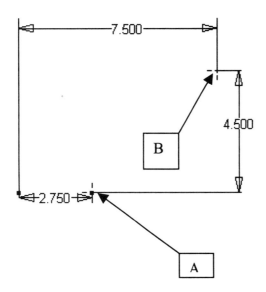

Project the Center Point and Point
A onto the New Sketch.

Place Point B.

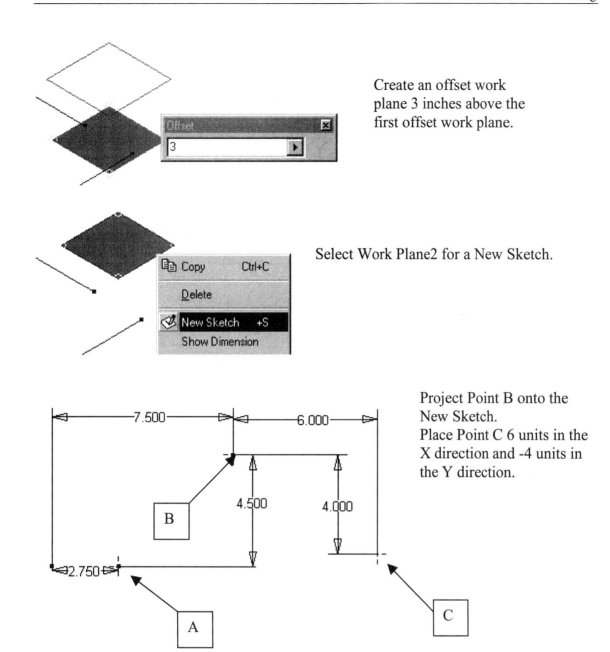

Create an offset work
plane 3 inches above the
first offset work plane.

Select Work Plane2 for a New Sketch.

Project Point B onto the
New Sketch.
Place Point C 6 units in the
X direction and -4 units in
the Y direction.

Place a Work Point at Points A, B, and C. Rename the Points to make it easier to keep track of them.

Place a fourth work point at the Center Point.

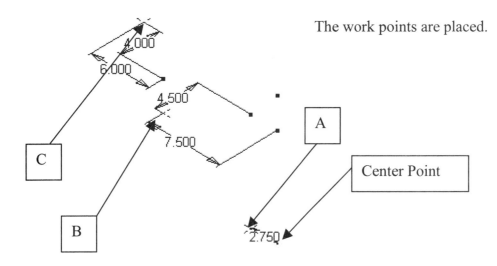

The work points are placed.

Select 3D Sketch from the Command Bar.

Right click in the graphics window.
Select 'Create 3D Line'.

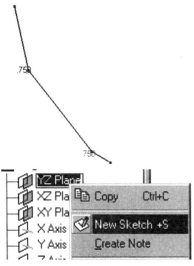

Draw a 3D Line from the Center
Point to A to B to C.

Set the Auto Bend Radius to 0.750.
Change the value of the bend radius
by double clicking on the radius
dimension.

Select the YZ Plane for a New Sketch.

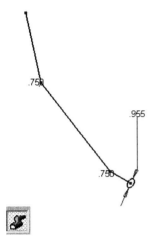

Project the Center Point.
Draw a 0.955 diameter
circle at the center point.

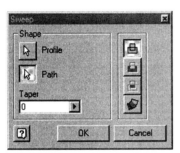

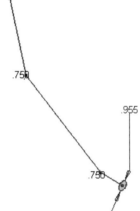

Create a Sweep using the circle as
the Profile and the 3D Sketch as the
Path.

The Handle Bars so far.

Create a work plane on the end of the
sweep.
To do this, make the 3D Sketch Visible;
select the end face and then the end point
of the 3D Sketch.

Mirror the sweep about Work Plane3.

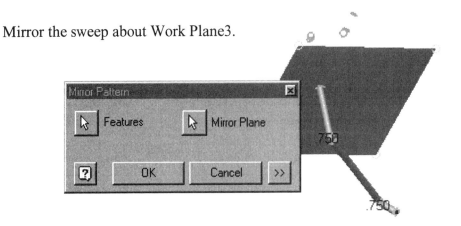

Our handle bar so far.

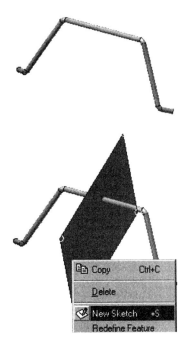

Select Work Plane3 for a New Sketch.

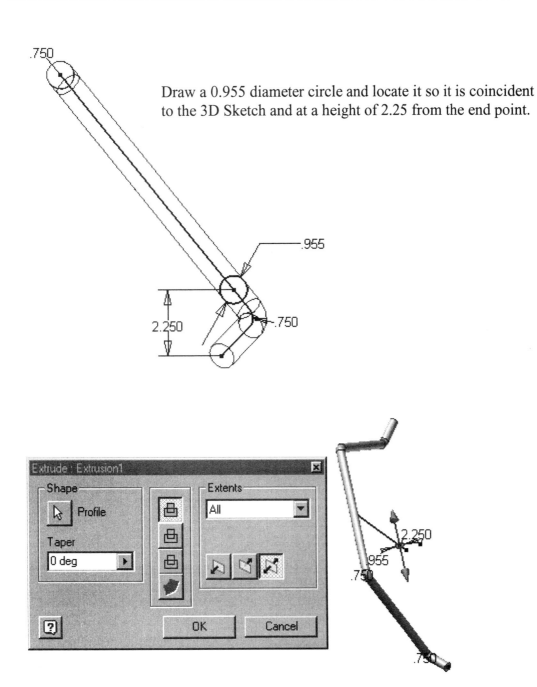

Draw a 0.955 diameter circle and locate it so it is coincident to the 3D Sketch and at a height of 2.25 from the end point.

Extrude the circle as mid-plane.
Set the Extents to All.

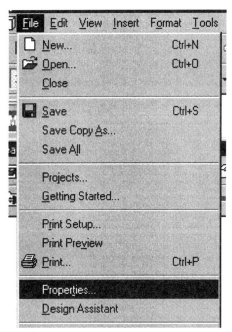

Our part is complete.
Go to File->Properties.

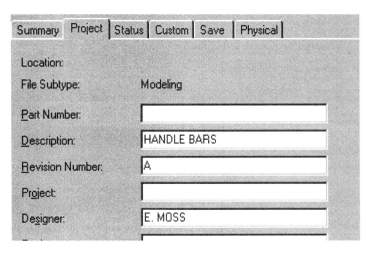

Fill in a Description and
Revision Number.
Save the part as Ex2-2.ipt.

Lesson 3
Adaptivity

One of the more intriguing features in Inventor is adaptivity. The idea that parts will automatically change so that they continue to fit and work together is very powerful.

There are a few key ideas you need to understand before we can proceed.

Adaptivity only works if:

1) The sketch and the part must be UNDER constrained. If you place dimensions, then the part will not change those dimensions.

2) You have to place constraints between the adaptive part and the non-adaptive part.

3) Do not make too many parts adaptive in any assembly. Inventor will get confused if the constraints begin conflicting and your system could crash.

Learning Objectives:

- Use of Adaptivity

Exercise 3-1
Adaptive Box

Drawing Name: Start a New Assembly file using Standard (Inches)
Estimated Time: 60 minutes

Use Create Component to create the bottom part of the box.

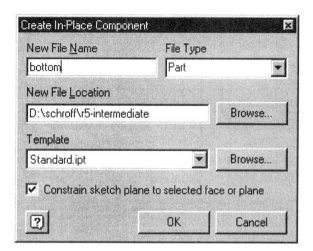

Name the new part bottom and locate it in your project director. Set the template to Standard.ipt. Press 'OK'

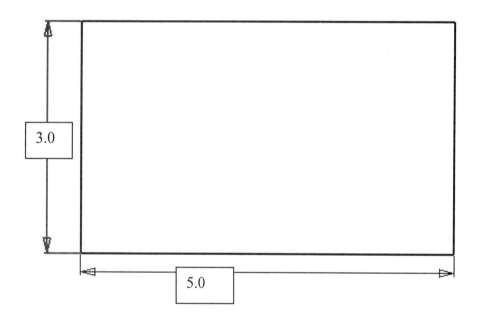

Create a sketch on the top (XZ) plane.
Draw a 5 x 3 rectangle.

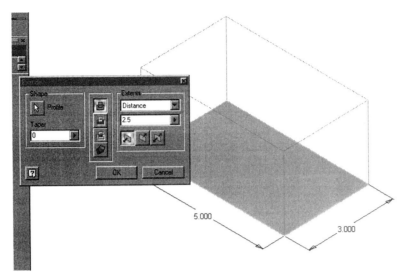

Extrude it 2.5".

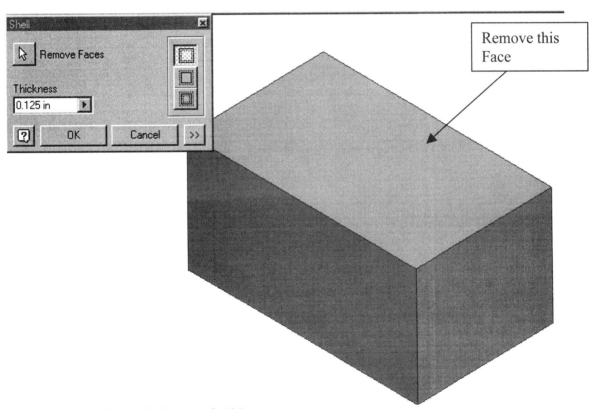

Remove this Face

Shell the box with a thickness of .125.

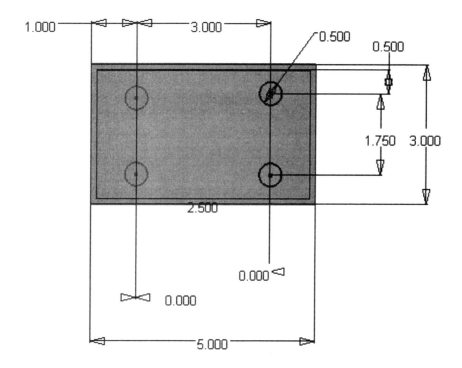

We create four bosses. Select the bottom of the box.
Draw four circles. Use equations to locate the circles or they will not shift when we modify the bottom.

Dimension the circles as shown.

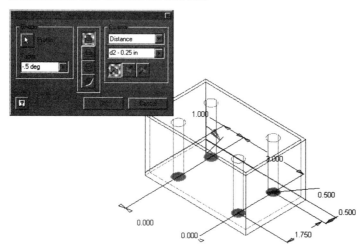

Extrude as a Join.
Select the four circles.
Set the Taper to –.5.
Set the Distance by selecting the 2.5 height dimension and subtracting .25.

TIP: Use 'Show Dimensions' in the Edit box to reveal the dimensions so they can be used.

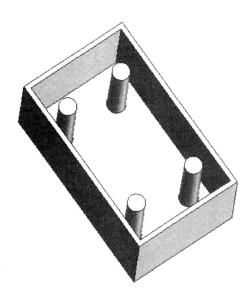

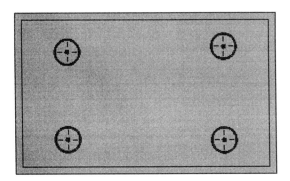

Place hole center points in the center of each boss.

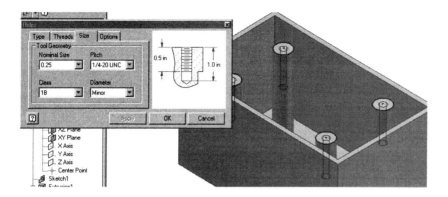

Place four holes ¼-20 x 1 inch in depth.

We are now finished with the bottom of the box and are ready to create the top.
Exit the Edit Part mode.
Select the Create Part tool.

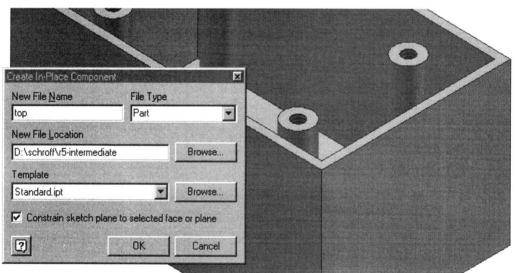

Name our new part 'top'.

Select the top of the box for the sketch plane.

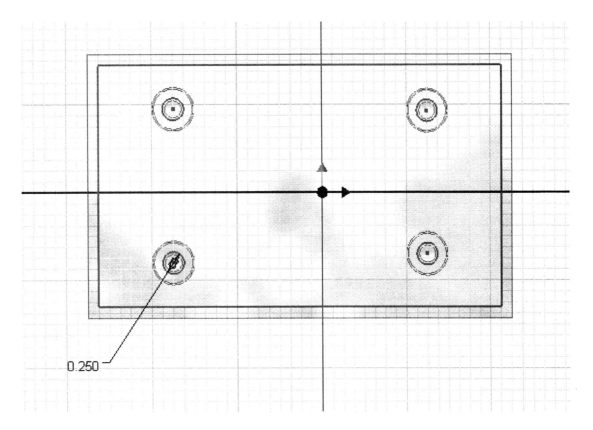

Draw a rectangle with four circles as shown.

The only dimension needed is the diameter of the holes. Set the holes equal.
Do not add any location dimensions for the holes or overall dimensions for the lid.

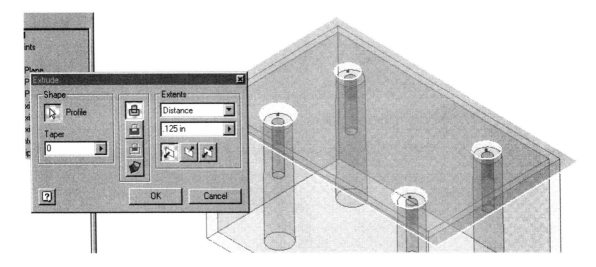

Extrude the profile a distance of .125.

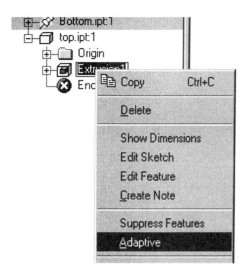

Locate the Extrusion for the top in the browser and set it to be adaptive.

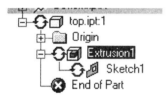

You will see the adaptive indicator next to the part, the extrusion and the sketch.

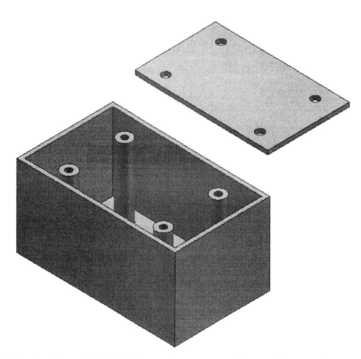

Exit the Part Edit Mode and return to Assembly mode.

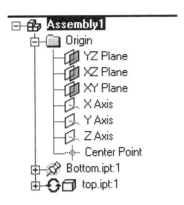

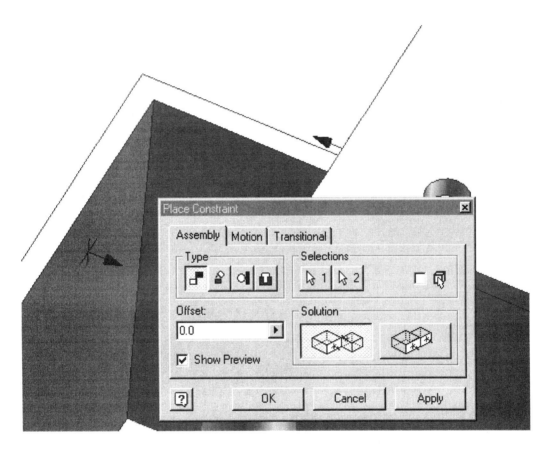

Add mate constraints to the inside wall of the box and the outside of the lid.
Watch as the top adjusts with each constraint.

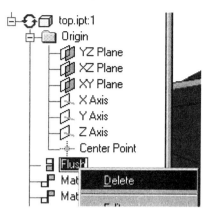

Delete the Flush constraint added when you created the part.

Rotate the lid to make it easier to select the holes and then add an insert constraint between each hole and each boss in the bottom.

Observe as the holes shift location to adapt to the box bottom.

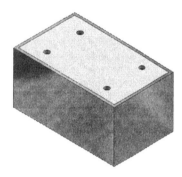

Our parts fit together.

But the real test is if the lid will adapt if the bottom changes.

Edit the bottom.
Select the part in the browser, right click and select 'Edit'.
You can also enter Edit Part Mode by double left clicking on the part name in the browser or the part in the graphics window.

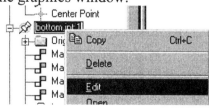

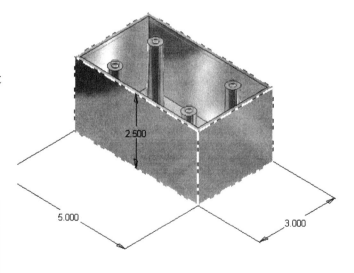

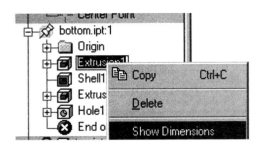

Right click on the first Extrusion
and select 'Show Dimensions'.
Change the 5.0 dimension to 6.
Change the 3.0 dimension to 4.

Press the Return button to exit Edit Part mode and return to Assembly
mode.

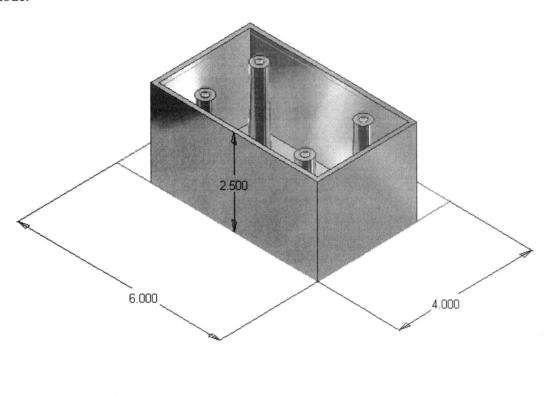

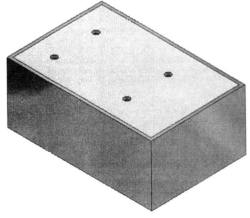

Observe how the lid updates with the bottom of the box.

Exercise 3-2:
Card Cage

Drawing Name: Start a new assembly using Standard (inches)
Estimated time: 60 minutes

Reviews the following commands and concepts:

- Adaptivity
- Pattern Components
- Extrude
- Create In-Place Component
- Show Dimensions

In this exercise, we create a rack system with a series of cards. We will make the cards adaptive and note how we can control their height if the height of the box changes.

First we create the rack.

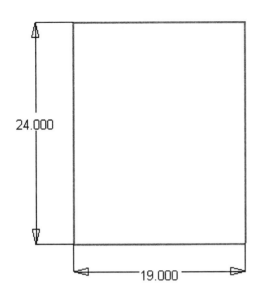

Create a 24 x 19 inch rectangle on the top (XZ) plane.

Rack systems come in 1.75" height increments. We'll start with a 2U box, which is 2*1.75. Extrude the rectangle a Distance of 2*1.75.

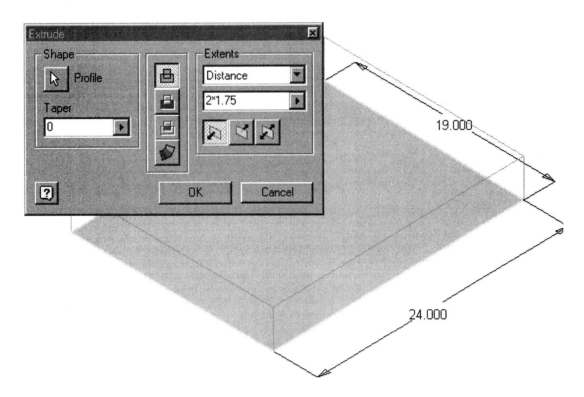

Shell out the rack with a .063 thickness.

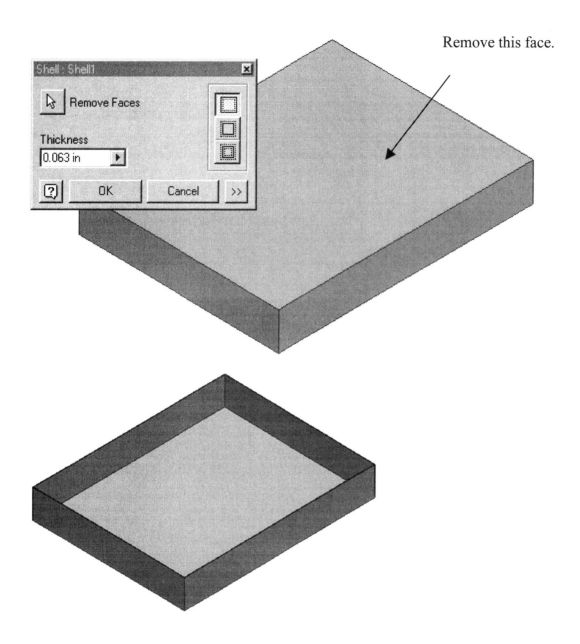

Remove this face.

Exit Part Edit Mode.

Start a New Part that will be a computer card.

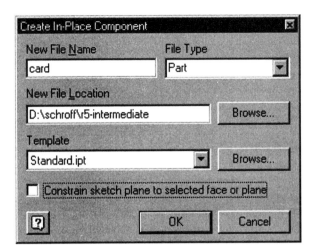

Call the new part 'card'.
Disable the constrain sketch plane option.
Select the bottom of the box to start your first sketch.

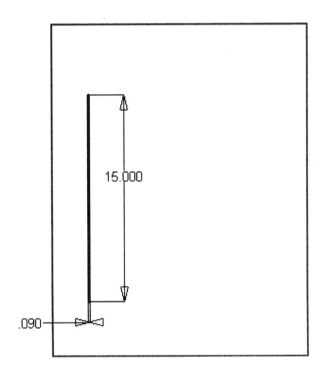

Draw a 15 x 0.09 rectangle.

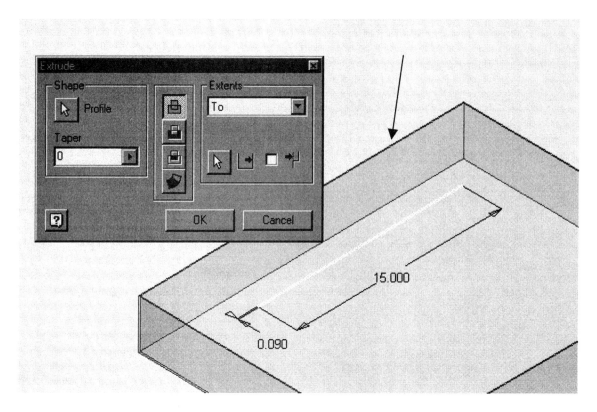

When you extrude, set the Distance to 'To' and select the top edge of the rack.
Return to Assembly mode.

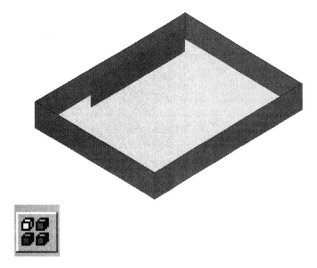

Create a rectangular array of the card.

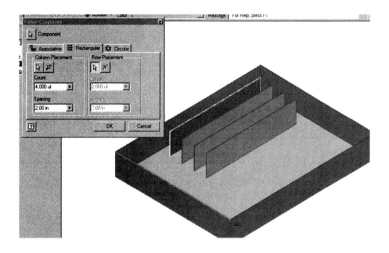

Select the card as the component to be patterned.
Set the Count to 4.
Set the Spacing to 2.
Press 'OK'.

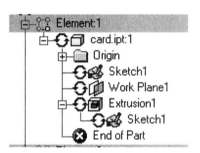

Set the extrusion of the card as Adaptive.

TIP: If you set the first element as adaptive, then all the parts in the pattern will be adaptive.

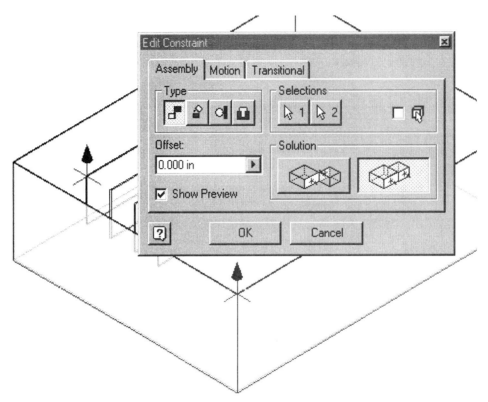

Add a Flush constraint between the top edge of the card and the top edge of the rack.

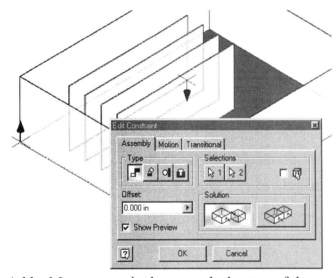

Add a Mate constraint between the bottom of the card and the bottom of the rack.

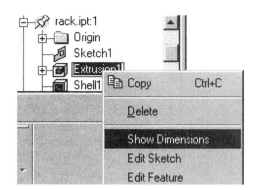

Select the rack in the browser.
Right click and select 'Edit'.

Select the first Extrusion. Right click and
select 'Show Dimensions'.

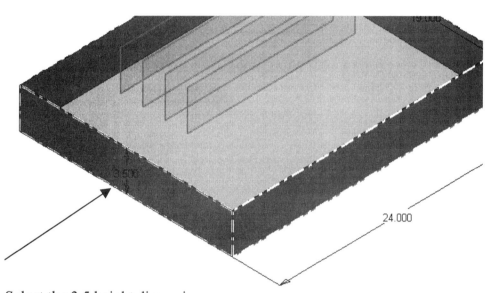

Select the 3.5 height dimension.

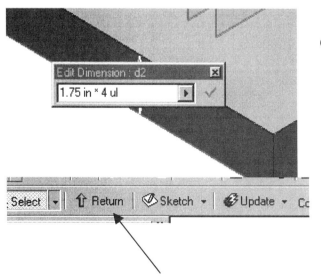

Change the height dimension to 1.75 * 4.

Press Return to exit Edit Part
mode.

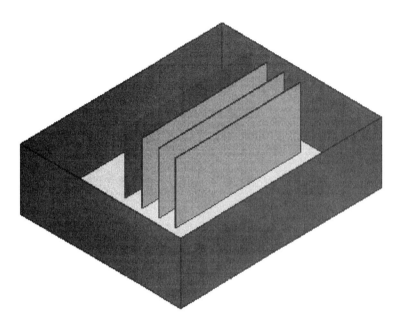

The cards automatically update to the same height as the box.

Save as Ex3-2.iam.

QUIZ 1

T F 1. When you are in 3D Sketch mode, you can access all the tools on the Sketch toolbar.

card.ipt:
2. The icon that appears in front of the card in the figure shown indicates the part is:
A. adaptive
B. grounded
C. invisible
D. recyclable

3. A type of part that may require a 3D Sketch is:
A. pipes
B. wires
C. cables
D. all of the above

4. In order for you to place a 3D Sketch, you need to:

A. Place work points, the sketch can snap to
B. Select a set of work planes
C. Place a set of center points
D. Draw a sketch in free space

T F 5. Once a loft is created, the user cannot reuse any of the consumed sketches.

6. 3D Sketch mode allows the user to draw a sketch using a:

A. circle
B. arc
C. line
D. all of the above

T F 7. It is a good idea to have as many parts in an assembly adaptive in order to keep your design fluid.

T F 8. 3D Sketches must be placed on a selected work plane.

9.   In order for parts to be adapted, they must be:

    A.   OVERCONSTRAINED
    B.   UNDERCONSTRAINED
    C.   FULLY CONSTRAINED
    D.   ANY OF THE ABOVE

10.   When creating a loft, the user needs to create:

    A.   more than one work plane
    B.   more than one sketch
    C.   more than one axis
    D.   A & B but not C

11.   To access 3D Sketch mode:

    A.   Select 3D Sketch under the Sketch dropdown in the Command toolbar
    B.   Select the 3D Sketch tool on the Sketch toolbar
    C.   Select Insert-> 3D Sketch in the menu
    D.   none of the above

T F 12.   When creating a loft, you can use an existing face as a profile for a loft.

13.   3D Sketches are used for:

    A.   Sweeps
    B.   Revolves
    C.   Extrusions
    D.   Lofts

14.   Adaptivity of parts is controlled by:

    A.   Dimensions
    B.   Tolerances
    C.   Assembly Constraints
    D.   magic threads

T F 15.   Parts are only adaptive in the Assembly environment.

ANSWERS:
1) F; 2) A; 3) D; 4) A; 5) F; 6) C; 7) F; 8) F; 9) B; 10) D; 11) A; 12) F; 13) A; 14) C; 15) T

Lesson 4
Surface Modeling

Construction surfaces provide ways to describe shapes when creating extruded, revolved, swept, and lofted parts. For each of these features, you can choose to create a surface instead of a cut, join, or intersection.

You can use an open or closed profile to create a surface. The surface can then be used as a termination face for other features or used as a split tool to create a split part.

Unlike work features, surfaces are not consumed by features.

⊕◀⬚ ExtrusionSrf1

A surface is represented in the browser as a suffix to the feature tool used to create it (for example, ExtrusionSrf1, SweepSrf1, and so on).

In the graphics window, a surface is translucent, similar to a work plane. You can right-click a surface in the browser or graphics window and turn its visibility off.

If desired, you can use Fillet and Chamfer tools to modify sharp edges of surfaces.

You can also edit the profile shape. Expand the surface in the browser, then right-click the sketch icon and select Edit Sketch.

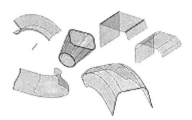

Examples of surfaces are shown clockwise from the top left corner:

- A revolved surface created from a sketched line rotated around an axis.
- A lofted surface created from two closed profiles.
- Extruded surfaces created from line segments extruded a specific distance. One uses fillets to round corners.
- A swept surface created by a profile containing lines and arcs swept along an arc.
- A revolved surface created by a spline rotated around an axis.

The Surface operation is available for the Revolve, Loft, Extrude, and Sweep tools on the Feature toolbar. Specific requirements for creating a surface depend on the feature tool you use.

A construction surface is created from an open or closed profile. When used as a termination plane, you can use it to refine shapes. A surface can also be used as a split tool when creating a split part.

After you use the surface as a termination plane or a split tool, you can turn its visibility off.

To begin, click the Sketch tool on the Command bar and select a face or work plane as the sketch plane.

1. Use tools in the Sketch toolbar to create an open or closed profile to represent the surface shape.
2. Create other geometry as required by the tool you will use to create the surface (such as an axis or second profile for a loft).
3. On the Feature toolbar, click the Extrude, Revolve, Loft, or Sweep tool.
4. When a profile is detected, the Surface operation is automatically selected. Select other geometry as required by the tool.
5. If desired, enter additional values to define the surface for the tool (such as a taper angle and distance, revolution angle, or point mapping, if available).
6. Click OK.

Create one or more features, selecting the construction surface when a termination plane is required or as the cutting line to split a part. If desired, you can use multiple construction surfaces as the beginning and ending termination planes.

TIP: A construction surface cannot be used as a sketch plane because of its irregular shape.

Exercise 4-1:
Thin Wall

Drawing Name: Start a new part using Standard (inches)
Estimated time: 15 minutes

Start a new part file and create the sketch shown on the Front (XY) plane.
Project the Center Point and X axis onto the current sketch.

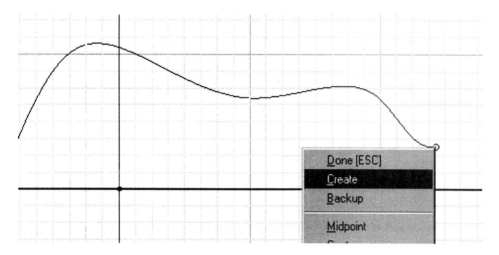

Using the spline tool, create a spline. Right click and select 'Create'.

TIP: The Spline tool is located on the Sketch toolbar under the Line dropdown.

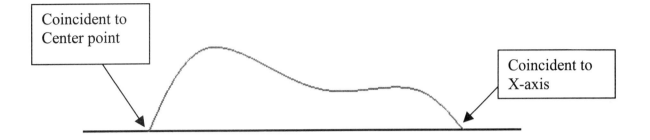

Coincident to
Center point

Coincident to
X-axis

Switch to an isometric view.

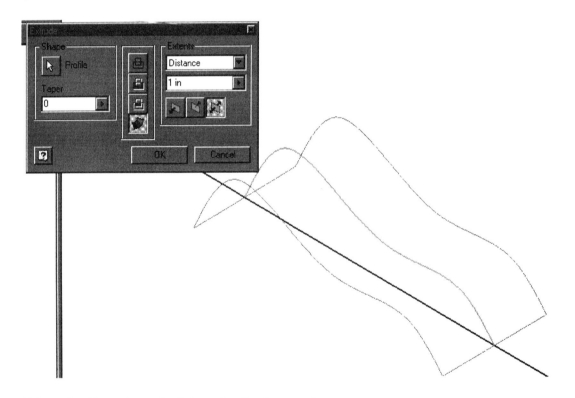

Select the Extrude tool. Select the Surface option.
This is the bottom button in the middle of the dialog.
Select the spline as the profile.
Set the Distance to 1 in Midplane.
Press 'OK'.

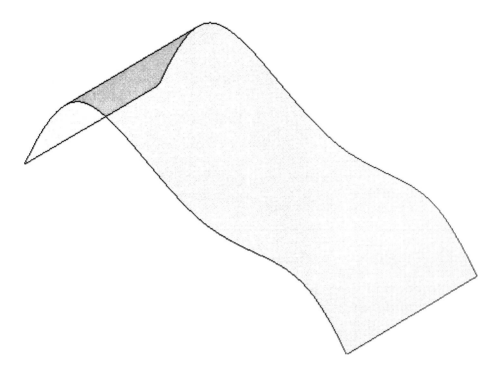

Our surface.

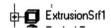 ExtrusionSrf1

Note how the surface is indicated in the Browser as an ExtrusionSrf.

Save as Ex4-1.ipt.

Exercise 4-2:

Thin Container

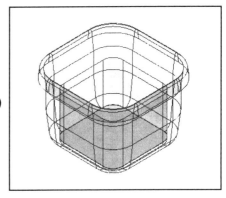

Drawing Name: Start a new part using Standard (inches)
Estimated time: 30 minutes

Select the XY (Front plane) for your sketch.

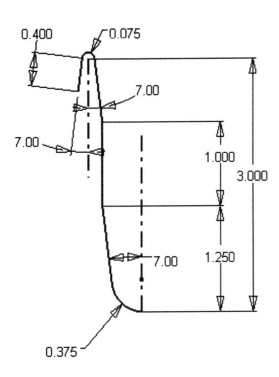

Use Project Geometry to project the Center Point onto the current sketch.

Create the following sketch.
The sketch should be fully constrained.

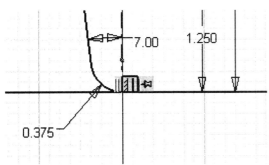

Add a vertical constraint between the center point of the arc and the center point of the sketch.

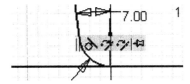

Add a tangent constraint between the angled line and the arc.

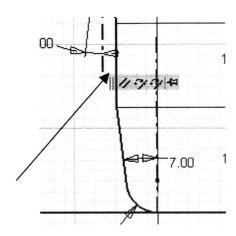

Add a parallel constraint between the straight line and one of the centerlines.

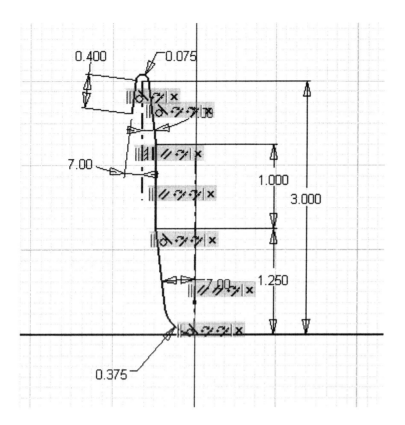

All the sketch constraints are shown here.
Exit sketch mode.

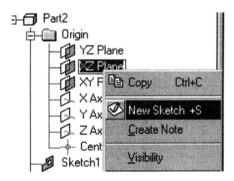

Select the XZ (top) plane. Right click and select New Sketch.

Project the center point onto the current sketch.

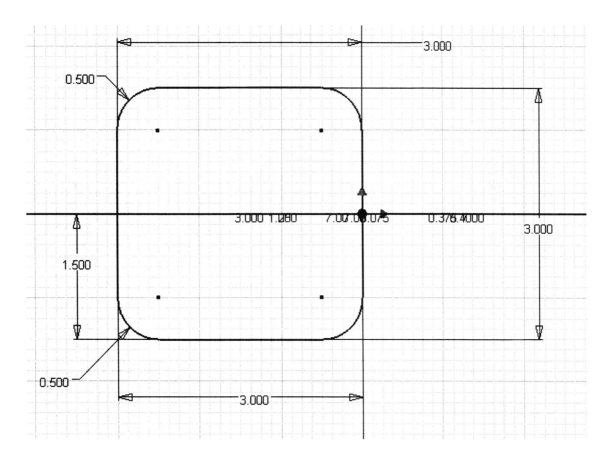

Draw a 3 x 3 square.

Fillet each corner with a radius of 3.0.

Position the rectangle so that one vertical side is coincident with the center point and it is centered horizontally.

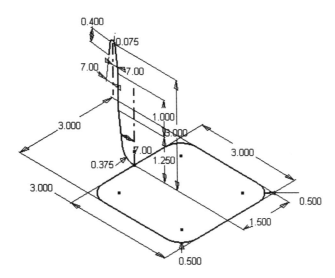

Exit sketch mode.

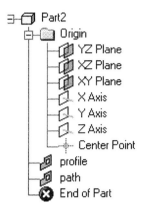

Rename the first sketch profile.
Rename the second sketch path.

Sweep the profile along the path using surface.

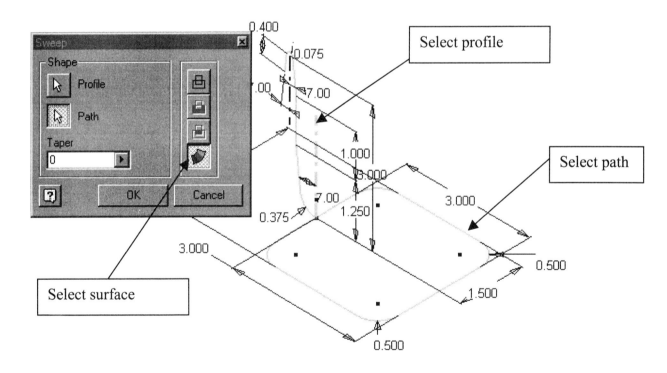

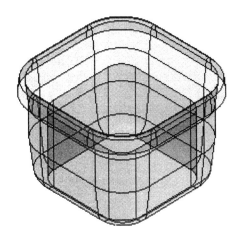

Create an offset work plane 0.10 from the top plane.

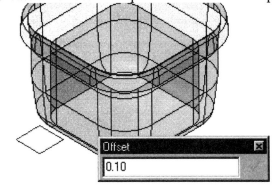

Select the offset work plane for a New Sketch.

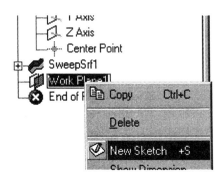

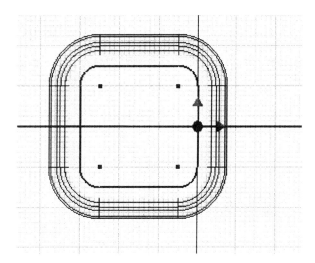

Use Project Geometry to select the inside edges of the bottom opening as shown.

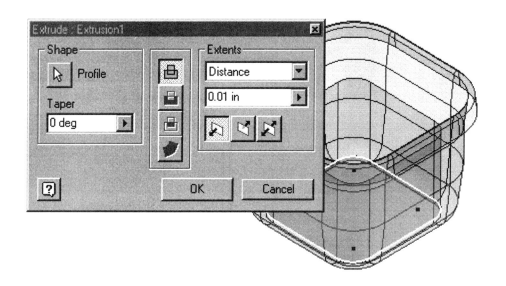

Select the Extrude tool.
Select the Profile we just created.
Set the distance to 0.01.
Extrude as a Join.

Save the part as Ex4-2.ipt.

Lesson 5
Derived Parts

To capture design intent, you can use selected sketches, an entire part, or selected parts from an assembly as the basis for a feature in an entirely new model. A derived part is a new part that uses an existing part or assembly as its base feature. You can add features to the derived part (the base feature), and update it to incorporate changes made to the original part or assembly.

After choosing the part or assembly to use, you can select geometry in a dialog box to include or exclude in the derived part. By selecting different combinations of sketches and features in a part or combinations of parts in an assembly, you can create multiple derived parts from one part or assembly.

A derived part from an assembly is represented as one item in a bill of materials.

You can use a derived part to explore design alternatives and manufacturing processes.

For example:

- A casting blank can be machined several different ways.
- A standard length of tubing can be machined in different configurations.
- A weldment can be configured several ways, including post-assembly operations such as cuts and holes.
- From an assembly, groups of parts can be subtracted or joined with other parts to create a single part with the desired shape.
- From a part that contains only work features and sketch geometry, derive one or more parts. In an assembly, use the derived parts as a layout when designing a framework for an assembly. Edit the original part and update the derived parts to automatically incorporate changes in the layout.

When creating a derived part, you can scale it larger or smaller than the original part or create a mirror of the original part using any of the origin work planes. You can update the derived part when changes are made to the original part.

Derived parts that originated from an assembly cannot be mirrored or scaled.

Changes made to the original part or assembly are reflected in the derived part after an Update is performed. The derived feature will show a red lightning bolt in the feature browser to indicate that it needs to be updated. Because an assembly checks component status when the file is opened, parts, which were derived from other parts or assemblies, are automatically updated when you update the assembly.

You can break the link to the original part or assembly if you no longer wish to update the derived part. Right-click on the derived part in the browser and select Break Link. The derived part becomes a regular feature (or component in an assembly) and its changes are saved only in the current file.

Create a new part file and click Return to exit the sketch. Click the Derive Component tool on the Feature toolbar and select the part or assembly file from which to derive a part. The following tips describe which geometry is allowed in the new file before you select a part or assembly to derive:

- In order to derive the base part's solid body, the part you are creating cannot currently contain solid features. The file can contain only sketch geometry and work features.
- Only visible, unconsumed, sketch geometry can be selected for inclusion in the new part.
- Only visible work features can be selected for inclusion in the new part.
- Only visible surfaces can be selected for inclusion in the new part.
- Two or more derived part features can be created within a part, using the same or different base parts. However, only one of them can derive a solid body.

All of the features of the selected part will be combined into a single feature in the browser of the derived part. By selectively including individual sketches from your selected part, you can define individual features from those sketches in the new part.

A common workflow for deriving a part from an assembly is:

- Model the individual parts of the assembly.
- Apply assembly constraints to position the parts.
- Save the assembly.
- Open a new part file.
- Select the Derived Component tool.
- Select the assembly to insert.

You can select or more parts to include in a derived part. From a single assembly, you can select different combinations of parts, resulting in multiple derived parts.

A derived part feature originates from a part file. You select features, surfaces, visible sketches and work features to include or exclude from the resulting derived part. Sketches that are not shared or consumed by features are included in the base feature.

To begin, create a new part file, and then click Return on the Command bar to close the default sketch.

1. On the Feature toolbar, click the Derived Component tool.
2. In the Open dialog box, browse to the part file (.ipt) to use as the base feature, then click Open.
3. In the Derived Part dialog box, model elements are displayed in a hierarchy. Accept the default (all geometry is included in the derived part) or click to cycle through options for one or more elements.

   Selects element for inclusion in the derived part.

   Excludes element in the derived part. Items marked with this symbol are ignored in updates to the derived part.

4. Specify scale factor and mirror plane:
   o Accept the default scale factor of 1.0 or enter any positive number.
   o If desired, select the check box to mirror the derived part feature from the base part. Click the down arrow to select an origin work plane as the mirror plane.
5. Click OK.

Note: If you select a geometric group, such as surfaces, for inclusion in the derived part, any visible surface later added to the base part is derived when you update. After placing the derived part in an assembly, click Local Update to regenerate only the local part and click Full Update to update the entire assembly.

A derived part that originates as an assembly file may contain parts, subassemblies, and derived parts. You select geometry to add or subtract from the resulting derived part.

TIP: The Derived Part tool is an easy way to mirror a Part.

To begin, create a new part file, and then click Return on the Command bar to close the default sketch.

1. On the Feature toolbar, click the Derived Component tool.
2. In the Open dialog box, browse to the assembly file (.iam) to use as the base feature, then click Open.
3. In the Derived Assembly dialog box, geometric elements are displayed in a hierarchy. Accept the default (all geometry is included in the derived part) or click to cycle through options for one or more elements.

Selects element for inclusion in the derived part.

Excludes element from the derived part. Items marked with this symbol are ignored in updates to the derived part.

Subtracts element from the derived part. If the subtracted element intersects with the part, the result is a cavity.

4. Select the check box to keep seams between planar faces, if desired.
5. Click OK.

Note: If a subassembly is selected for addition or subtraction, any component later added to the subassembly will automatically be reflected when you update. After placing the derived part in an assembly, click Local Update to regenerate only the local part and click Full Update to update the entire assembly.

Exercise 5-1
Stacking Dolls

Drawing Name: Start a new Part file
                    using Standard (inches)
Estimated Time: 60 minutes

Learning Objectives:

- Derived Parts
- Split Parts
- Revolve
- Shell

Most users can recall playing with stacking dolls as young children. In this exercise, we create a set of three stacking dolls using derived parts.

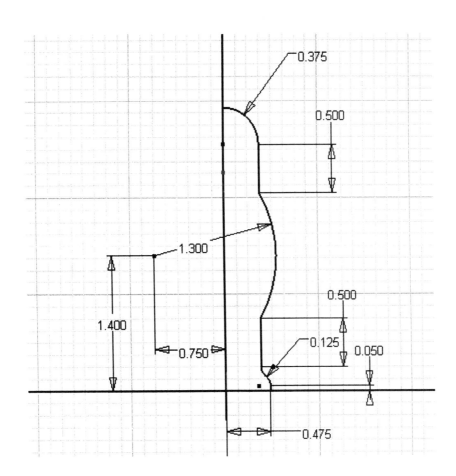

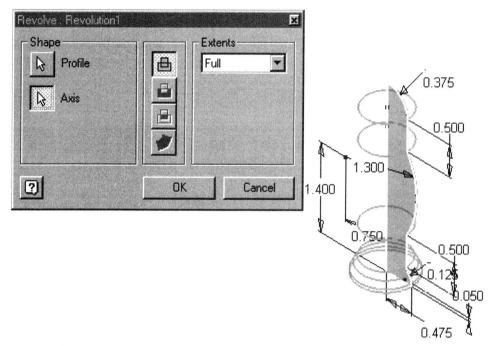

Create a full Revolve.

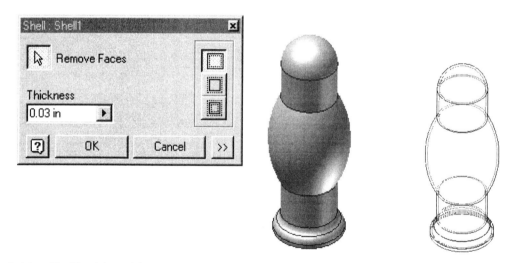

Add a Shell with a thickness of 0.03.
Do not select any faces to remove.
If you switch the View Mode to Wire Frame, you will see the shell.

Create an Offset Work Plane .625" above the top plane.

Select the Split Part tool from the Features toolbar.

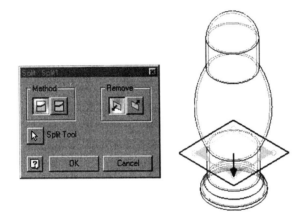

Select the 'Split Part' button.
Select the Offset Work Plane.
The Arrow indicates the section that will be removed.
Press 'OK'.

Save a copy of the part as 'doll-bottom.ipt'.

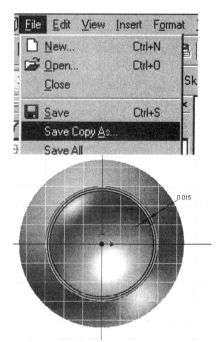

Select the
bottom lip for a
New Sketch.

Project the inner edge of the bottom flange.

Select the Offset Sketch tool and offset a circle between the inner edge and outer
edge.

Add a 0.015 dimension between
the offset and the inner edge.

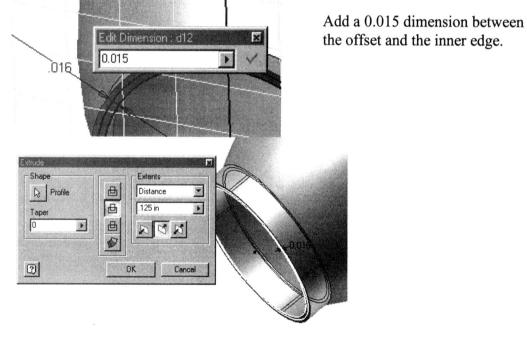

Create a Cut a distance of 0.125.
Save the part as 'doll-top.ipt'.

Open the 'doll-bottom' part we created as a copy.

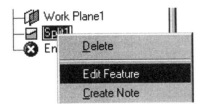

Locate the Split in the Browser. Right click and select 'Edit Feature'.

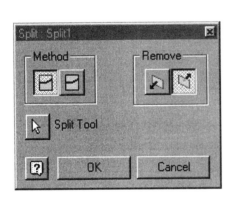

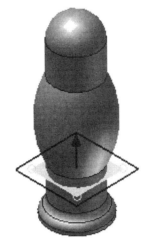

Edit the Part Split feature and change the section to be removed to be the top.

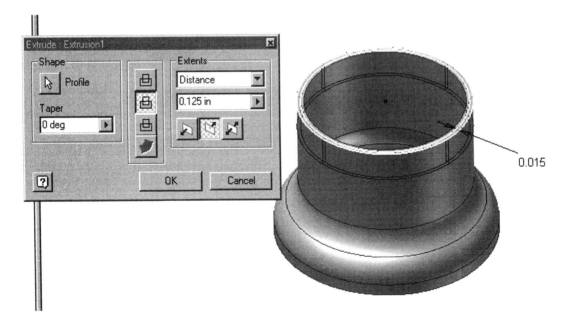

0.015

Add an extrude cut a Distance of 0.125 using the outer edge of the flange and an offset between the edges.

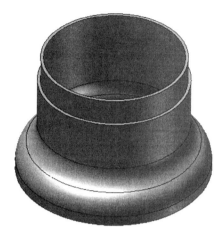

Save the file as 'doll-bottom.ipt'.

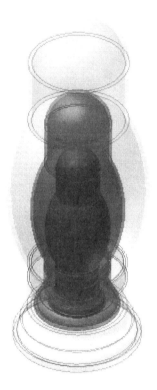

Create a derived part of the top and bottom pieces. Each derived part is 1.5X scale of the source part.

Start a New Part File Using Standard.ipt.

Exit Sketch Mode.

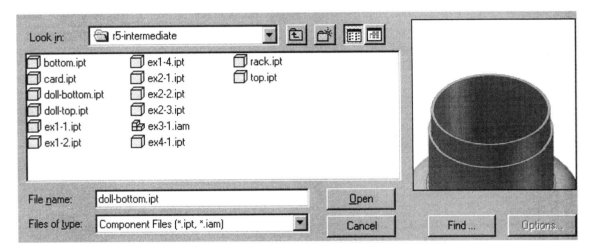

Select the Derived Component tool from the Features toolbar.

Locate the 'doll-bottom.ipt' file.

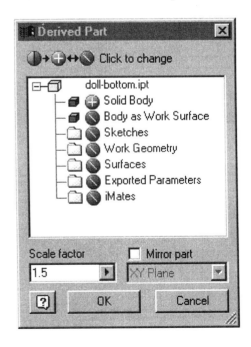

Set the Scale Factor to 1.5.

Press 'OK'.

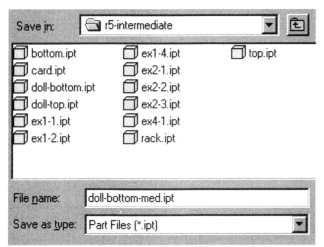

Save the doll-bottom.ipt as 'doll-bottom-med.ipt'.

Start another part file using Standard.

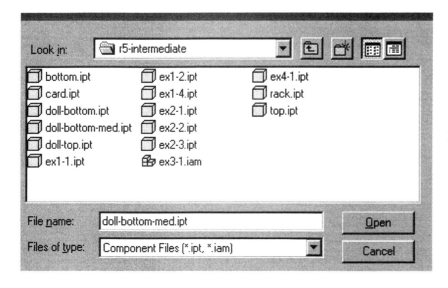

Select the Derived Component tool and located the doll-bottom-med.ipt file.

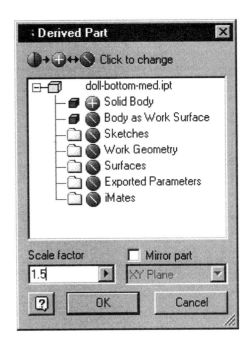

Set the Scale Factor to 1.5.

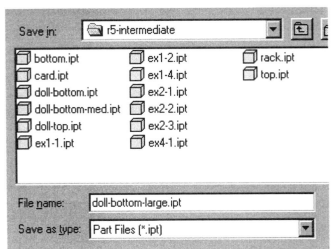

Save the file as
doll-bottom-large.ipt.

Repeat the process for the 'doll-top.ipt'.

Create an assembly file with all the parts.
See if you can stack the dolls.

Save the assembly as 'stacking dolls.iam'.

Lesson 6
Parameters

Each time you add a dimension or other measurement to a model, that value is established as a parameter for the model. You can use parameters in equations to derive other parameters or define user parameters that you call by name when entering values.

Using an Existing Part

When you add a dimension or other value, it is assigned a default parameter name, such as d0, d1, or d2. You can assign a meaningful name to a parameter. You can also change the value of a parameter by changing its equation.

1. On the Standard toolbar, click the Parameters button.
2. In the Parameters dialog box, locate the parameter to change.
3. To change the Parameter Name, Equation, or Comment, click in the corresponding box to select the existing value and then enter the new value.
4. Press Enter to save the change.
5. To update the model, click the Update button on the Command toolbar.

TIP: You can also change the value of an existing parameter by editing the sketch dimension or the feature.

Using an Excel Spreadsheet

You can define parameters in a Microsoft Excel spreadsheet and then link to the spreadsheet to use those parameters in a part or assembly.

1. On the Standard toolbar, click the Parameters button.
2. In the Parameters dialog box, click the Link button to find and select the Microsoft Excel (.xls) file.
3. Specify the starting cell in the spreadsheet for the parameters. Do not include any column or row headings or other content from the spreadsheet.
4. Specify whether the spreadsheet is to be embedded or linked.

When you link to or embed a spreadsheet, a table showing the parameters is added to the Parameters dialog box. You cannot edit the parameters in the spreadsheet from the Parameters dialog box. You must open the file in Microsoft Excel to make changes.

Parameter values can be made to appear in component properties and are then available for display in the bill of materials and the parts list.

1. In the parameters dialog box locate the export parameters column as indicated by the export parameters icon.
2. Check the box next to the parameter that you wish to export.
3. Click Done.

The exported parameters will then appear on the Custom tab of the component properties dialog box and will also be available in the bill of materials and parts list Column Chooser dialog boxes.

1. Exported parameter values are available for display in the bill of materials and the parts list. In the Bill of Materials or Parts List dialog boxes click the Column Chooser.
2. Select the Custom Properties field.
3. From the Available Properties field select the parameters that you wish to appear in the bill of materials or parts list.
4. Click Done. The selected parameter appears as a new column.

When you use the Parameters tool to define or edit a parameter, changes you make are not applied until you click the Update button. When you edit a feature, all dependent parameters change with the feature.

Follow these guidelines to make sure parameters and parts update predictably:

• Assign meaningful names to parameters.
• Equations cannot be recursive.
• Parameter names cannot include spaces, mathematical symbols, or special characters.
• If you link a spreadsheet to the parameters, you cannot edit its values or equations inside Autodesk Inventor (instead you must open and edit the spreadsheet in Microsoft Excel).

If you use the same parameters in many models, you can define parameters in a Microsoft Excel spreadsheet. You can embed or link to the spreadsheet from assembly or part models.

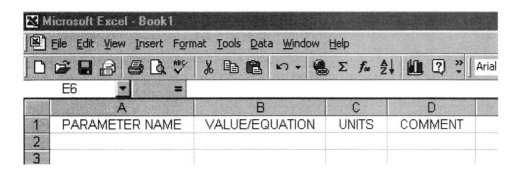

Use Microsoft Excel to create a spreadsheet with the following format:

- The data can start in any cell of the spreadsheet.
- The data items can be in rows or columns, but they must be in the correct order: parameter name, value or equation, unit of measurement, comment.
- The parameter name and value are required; the other items are optional.
- If you do not specify the units of measurement for a parameter, the default units for the model are assigned when you use the parameter. To create a parameter without units, enter UL in the units cell.
- You can include column or row headings or other information in the spreadsheet, but they must be outside the block of cells that contains the parameter definitions.

After creating and saving the parameters spreadsheet you can use it in any part or assembly model.

1. Open the model file in Autodesk Inventor.
2. On the Standard toolbar, click the Parameters button.
3. In the Parameters dialog box, click the Link button to find and select the spreadsheet.
4. In the Open dialog box, specify the starting cell for the parameter data in the spreadsheet.
5. Select Link or Embed. Select Link to share the same spreadsheet parameters across multiple files, select embed to use and edit the spreadsheet parameters in the active model without affecting other files.

You cannot edit the parameters in a spreadsheet from the Parameters dialog box. If the spreadsheet file is linked, you can open the spreadsheet in Microsoft Excel and edit it. You can use the following procedure to edit either a linked or an embedded spreadsheet.

1. In Autodesk Inventor, open the model that uses the spreadsheet.
2. In the browser, expand the 3rd Party folder.
3. Double-click the spreadsheet to edit. The spreadsheet will open in a Microsoft Excel window for editing.

The Parameters tool displays and defines the parameters in a model. You can rename, change values of, or add comments to existing parameters. You can also define user parameters for use in the part.

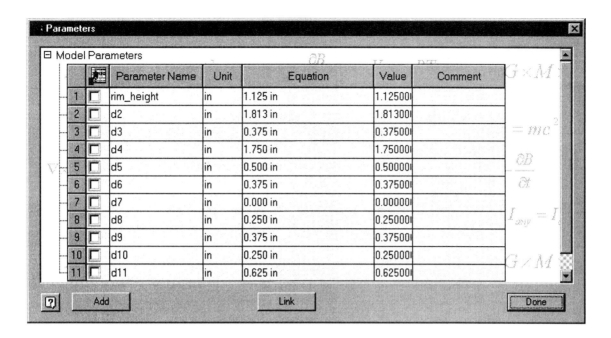

Model Parameters

Displays the names and values of the parameters automatically created during the modeling process. Each time you add a dimension or feature to the model, parameters are assigned.	
Parameter Name	The name of the parameter. To change the name of a parameter to a descriptive name, click in the box and enter the new name. When you update the model, all dependent parameters update to reflect the new name.
Units	The units of measurement for the parameter.
Equation	The equation that generates the value of the parameter. If the parameter is a discrete value, the value is displayed, rounded to match the precision setting for the model. To change the equation, click the existing equation and enter the new equation.
Value	The calculated value of the equation (displayed in full precision).
Comment	The comment, if any, about the parameter. To add a comment, click in the box and enter the comment.

User Parameters

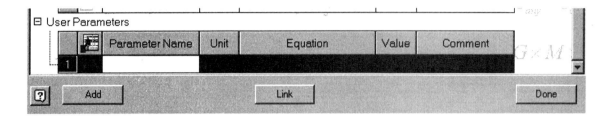

User parameters display parameters that you define to drive dimensions and features in the model. To add a parameter, click the Add button to add a new row to the table, and then enter the values for the parameter.

Parameter Name	The name of the parameter. Click in the box and enter the name.
Units	The units of measurement for the parameter. To set the units, click in the box to open the Unit Type dialog box and select the desired units.
Equation	The equation that generates the value of the parameter. Click in the box and enter the equation or value for the parameter.
Value	The calculated value of the equation (displayed in full precision).
Comment	The comment, if any, about the parameter. To add a comment, click in the box and enter the comment.
Add	Adds a new row to the table of User Parameters so that you can define a parameter.
Link	Displays the Open dialog box so that you can locate and specify an external spreadsheet that defines parameters. Click the button to add a link to the spreadsheet file.

When you link to a spreadsheet, a table showing parameters in the spreadsheet is displayed in the Parameters dialog box. You cannot change the spreadsheet from the Parameters dialog box; you must open the file in Microsoft Excel to make changes.

Exercise 6-1:

Naming Parameters

Drawing Name: Start a New Part file using Standard (inches)
Estimated Time: 30 minutes

Learning Objectives:

- Parameters
- Revolve
- Pattern Feature
- Textures
- Suppress Features
- Thread

Create the sketch on XY plane.

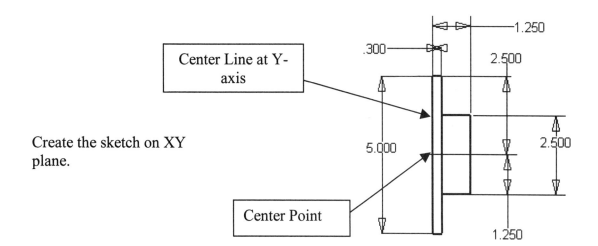

Center Line at Y-axis

Center Point

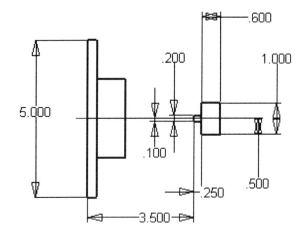

Add two small rectangles to the right.
The first rectangle is 0.250 x 0.100.
The second rectangle is 0.600 x 1.00.
Both rectangles are centered on the X axis.

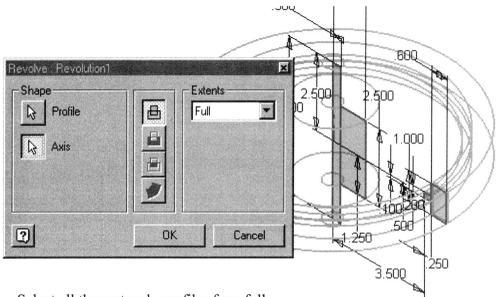

Select all the rectangle profiles for a full
revolve.
Select the Y-axis for the Axis.

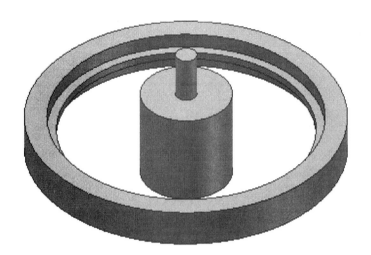

Our model so far.

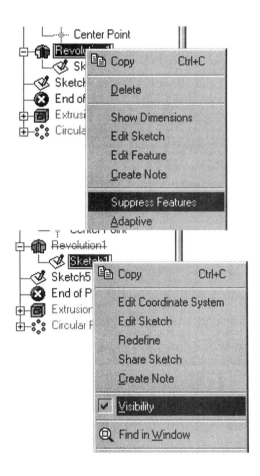

Suppress the Revolution feature.

Locate the sketch under the Revolution.
Enable the Visibility.

Select the XZ plane for a New Sketch.

Select the XY Plane for a sketch.
Add a 1.7 x 2.5 rectangle to the
right side of the first sketch.
Add 1.0 fillets to the right corners.
Add 0.5 fillets to the left corners.

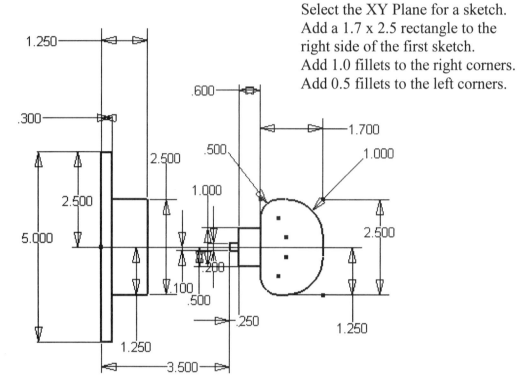

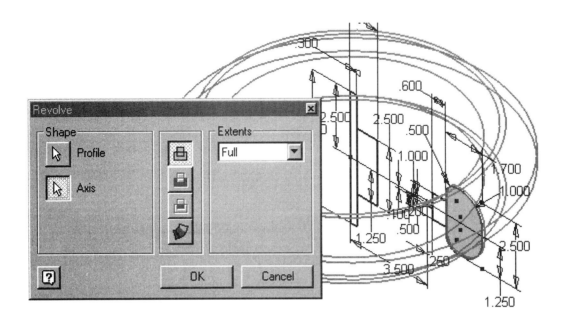

Revolve the sketch around the Y axis.

Turn off the sketch
visibility and
unsuppress the
Revolution feature.

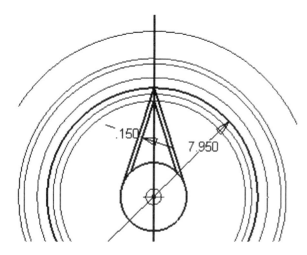

Project the larger inner circle.
Draw a 7.95-diameter concentric circle.
Draw two lines with one end coincident to the 7.95 diameter circle and one end tangent to the projected edge.
Offset the two lines in a distance of 0.150.
Draw two small arcs to close the profiles.

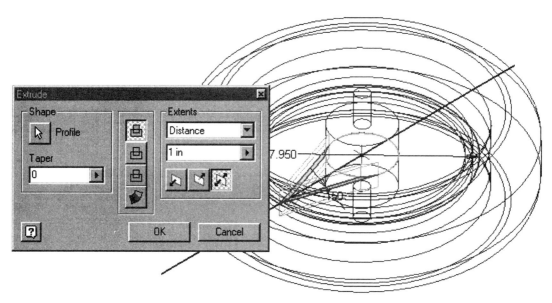

Extrude the spoke 1 inch using Mid-Plane.

Our wheel so far.

Create a circular pattern of the spoke.
Select the center cylinder for the Rotation Axis.

Set the Count to 7.
Set the Angle to 360.
Press the 'More' button.
Enable 'Adjust to Model'.
Press 'OK'.

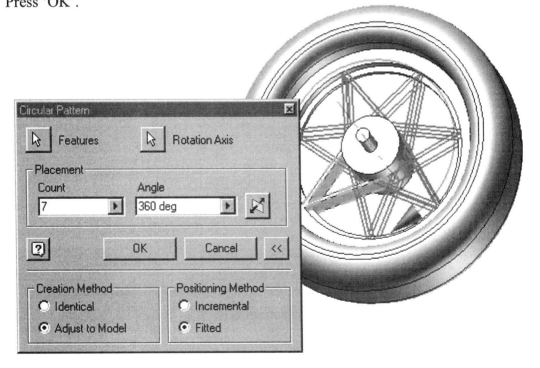

Go to Format->Colors.

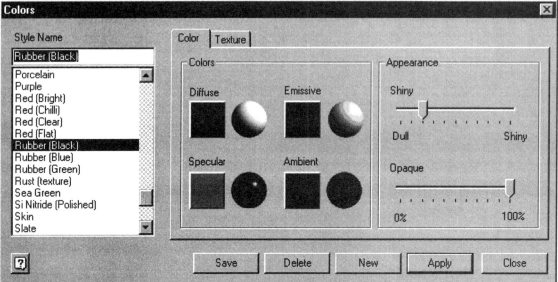

Locate Rubber (Black) under Style Name.
Select the Texture Tab.

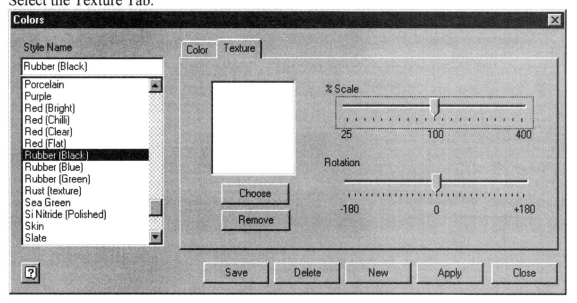

Select the Choose button.

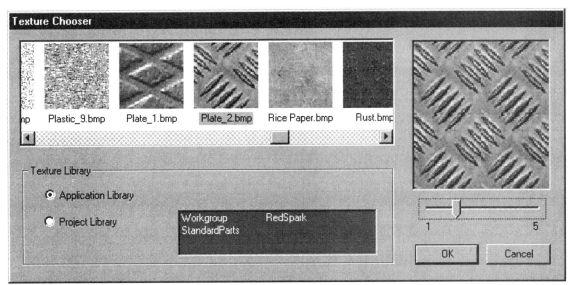

Locate 'Plate_2.bmp'. Set the scale to 2.
Press 'OK'.

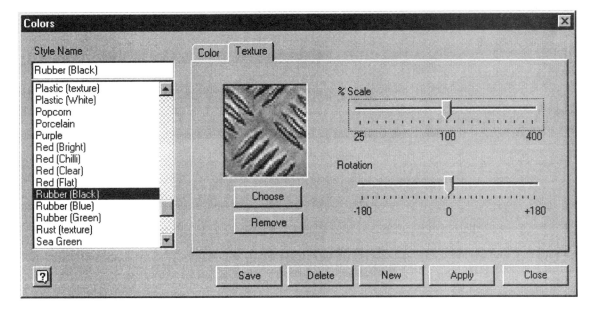

Press 'Save'.

The Rubber (Black) color will now use that texture.

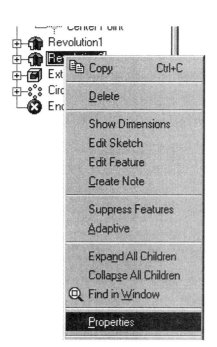

Highlight the second Revolution in the browser.
Right click and select 'Properties'.

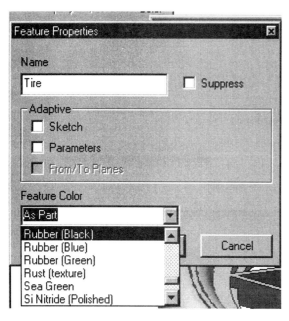

Change the Name of the Revolution to Tire.
Under Feature Color, select Rubber (Black).
Press 'OK'.

Your wheel tire now shows treads.

TIP: It is easier to see the treads if you apply a contrasting color/material to the wheel.

    Select the Thread tool.

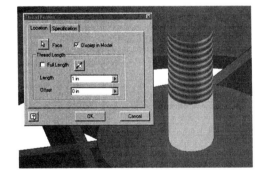

Select the face of the axle.
Disable Full Length.
Set the Length to 1 in.
Set the Offset to 0.

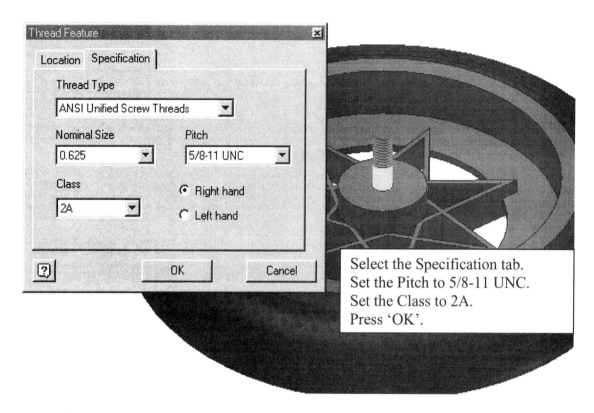

Select the Specification tab.
Set the Pitch to 5/8-11 UNC.
Set the Class to 2A.
Press 'OK'.

Repeat for the axle end on the other side.

Save the part as 'Ex6-1'.

Start the Parameters tool.

⊟ Model Parameters

Parameter Name	Unit	Equation	Value		Comment
AXLE_RADIUS	in	0.30 in	0.300000	☐	
AXLE_LENGTH	in	5 in	5.000000	☐	
d2	in	AXLE_LENGTH / 2 ul	2.500000	☐	
SPOKE_RADIUS	in	3.5 in	3.500000	☐	
RIM_THICKNESS	in	0.2 in	0.200000	☐	
d5	in	0.1 in	0.100000	☐	
RIM_HEIGHT	in	0.25 in	0.250000	☐	
OUTER_RIM_HT	in	1.0 in	1.000000	☐	
d8	in	0.5 in	0.500000	☐	
d9	in	0.6 in	0.600000	☐	
d16	in	2.5 in / 2 ul	1.250000	☐	
d17	in	2.5 in	2.500000	☐	
d18	in	1.25 in	1.250000	☐	
SPOKE_RAD	in	7.95 in	7.950000	☐	
SPOKE_WIDTH	in	0.15 in	0.150000	☐	
d57	in	1 in	1.000000	☐	
d58	deg	0 deg	0.000000	☐	
SPOKE_NO	ul	7 ul	7.000000	☐	
d61	deg	360 deg	360.000000	☐	
tIRE_THKNESS	in	1.7 in	1.700000	☐	
TIRE_DIA	in	2.5 in	2.500000	☐	
d64	in	1.25 in	1.250000	☐	
INNER_FILLET	in	0.500 in	0.500000	☐	
OUTER_FILLET	in	1 in	1.000000	☐	

Rename the parameters as shown.

TIP: Parameter names cannot have spaces or punctuation marks.

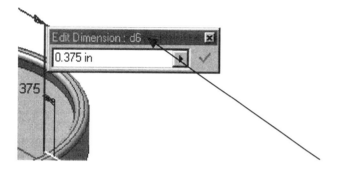

If you are not sure which parameters belong to which dimension, switch to the graphics window, Show Dimensions, and select the dimension.
The dimension parameter name will appear in the top of the Edit Dimension box.

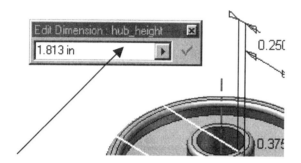

When you change the Parameter name of the dimension, it will be reflected in the Edit Dimension box.

When you are finished defining your parameters, select 'Done'.

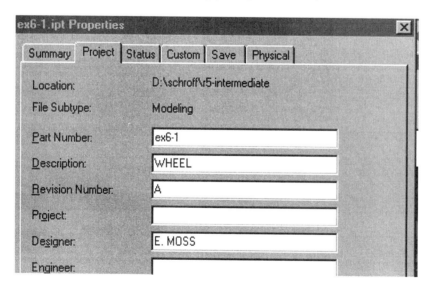

Assign file properties.

Save the file as EX6-1.ipt.

Exercise 6-2
Using an Excel Spreadsheet

Drawing Name: Start a New Part file using Standard (inches)
                      Ex6-2.xls
Estimated Time: 30 minutes

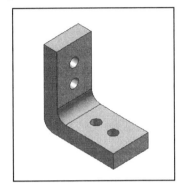

Learning Objectives:

- Parameters
- Use of Spreadsheet

	A	B	C	D	E	F	G
1	LENGTH	HEIGHT	WIDTH	FILLET	THICKNESS	HOLE_DIA	HOLE_DIST
2	4.00	4.00	2.00	0.50	0.75	0.50	1.00
3							
4							
5							

Ex6-2.xls

Create an Excel Spreadsheet as shown.
Note that the Parameter Name should be the first row.
Values should be the second row.
Units should be the third row (optional).
Comments should be the fourth row (optional).

TIP: You can use the Ex6-2.xls file that can be downloaded for free from www.shroff1.com/inventor.

Start a New Part file.

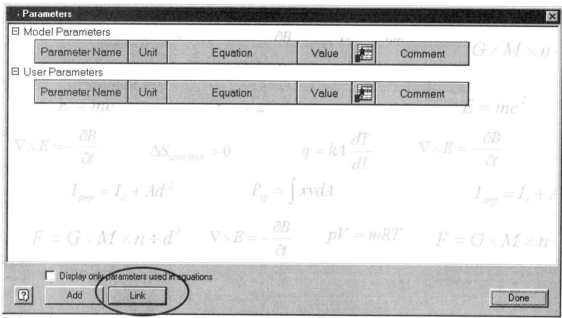

Select the Parameters tool.

Press the Link button.

Locate the xls file you just created. Press 'Open'.

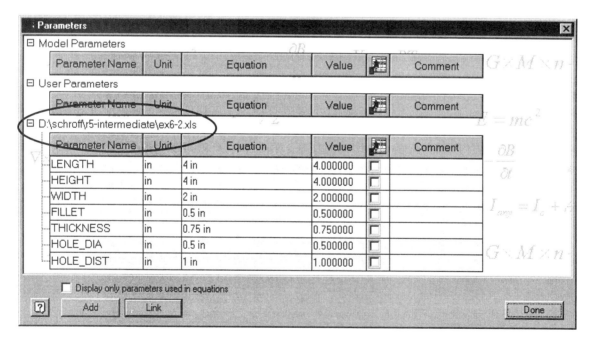

The Excel spreadsheet will appear in the Parameters dialog. Press 'Done'.

If you do not see the values and parameter names you created than the format of your spreadsheet is wrong.

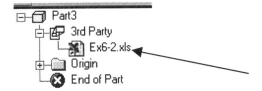

The spreadsheet will appear in the browser.

Start a new sketch on the Front (XY) Plane.

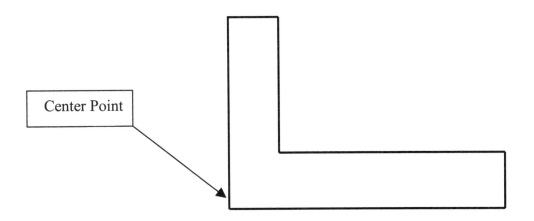

Draw the L figure shown.

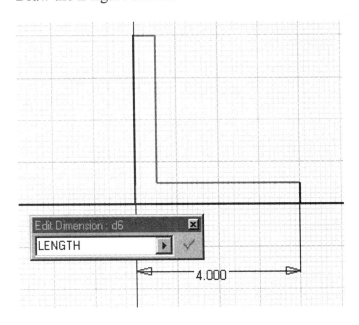

Place dimensions, but when entering in values use the parameters instead.

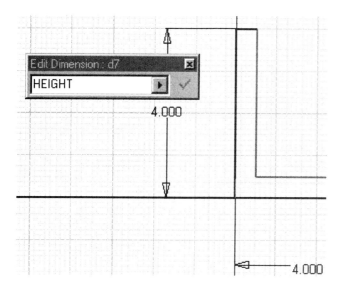

TIP: The parameters are case-sensitive, so if you defined your parameters as all capitals, you need to enter them as all capitals.

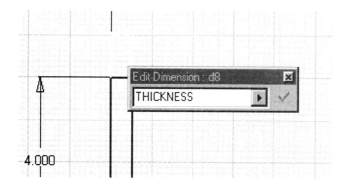

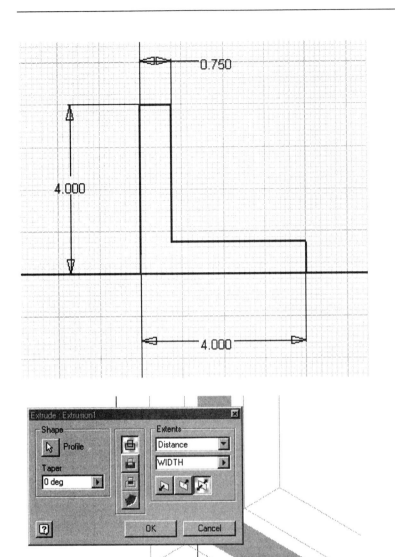

Create the extrusion mid-plane with a distance of WIDTH.

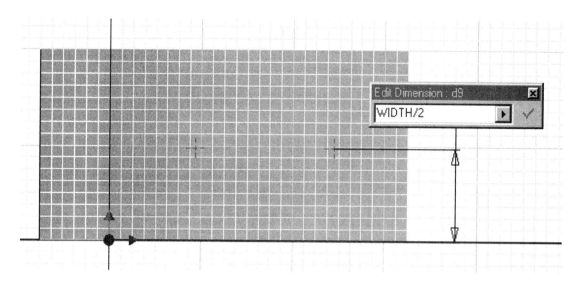

Place two hole center points.
Set the vertical dimension as WIDTH/2.

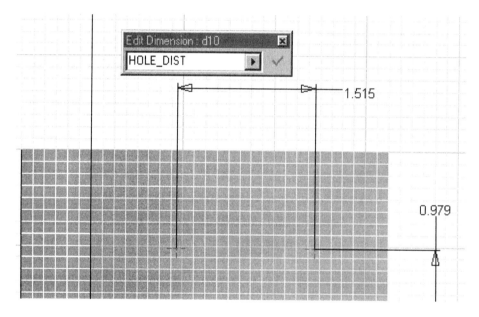

Set the distance between the points as HOLE_DIST.

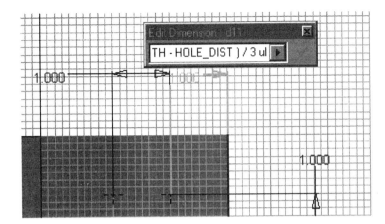

Set the horizontal distance
from the edge to be
(LENGTH – HOLE_DIST)/3.

Exit this sketch and select the
vertical face for a new sketch.

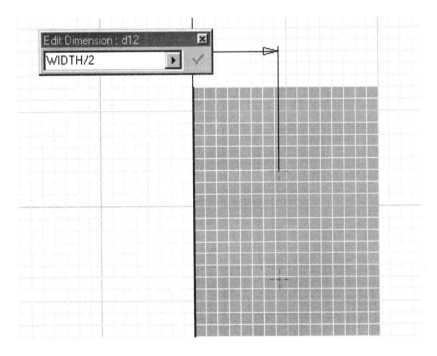

Place two more hole points on the vertical bend.
Set the horizontal dimension to WIDTH/2.

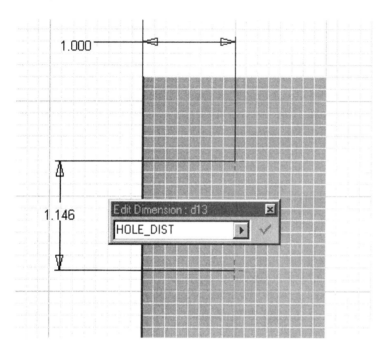

Set the spacing between the points to HOLE_DIST.

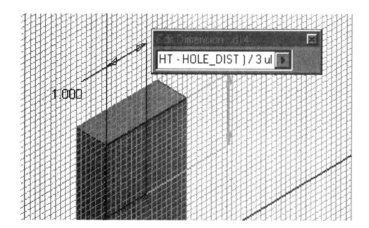

Set the vertical distance from the top to the hole point to (HEIGHT – HOLE_DIST)/3.

Exit Sketch Mode.

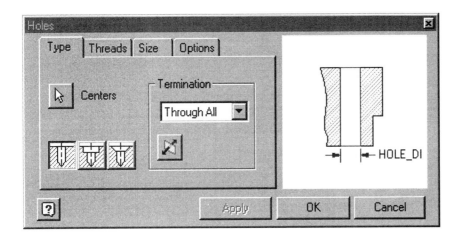

Select the Hole tool.
Define the hole diameter in the dialog box by typing HOLE_DIA instead of a value.
Set Termination to Through All.

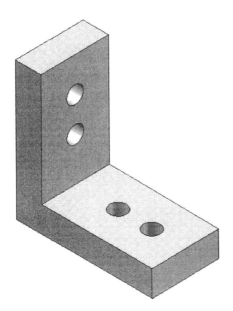

Add a fillet using the parameter.

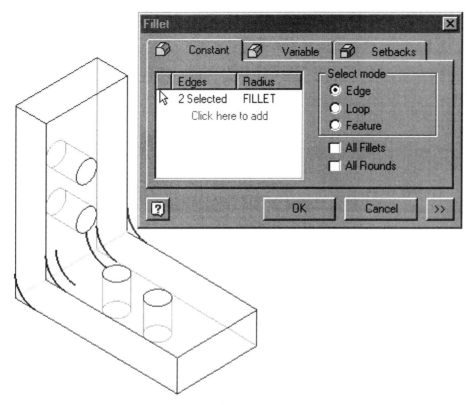

Select the FILLET tool. Instead of a radius value, type the word FILLET.

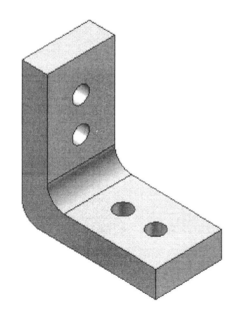

Save as Ex6-2.ipt.

Exercise 6-3
Using Parameters

File: Ex6-1.ipt
Estimated Time: 15 minutes

Open the file called Ex6-1.ipt.

        Select the Parameters tool.

d58	deg	0 deg	0.000000	
SPOKE_NO	ul	5 ul	5.000000	
d61	deg	360 deg	360.000000	

Change the value of the SPOKE_NO to 5.
Press 'Done'.

Press 'Update'.

The number of spokes changes to 5.

Save the file as Ex6-3.ipt.

Replaying a Transcript

Inventor Release 4 and below allowed you to save a transcript of how a part is created or how an assembly is built.

To create a transcript for a part or assembly:

Go to Tools-> Options.
Select the General tab.
Enable Transcripting so it is ON.

To play your transcript:

1. Go to the directory where you are saving your transcripts, usually your Temp directory
2. Identify the transcript file you want to play and rename it (not required but useful)
3. Start Inventor and cancel the opening dialog
4. Make the Inventor window smaller so you can see other applications
5. Load Windows Explorer, find the transcript and drag and drop it into the Inventor window
6. Sit back and watch your part or assembly re-build.

Lesson 7
iParts

iParts are used to create a family of parts from a single part design.

We can use an existing part to create the iPart. It is usually easier to create the parent part and then develop the additional configurations.

A good way to think of iParts is as an extension of using parameters, except more powerful. With iParts, we can modify dimensions and suppress features.

Use the iPart Author tool on the Standard toolbar to transform a part into an iPart Factory, a part that has multiple configurations whose parameters, properties, and other values are maintained in an embedded spreadsheet. You select values to include in the iPart table, adding rows and editing cell values to create unique configurations of the iPart.

You can create a Standard iPart Factory or a Custom iPart Factory.

- Standard iPart factories are not edited (an example is a bolt factory). Because bolts are parts that do not change, you select the individual iPart to use, but do not edit any values.
- Custom iPart factories are not edited directly, but allow you to make some modifications to the published iPart (an example is an angle iron factory). You select the individual custom iPart to use, and then modify certain types of values (such as length, width, or thickness) specified by the designer of the custom iPart factory.

Turning a Part into an iPart Factory

To begin, open a part to use as the iPart Factory.

1. Click the iPart Author tool on the Standard toolbar. Part data is listed in the left window of the dialog box.
2. On one or more tabs, use the direction arrows to add or remove items on the selected values list. Each value creates a column in the spreadsheet.
3. In the selected items list, click a key symbol on items to use as defining interface items when placing the iPart. One primary key (Key [1]) is required, but you can add up to eight secondary keys (whose values are restricted by values allowed by Key [1]).
4. In the iPart table, right-click in a row and select Insert Row to create another configuration of the iPart. Edit cell contents as necessary to create needed values for each configuration.
5. Right-click in a row and use options to customize the iPart configuration:
    o Select Delete Row to remove a configuration of the iPart.
    o Select Set as Default to make the row the default iPart configuration.
    o Select Custom Parameter Cell to allow the designer placing the iPart to specify its value.
6. Right-click in a column and use options to customize a defining value of an iPart:
    o Select Delete Column to remove a defining value of an iPart.
    o Select Custom Parameter Column to allow the designer placing the iPart to specify the value.
    o Select Key to specify the column as a defining interface when placing the iPart. You can add, delete, or change the order set in the selected items list.

When you finish defining the contents of the table, click OK to convert the part to an iPart Factory and place a table icon representing the embedded Microsoft® Excel spreadsheet in the browser.

Standard iPart Factories and Custom iPart Factories contain unique configurations of iParts managed in an iPart table. Each row in the iPart table contains a configuration of a standard iPart or a custom iPart, respectively.

- A Standard iPart Factory has all values defined in columns. When you use a Standard iPart Factory to publish a part, its parts cannot be modified after placement.
- A Custom iPart Factory contains at least one column identified as a Custom Parameter Column. When you use a Custom iPart Factory to publish a part, its parts contain some values that can be modified when placed. You can add features to a custom iPart after placement.

Use primary and secondary keys defined in the iPart Factory to identify a unique configuration of an iPart.

TIP: Add the file locations to the active project. Autodesk Inventor determines where to store the iParts generated by iPart factories based on how you set the search paths in the active project.

Using Standard iParts in an Assembly

1. Click the Place Component tool on the Assembly toolbar.
2. Browse to the folder that contains the component and click to Open. Autodesk Inventor detects which components are iPart Factories.

   The default configuration of the iPart is attached to the cursor. On the Standard iPart Placement dialog box:

3. The Keys tab lists primary and secondary keys in the order specified in the iPart Factory. Select the values of the key to specify a unique iPart configuration:
   - Click the first key to insert the value listed. If multiple key values were defined, click All Values and select from the list.
   - Click the next key value, if available, to select from the values listed. Notice that the value of the primary key changes to match an allowable value for the selected key.
   - Continue to select key values until the part parameters are as desired.
   - Click in the graphics window to place an instance of the standard iPart.
4. If you prefer, use the Table tab to identify an iPart configuration by selecting a row in the table:
   - If desired, right-click and select Sort Ascending or Sort Descending to reorder the rows.
   - Click in a row to select a configuration of the iPart.
   - Click in the graphics window to place an instance of the standard iPart.
5. Continue to place multiple instances of different configurations of the iPart, if desired.
6. When finished, click Dismiss to close the dialog box.
7. To change configurations of a standard iPart, click to expand the table icon in the browser. Right-click a version and select Change Member.

Using Custom iParts in an Assembly

1. Click the Place Component tool on the Assembly toolbar.
2. Browse to the folder that contains the component and click to 'Open'. Autodesk Inventor detects which components are iPart Factories.

   The default configuration of the iPart is attached to the cursor.

3. On the Place Custom iPart dialog box, use the Keys tab to set values. The left column lists primary and secondary keys in the order specified in the iPart Factory. The right column lists custom parameter keys.
   1. In the left column, select the values of the key to specify a unique iPart configuration:
      - Click the first key to insert the value listed. If multiple key values were defined, click All Values and select from the list.
      - Click the next key value, if available, to select from the values listed. Notice that the value of the primary key changes to match an allowable value for the selected key.
      - Continue to select key values until the part parameters are as desired.
   2. In the right column, enter custom values for the keys.
      - Click the first key and enter the desired value.
      - Continue to select keys, if available, and enter desired values.
4. When you have finished defining the custom iPart, click in the graphics window to place an instance.
5. If you prefer, use the Table tab to identify an iPart configuration by selecting a row in the table:
   1. Click in a row to select a configuration of the iPart.
   2. Click in the graphics window to place an instance of the standard iPart.
6. Continue to place multiple instances of different configurations of the iPart, if desired.
7. When finished, click Dismiss to close the dialog box.
8. To change configurations of a custom iPart, click to expand the table icon in the browser. Right-click a version and select Change Member.
9. To change custom values, open or edit in place the custom iPart. Right-click on the table or a configuration in the table, and click Compute Row.

TIP: You can accept the default name of the custom iPart or specify a different name.

An iPart Factory can be edited, but the changes do not automatically update iParts that have been placed in assemblies.

1. In an assembly, click the Full Update tool on the Standard toolbar.

   In the browser, iParts that need to be updated are marked with an update symbol.

2. Right-click the table icon in the browser, then choose Change Member to get the proper configuration of the revised iPart Factory.

Keep these tips in mind as you create an iPart Factory:

- Use the Parameters tool on the Standard toolbar to rename system parameters and to create unique parameter names before you use the iPart Author tool. Named parameters are automatically added to the table-driven list when you create the iPart Factory.
- If no unit of measurement is specified in a cell, the default document units are used.
- If you select the Material property from the Design Tracking Properties list, you must use the Material Column option on the 'Other' tab to ensure that the current color is set to As Material.
- In order for part properties to be used in drawings and bills of materials, you must include them in the iPart table, even if their values do not vary between configurations.

TIP: Double-click in the browser to add or remove items in the iPart list.

   o   On the Parameters tab, select one or more parameters.
   o   On the File Properties tab, select one or more properties.
   o   On the Suppression tab, select one or more features. Features will be computed if the status is Compute and will be suppressed if the status is Suppress.
   o   On the Other tab, create custom values such as Color, Material, or Filename, if desired.

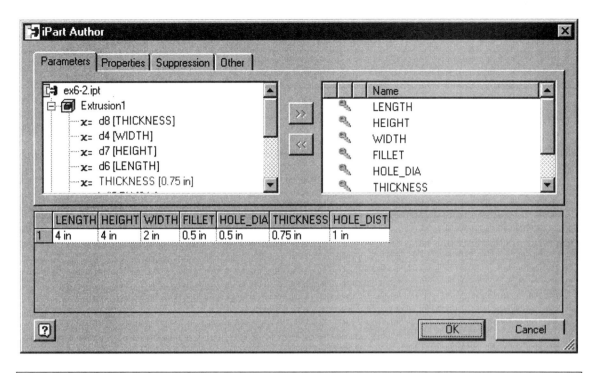

The iPart Author shows the Parameter, Feature, Property, and Other data in the table.
Click in the cell to edit its value.

A spreadsheet cell may contain an equation, in which case the cell contains text, or an
Microsoft® Excel formula. Cells with Microsoft® Excel formulas are shown in red.

	Represents a row in the spreadsheet (which defines the iPart Factory). Each row is a configuration of the iPart. Right-click in the row and select options to edit the table:
Row	• Click Insert Row to add another iPart configuration, and then edit the cell values as required to create a unique configuration. • Click Delete Row to remove the iPart configuration from the table. • Click Set as Default Row to set this row as the default iPart configuration. • Click Custom Parameter Cell to allow the designer placing the iPart to enter a custom value in the cell. After designation as a Custom Parameter Cell, you can set a minimum and maximum range of values. Right-click and select Specify Range for Cell.

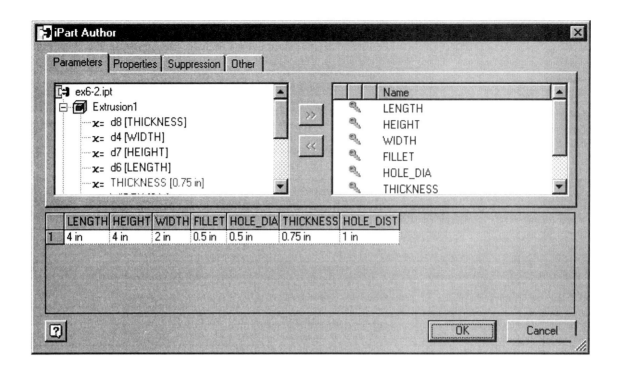

	Represents a property named in the Selected properties list. A column represents the same type of information for each version of an iPart in the iPart Factory. Right-click in the column and select options to edit the table: • Click Custom Parameter Column to allow the designer placing the iPart to enter a custom value for the property. • Click Material Column to define the material of the iPart when it is published. Material names must match a material type in the factory. • Click Delete Column to remove it from the table. This action is equivalent to clicking the Remove button to remove a property from the Selected properties list.
Column	

Exercise 7-1

Creating a Standard iPart

Drawing Name: ex6-1.ipt
Estimated Time: 30 minutes

Open the 'ex6-1.ipt' file created in Lesson 6.

Select the iPart Author tool.

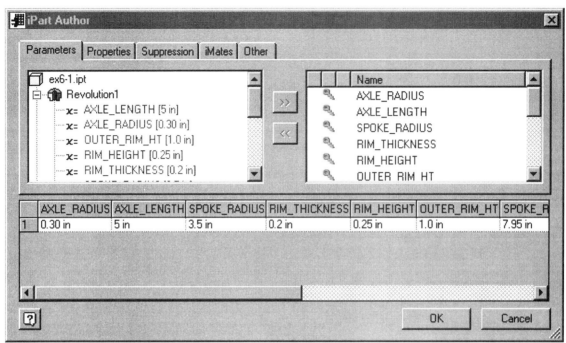

You should see the parameters you defined in Lesson 6.

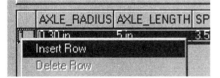

Highlight the row as shown.
Select 'Insert Row'.

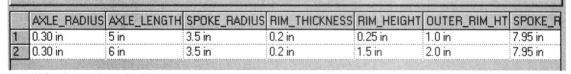

Modify the values in Row 2.
Set the AXLE_LENGTH to 6.
Set the RIM_HEIGHT to 1.5.
Set the OUTER_RIM_HT to 2.0.
Set the SPOKE_NO to 5.
Press 'OK'.

Check out the browser.

Notice that the part icon has changed to indicate the part is now an iPart.

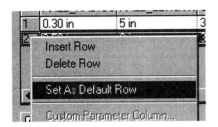

Go back into the table.
Highlight the second row.
Right click and Set As Default Row.

 Press Update for the changes to take effect.

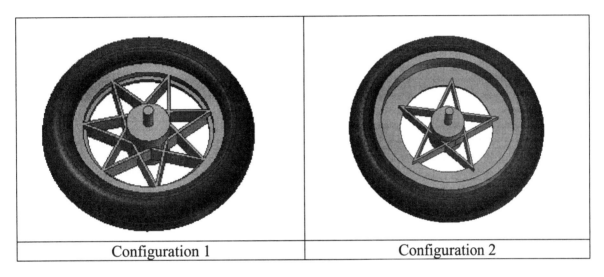

| Configuration 1 | Configuration 2 |

Highlight the SPOKE_NO = 7 in the browser.
Double click on it. The part changes back.

Activate the iPart Author again.

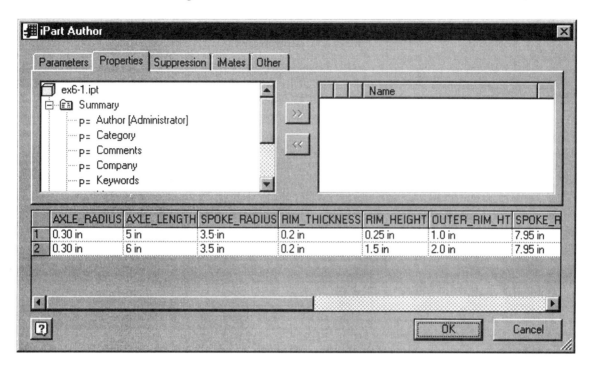

Select the Properties tab.
Expand the Project area in the tree in the left window.

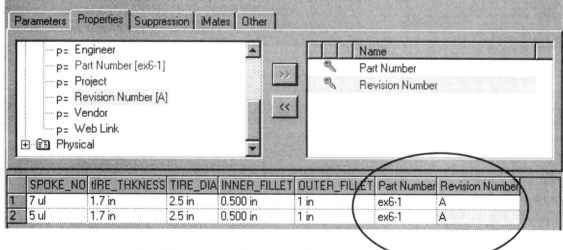

Locate where it says Part Number and Revision Number.
Select the >> button to add those columns to the configuration.
Notice the columns are added to the row.

Change the Part Number to the values shown.
To modify, just left click in the column and start typing.

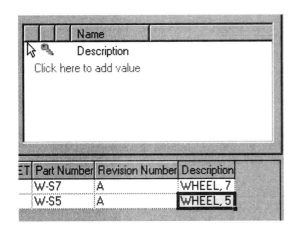

Select the 'Other' tab.
Type 'Description' under the Name.
Modify the descriptions for the configurations.
For the first part, enter
WHEEL, 7 SPOKES.
For the second part, enter
WHEEL, 5 SPOKES.

Exit the table.

Select the iMate tool. (iMates are discussed in detail in Lesson 8)

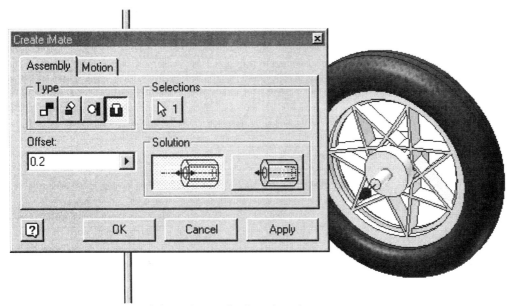

Place an Insert Constraint at the end of each axle.
Set the Offset to 0.2

You will see an iMate icon at the two insert points.

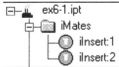

In the Browser, you see the iMates added.

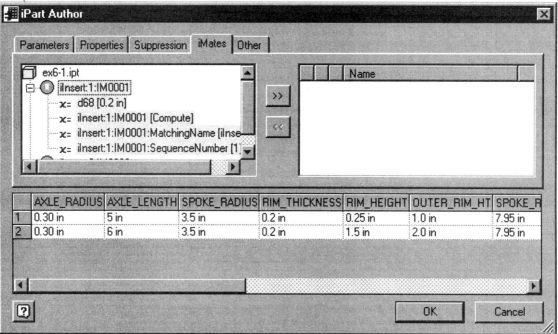

Now when you enter the table, select the iMates tab.
(This tab was added in Release 5)
We can now set different iMates for different part configurations.

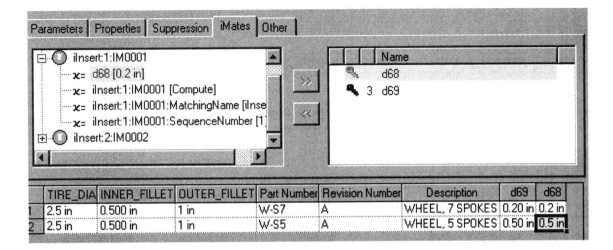

Place both iMate offsets in the configuration list.

Note that the offsets have been assigned a dimension value.

Your number will probably be different but the values will be the same.

Change the values of the Offset to 0.50 for the second configuration.

The Part Number, Revision Number, and Description can be used in Design Assistant, in a Drawing Title block, or in a Bill of Materials.

TIP: Setting Properties in the iPart Author is similar to setting File Properties for parts and assemblies. It is a good habit and saves time when you create the part and assembly documentation.

If you highlight the iPart table and right click, you can Edit the Table using the iPart Author or Edit Via Spread Sheet.

Select 'Edit Via Spread Sheet'.

A work sheet in Excel will pop up with the values and configurations you defined in the iPart Author.

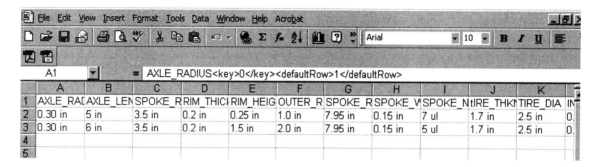

	A	B	C	D	E	F	G	H	I	J	K	
1	AXLE_RAI	AXLE_LEN	SPOKE_R	RIM_THICI	RIM_HEIG	OUTER_R	SPOKE_R	SPOKE_V	SPOKE_N	tIRE_THKI	TIRE_DIA	IN
2	0.30 in	5 in	3.5 in	0.2 in	0.25 in	1.0 in	7.95 in	0.15 in	7 ul	1.7 in	2.5 in	0.
3	0.30 in	6 in	3.5 in	0.2 in	1.5 in	2.0 in	7.95 in	0.15 in	5 ul	1.7 in	2.5 in	0.
4												
5												

Save the file as Ex7-1.ipt.

Exercise 7-2
Creating a Custom iPart

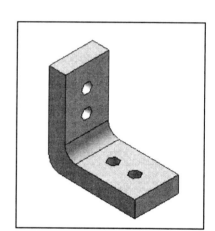

Drawing Name: ex6-2.ipt
Estimated Time: 30 minutes

Use the bracket created in Lesson 6, Exercise 6-2.
Custom iParts allow the user to enter dimension values on the fly.

Select the iPart Author tool.

Select the first configuration.
Right click and select 'Insert Row'.

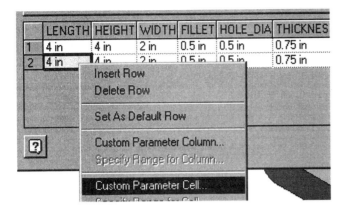

Select the lower Length cell.
Right click and select 'Custom Parameter Cell'.
Set Height, Width, Hole_Dia, and Thickness all as Custom Parameter Cells for the second configuration.

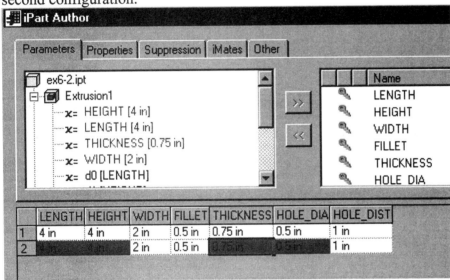

Notice that the cells defined as Custom Parameters have a different color.

Select the Suppression tab.

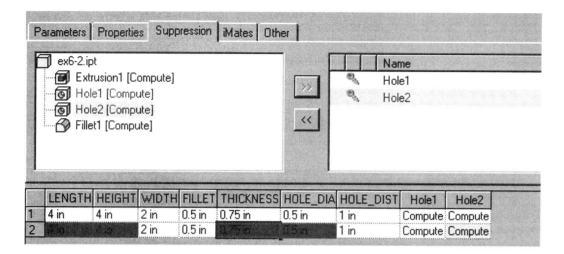

Select both hole features and move over to the selected column window.

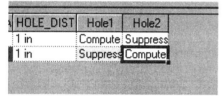

For configuration 1, edit the column for Hole2 and type 'Suppress'.
For configuration 2, edit the column for Hole1 and type 'Suppress'.

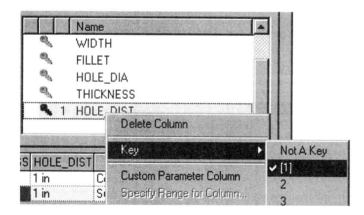

iParts require that a minimum of one parameter be identified as a Key.
Select the HOLE_DIST parameter.
Left click on the key.
The key in the window next to HOLE_DIST will darken and the number 1 will appear.

Press 'OK'.

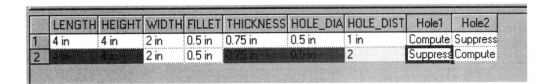

	LENGTH	HEIGHT	WIDTH	FILLET	THICKNESS	HOLE_DIA	HOLE_DIST	Hole1	Hole2
1	4 in	4 in	2 in	0.5 in	0.75 in	0.5 in	1 in	Compute	Suppress
2		4 in	2 in	0.5 in	0.75 in	0.5 in	2	Suppress	Compute

Change the values for Configuration 2:

HOLE_DIST	2

Press 'OK'.

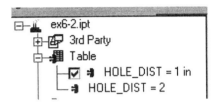

In the browser, you will see that the first configuration is active.
Activate the second configuration by double clicking on it.

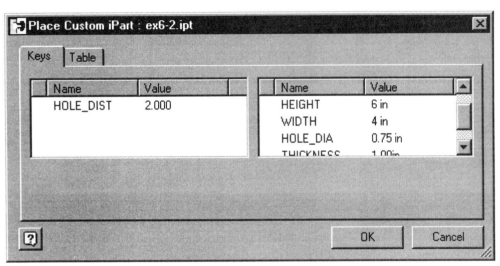

A dialog box will pop up.

Change the values as follows:

LENGTH	6
HEIGHT	6
WIDTH	4
HOLE_DIA`	0.75
THICKNESS	1.0

To modify the values, just place your mouse in the Value column and start typing.
Press 'OK'.

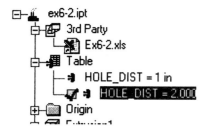

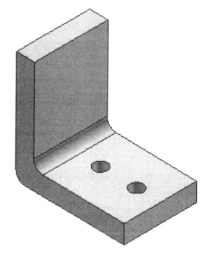

Configuration 2 activated

Save the file as Ex7-2.ipt.

QUIZ 2

T F 1.   You cannot edit the parameters in a spreadsheet from the Parameters dialog box.

T F 2.   You can not place a Derived Part and it's parent part in the same assembly drawing.

3.   The tool shown is:
   A.   Parameters
   B.   iParts
   C.   Excel
   D.   Spreadsheet

4.   Besides the Parameter dialog box, parameters can be assigned and named using:
   A.   Excel
   B.   Word
   C.   NotePad
   D.   Access

T F 5.   When you mirror a Derived Part, you must select the plane to mirror about from the browser.

T F 6.   Derived parts that are originated from an assembly cannot be mirrored or scaled.

T F 7.   If you unlink a Derived Part, you can restore the link later.

T F 8.   Surfaces have no mass or volume.

T F 9.   After creating and saving a parameters spreadsheet, it can be used in any part or assembly model.

10.   User assigned Parameter names:
   A.   Cannot have spaces or punctuation marks
   B.   Cannot be lower case
   C.   Cannot be sentence case
   D.   Can be whatever the user wants

T F 11.   A construction surface cannot be used as a sketch plane because of its irregular shape.

T F 12.   A Derived Part can be mirrored or Scaled, but not both at the same time.

T F 13.   When you add a dimension to a sketch or feature, it is automatically assigned a parameter name.

T F 14.   Parameters are case-sensitive.

T F 15.   You can use open or closed profiles to create a surface.

T F 16.   iParts must be created from scratch, not using existing parts.

T F 17.   iParts are used to create a family of parts from a single part design.

18.   Automatically assigned Parameter names follow this format:
   A.   A1, A2
   B.   d0, d1
   C.   D1, D2
   D.   dim1, dim2

T F 19.   You must perform an update on a Derived to see any changes performed on the original part.

20.   The two types of iParts are:
   A.   Assembly and Model
   B.   Standard and Custom
   C.   Standard and User-Defined
   D.   Dynamic and Static.

ANSWERS:
1)T; 2) F; 3) A; 4) A; 5) F; 6) T; 7) F; 8) T; 9) T; 10) A; 11) T; 12) F; 13) T; 14) T; 15) T; 16) F; 17) T; 18) B; 19) T; 20) B

Lesson 8
iMates

Parts and subassemblies often use the same assembly constraints when placed in an assembly. You can define constraint pairs in parts, called iMates, which tell them how to connect when inserted in an assembly. iMates are identified by symbols that show the type and state of the iMate.

When you create or modify a component, use the Create Component IMate tool on the Standard toolbar to define an iMate constraint. You define half of a constraint pair on a part. The iMate is stored in the part file, and when the component is placed in an assembly, is positioned with an iMate with the same name.

You define iMates when you create or edit a component, attaching them to critical placement features. Components that will be constrained to one another in an assembly each have one half of an iMate pair. When the components are placed in an assembly, the iMate halves know how they are supposed to fit together.

You can retain constraints during component replacement by using common iMates in both components. The components with the common iMates are not required to share geometric definitions.

You define assembly constraints when you place a component in an assembly and match its position relative to another component. A component replacement without iMates retains assembly constraints only if the existing and new components were created from a common base. Each time you use a component, you must define how it fits together with other components.

iMates are ideal for components that are used repeatedly and constrained in the same way. You define an iMate once, saving time every time you place the component. You can automatically place a single key assembly constraint when you place the component:

- Constraint names must match on the placed component and the unconsumed iMate in the assembly.
- When the two matching iMate halves join in the assembly, a single consumed iMate is created. Because the relationship is specific to two parts with matching iMate halves, multiple occurrences cannot be placed.

An iMate symbol is shown in the browser and on the components in the graphics window.

Multiple iMates are classified by rank. You should determine which is the most important constraint to place first before you define iMates.

- The first iMate created for the component is assigned the rank of primary.
- Subsequent iMates are all ranked as secondary.
- Raising a secondary iMate to primary reduces the rank of the existing primary iMate to secondary.

When the Use iMate option is checked in the Place Component dialog box, the placed component's iMate will connect to an unconsumed iMate half with the same name.

Create Component IMate defines constraint pairs called iMates to specify how parts connect when inserted in an assembly. iMates are identified by symbols that show the type and state of the iMate, and can be renamed to correspond with a matching constraint in other parts.

Multiple iMates can be defined on a single part.

The Create Component IMate tool specifies one or more constraint types, geometry, and constraint names to define iMates. The first specified constraint is the primary iMate.	
Type	Specifies the constraint type to match when the part is inserted and constrained in an assembly. Mate constraint specifies that the selected face will be positioned face to face or adjacent and flush to another face on a component with a matching iMate. Angle constraint specifies the allowed angle of the selected edge or planar face when positioned relative to another component with a matching iMate. Tangent constraint requires contact of the selected face, plane, cylinder, sphere, or cone at a tangent point on a component with a matching iMate. Insert constraint requires a face-to-face mate constraint between planar faces and a mate constraint between axes on a component with a matching iMate.
Selection	Selects the geometry on the part to constrain to an iMate on another part.
Offset or Angle	Specifies distance or angle by which the iMate halves are offset from one another.
Solution	Shows the relationship defined when the part is constrained to a matching iMate in an assembly.

Create an iMate

1. Click the Create IMate tool on the Standard toolbar.

1. In the Create Component IMate dialog box, the Mate constraint is automatically selected. Use the default or click the Angle, Tangent, or Insert button.
2. In the graphics window, select the geometry you want to use as the primary position geometry.
3. Click Apply. An iMate symbol corresponding to the selected constraint type is attached to the geometry on the part.
4. If desired, continue to select constraints and geometry for additional iMates, clicking Apply after each one.
5. Save the file.

Note: If desired, rename iMates in the browser, choosing a name to correspond with the matching iMate in another part. For example, to identify the geometry, you could rename Mate1 to Axis1 and a secondary iMate named Mate2 could be renamed Face1.

Repeat this sequence for each part that you want to constrain to this part, making sure to give matching iMates the same name.

Placing an iMate Component in an Assembly

Use the Place Component tool to insert components with matching iMates in an assembly.

You can match iMate constraints three ways:

- Use the Place Constraint tool to match constraint symbols.
- Drag the selected iMate symbol over the corresponding symbol and drop in position.
- Use the Use IMate option on the Place Constraint dialog to automatically detect and match iMates.

TIP: When using the Drag and Drop method, you will hear a SNAP sound when the two parts connect. If you want to turn off the sound cue, delete the *connect.wav* file. The default location for this file is *C:\Program Files\Autodesk\Inventor 5\Bin*.

Method 1: Using the Place Constraint to match constraint symbols

To begin, open an assembly file.

1. Click the Place Component tool on the Assembly toolbar to choose a component with one or more defined iMate constraints.
2. Browse to the folder that contains a component, select it, and click Open.
3. The selected component is placed in the graphics window, attached to the cursor. Right-click and select 'Done'.
4. Repeat to select and place additional components with defined iMates.
5. Click the Place Constraint tool on the Assembly toolbar.
6. Click an iMate symbol on a component.
7. Click a matching iMate symbol on another component, and then click Apply.

Continue to apply iMates as desired, and then click OK to close the dialog box.

Method 2: Using Drag and Drop

To begin, open an assembly file.

1. Click the Place Component tool on the Assembly toolbar to choose a component with one or more defined iMate constraints.
2. Browse to the folder that contains and component, select it, and click Open.
3. The selected component is placed in the graphics window, attached to the cursor. Right-click and select Done.
4. Repeat to select and place additional components with defined iMates.
5. Click the Place Constraint tool on the Assembly toolbar.
6. Click an iMate symbol on a component.
7. Drag the selected iMate symbol over a matching iMate symbol on another component. When the second iMate symbol is highlighted, click to position the components.
8. Click Apply to complete the constraint.

Continue to apply iMates as desired, and then click OK to close the dialog box.

TIP: During component placement, you can use the primary iMate of a placed component to automatically create an iMate constraint. The names of the iMates on both components must match.

Method 3: Using the 'Use IMate' Option

To begin, open an assembly file.

1. Click the Place Component tool on the Assembly toolbar to choose a component with one or more defined iMate constraints.
2. Browse to the folder that contains and component, and select it.
3. Select the Use IMate check box and click Open.
4. The selected component is placed in the graphics window, attached to the cursor. Right-click and select Done.
5. Repeat to select and place a second component with a defined iMate, making sure to select Use IMate on the Open dialog box.

The second component is placed and a consumed iMate symbol is shown in the browser.

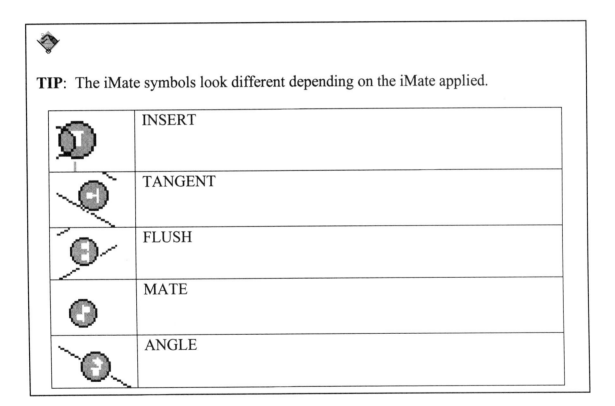

TIP: The iMate symbols look different depending on the iMate applied.

	INSERT
	TANGENT
	FLUSH
	MATE
	ANGLE

TIP: To turn off the visibility of the iMate symbol, go to View->iMate Glyph.

Exercise 8-1
Creating an iMate

Drawing Name: ex8-1.ipt (or create the part from scratch using Standard units)
Estimated Time: 15 minutes

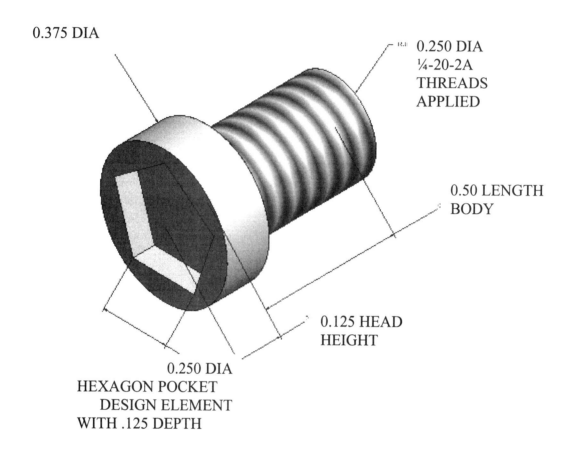

0.375 DIA

0.250 DIA
¼-20-2A
THREADS
APPLIED

0.50 LENGTH
BODY

0.125 HEAD
HEIGHT

0.250 DIA
HEXAGON POCKET
DESIGN ELEMENT
WITH .125 DEPTH

Either open the ex8-1.ipt file or create the part shown above.

Select the 'Create Component IMate' tool.

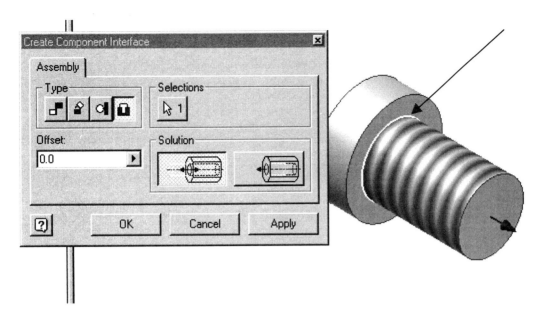

Select the Insert Constraint type.
Select the top edge of the body as shown.

Press 'Apply'.
Then close the dialog box.

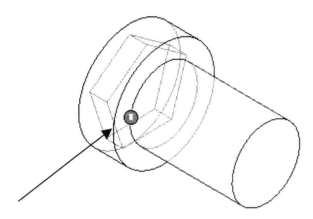

An iMate Symbol will appear on the part.

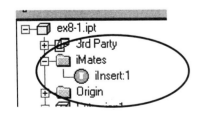

An iMate Symbol will appear in the browser.

Save the file as Ex8-2.ipt.

Exercise 8-2

Deleting an iMate

Drawing Name: ex8-2.ipt (or use the part file created in Exercise 8-1)
Estimated Time: 5 minutes

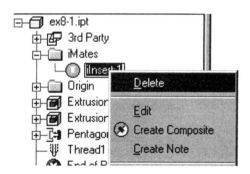

Highlight the iMate in the browser.
Right click and select 'Delete'.

Starting in R5, you have the ability to create a composite iMate.

Composite iMates

1. Create multiple single iMates in a part or assembly.
2. In the browser, click to expand the iMates folder.
3. Hold down the Ctrl key, then click each iMate you want to include in the composite iMate.
4. Right-click and select Create Composite.
5. If desired, click the composite iMate label and give it a name to describe its purpose or placement.
6. Save the file.

Note: Choose a name that corresponds with a matching composite iMate in another part or assembly. When you replace parts in an assembly that were positioned using a common composite iMate, the composite iMate automatically positions the replacement using the previously defined constraints.

Exercise 8-3
Method 1:
Using the Place Constraint to match constraint symbols

Drawing Name: Create a New assembly file using Standard (inches)
                  ex8-3a.ipt, ex8-3b.ipt (these are downloaded from
                  www.schroff1.com)
Estimated Time: 10 minutes

Open a new assembly file using Standard.

Using 'Place Component', insert ex8-3b.ipt and ex8-3a.ipt into the assembly drawing.
Place ex8-3b first, so it will be grounded.

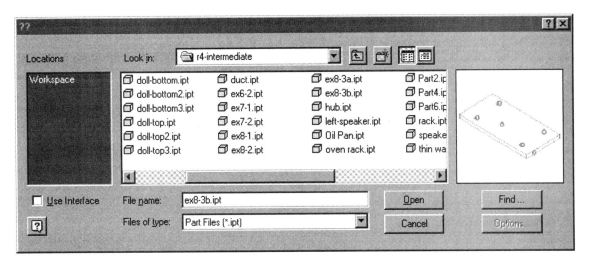

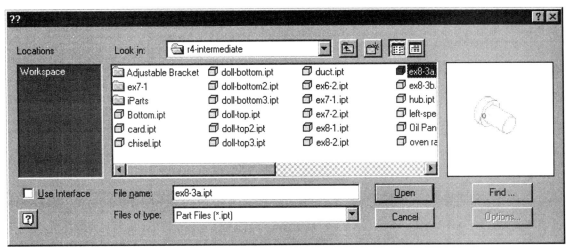

Place two instances of the fastener 8-3a.

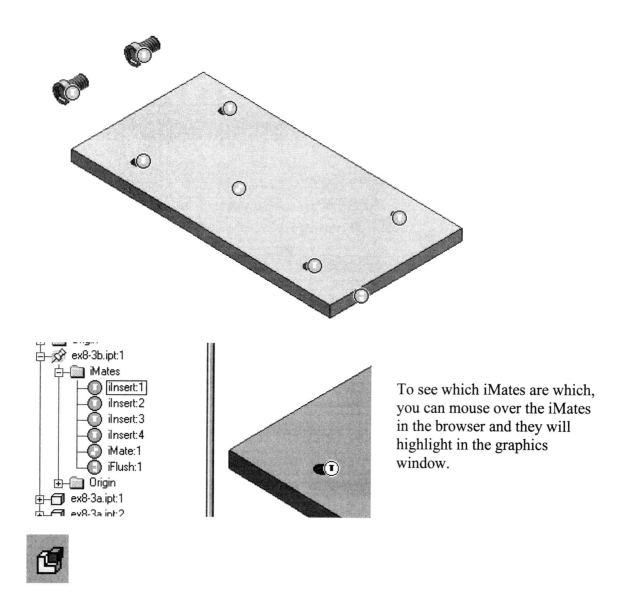

To see which iMates are which, you can mouse over the iMates in the browser and they will highlight in the graphics window.

Select the 'Place Constraint' tool.

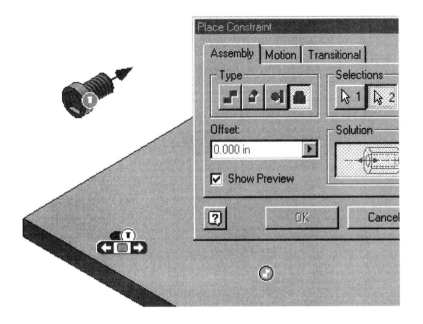

Select the type of constraint to be used – 'Insert'.
Select the 'Insert' iMate on one of the bolts.
Select the 'Insert' iMate on one of the holes in the board.
Press 'Apply'.

The bolt should pop into place.

Save as Ex8-4.iam.

TIP: To change the sound that happens when you connect two iMates:

1. Save the desired sound in the WAV format and name the file *connect.wav*.
2. Replace the default *connect.wav* file with the new file.

The default location of the *connect.wav* file is *C:\Program Files\Autodesk\Inventor 5\Bin*.

If you don't want to hear the connect sound, you can delete the connect.wav file or move it to a different location.

Exercise 8-4

Method 2: Using Drag and Drop

Drawing Name: Ex8-4.iam
Estimated Time: 10 minutes

Select the 'Place Constraint' tool.

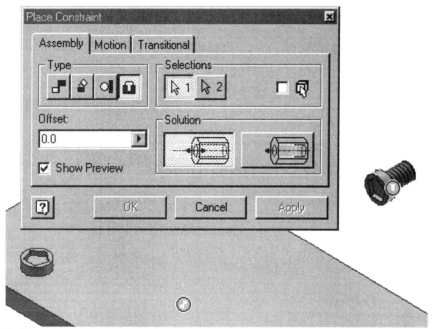

Select the Insert constraint as the type of constraint to be applied.

Select the iMate symbol on the second fastener and drag it over to an insert iMate symbol on the board. Release to place.

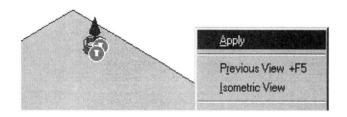

Right click and select 'Apply'.
Save as Ex8-4.iam.

Exercise 8-5

Method 3: Using the 'Use iMate' Option

Drawing Name: Create a New assembly file using Standard (inches)
ex8-3a.ipt, ex8-5b.ipt

Estimated Time: 10 minutes

Open a new assembly file using Standard.

Select 'Place Component'.

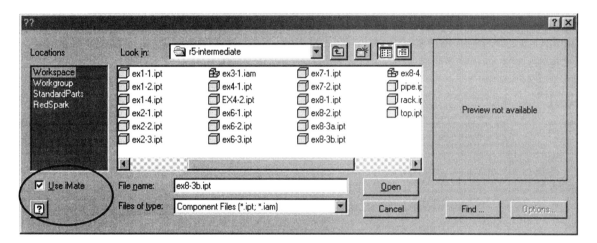

Locate the ex8-5b.ipt file. Enable 'Use IMate'.

Right click and select 'Done'.

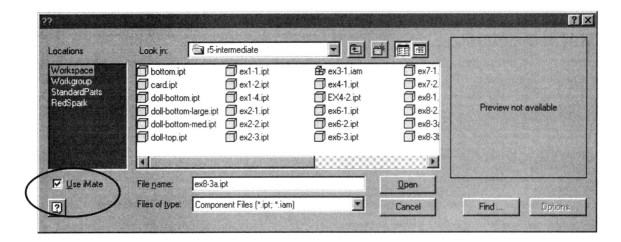

Select the Place Component tool again.
Locate the ex8-3a.ipt and select 'Open'.
Make sure the 'Use iMate' is enabled.

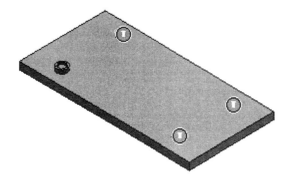

The bolt is automatically placed and your graphics window automatically zooms to the extents.

TIP: Composite iMates can only be activated by the 'Use iMate' option.

Exercise 8-6
Creating Composite iMates

File: Assembly using Standard
                         Ex8-6a.ipt
                         Ex8-6b.ipt

Estimated Time: 30 minutes

Start a New Part File using Standard.

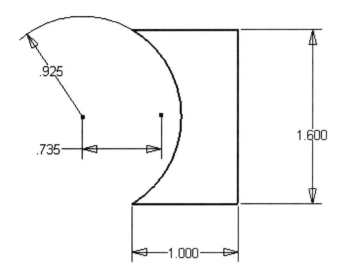

Create this sketch.

Extrude 1 inch.

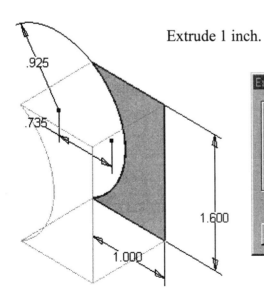

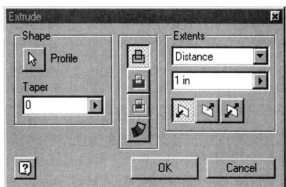

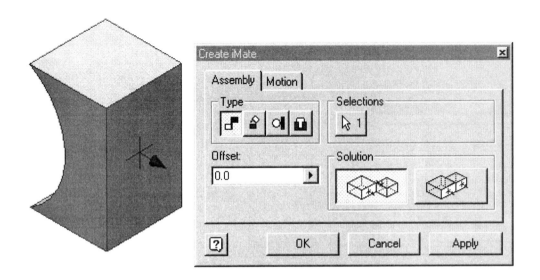

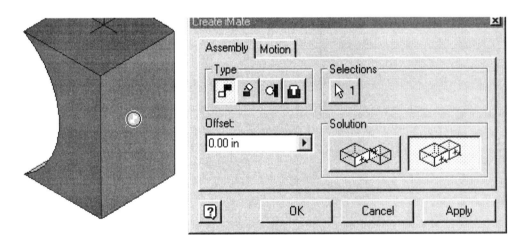

Use the iMate Offset = 0.

Place a Flush Constraint on the top with an Offset = 0.0.

Place a Flush Constraint on the curved side with an Offset = 0.0.

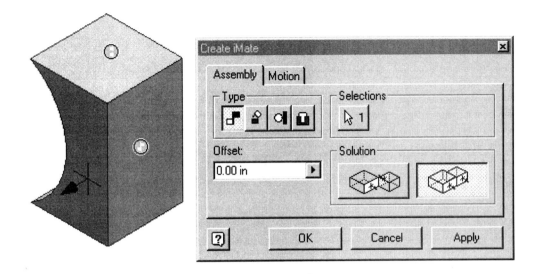

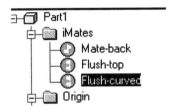

To make it easier for you to keep track of the iMates, you can rename the iMates in the Browser.

Save the file as 'Ex8-6a.ipt'.

Start a New Part file.
Exit out of Sketch Mode.

 Select the Derived Component tool from the Features toolbar.

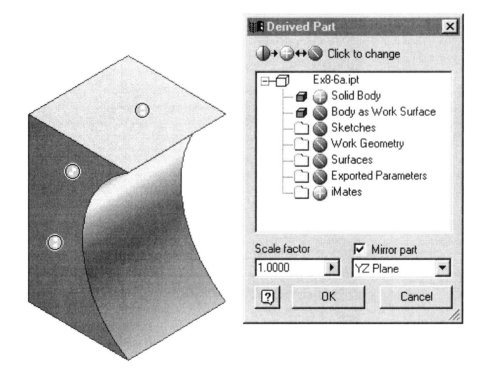

Mirror the part about the YZ Plane.

Notice that the iMates are included in the Derived Component definition.

If you highlight the iMates in the Browser, the faces defined for the iMates will highlight.
Go through the iMates so you can see how they are placed.

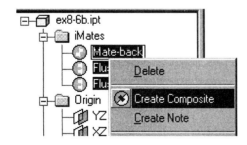

Highlight all the iMates in the Browser.
Right click and select 'Create Composite'.

Save the part as Ex8-6b.ipt.

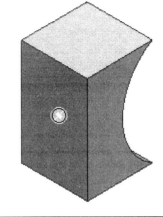

The three iMates are combined into one iMate.

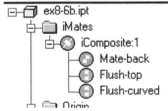

The iComposite appears in the Browser.

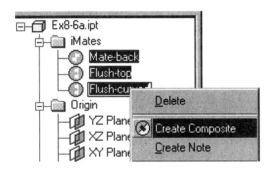

Switch to the Ex8-6a file (or open it if you closed it).
Create Composite iMate from the iMates.
Save the file.

Open an Assembly file.

 Use the Place Component tool.

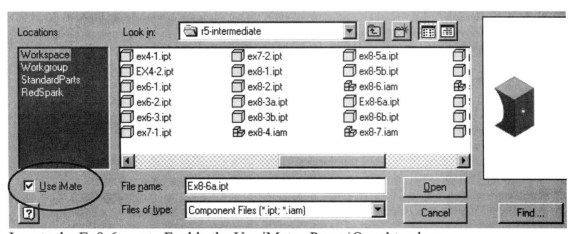

Locate the Ex8-6a part. Enable the Use iMate. Press 'Open' to place.

Place one instance of the part. Right click and select 'Done'.

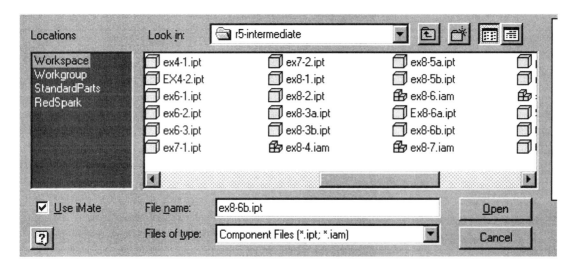

Locate the Ex8-6b.ipt part. Enable the 'Use iMate'. Press 'Open'.

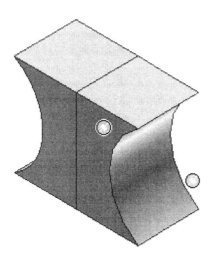

The two parts automatically mate properly.

Save the file as Ex8-6.iam.

TIP: Composite iMates do not fully support the use of Offsets for Release 5. Use Offset Distances sparingly with Composite iMates. You may get unanticipated results.

Lesson 9
Lighting, Materials, and Colors

Inventor allows user to create different Lighting, Colors and Materials using Organizer. The Organizer is located in the menu under Format.

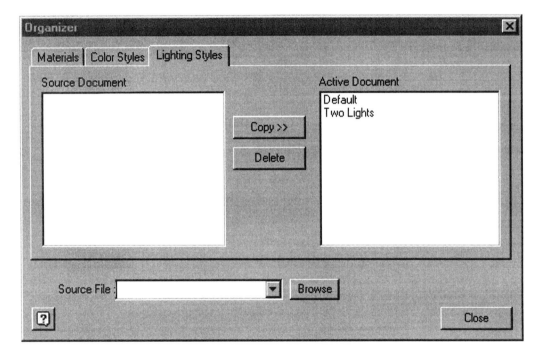

Style Organizer

The Style Organizer allows the user to copy color, lighting styles and material formats from one part, assembly, or template to another.

TIP: Lighting, Colors, and Materials are stored in each drawing. This can be annoying if you need to search for a color or material you like. Instead, store your favorite colors and materials in the standard templates. Then, they will always be available for you. But, remember – save a backup copy in case you need to reinstall or upgrade Inventor!

Lighting Styles

To create a new lighting style, use Format->Lighting.

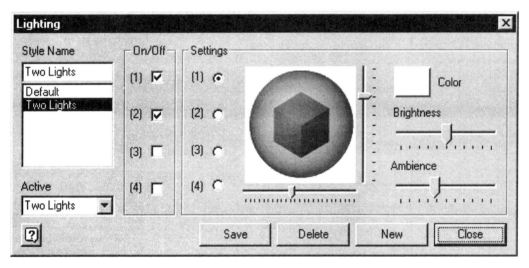

The Lighting dialog creates lighting styles and specifies the lighting attributes of each style. Lighting styles interact with color styles to control the online display of color in part and assembly.

Style Name lists the lighting styles in the active part or assembly model file or template file. To edit a style, select it in the list and change its attributes. To add a new style, click the 'New' button and enter the name of the new style in the box.

The Active Drop-down specifies the active lighting style for the model. To change the lighting style, click the arrow and select another style from the list.

On/Off specifies which settings to use. Select the check box to use a setting; clear the check box to suppress it. When multiple settings are selected, their effects are combined.

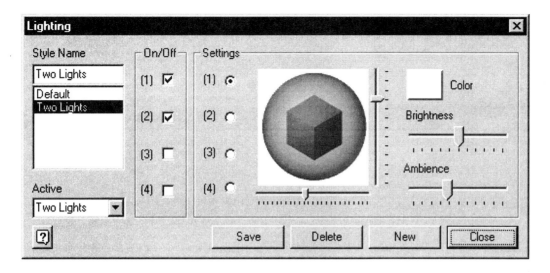

Setting sets the lighting effects for the selected style. You can define a single setting or multiple settings to use for each style. To define a setting, select its number and then make the changes. The effects of changes are shown in the view box.

	Sets the position of the light source for the selected setting. Move the vertical and horizontal sliders to specify the position.
Color	Sets the color of the light source for the selected setting. Click the color pad and select the color from the dialog box.

Brightness sets the intensity of all the directed light sources. Use the slider to increase or decrease the intensity.

TIP: To change the brightness of a single light setting, change its color.

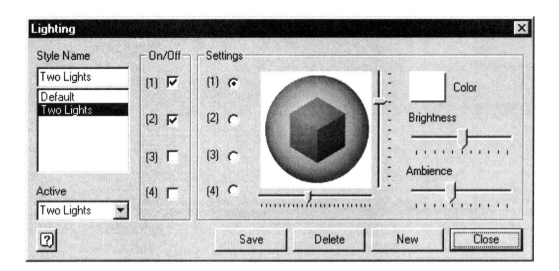

Ambience sets the level of ambient light in the scene, controlling the level of contrast between the lighted and unlighted areas of a face. Move the slider left to increase the contrast; move it right to decrease the contrast.

Material Styles

To create or modify a material, use Format->Materials.

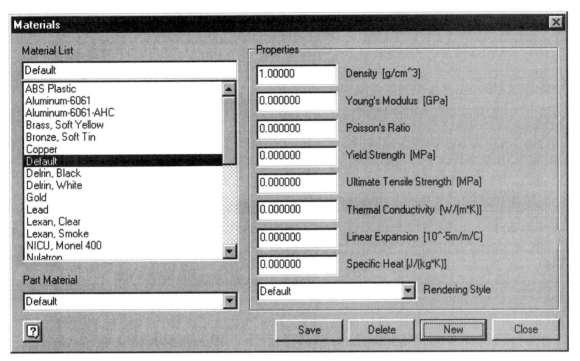

The Materials dialog creates material formats and specifies the physical characteristics of each material. Material formats control the physical properties of parts.

Material List	Lists the material formats in the active part or template file. To edit a format, select it in the list and change its properties. To add a new style, click the New button and enter the name of the new format in the box.
Part Material	Specifies the material currently applied to the model. To change the material, click the arrow and select another material from the list.
Properties	Specifies the thermo-physical and deformation attributes of the selected material. Material properties are used to calculate the physical properties of the model such as mass moments of inertia. When creating a custom material, enter metric values for the applicable properties.

Click to show the definition of a property, its units, and the commonly used symbol.

TIP: Material Styles can only be created inside part files.

You can create material formats and use them to calculate the physical properties of a part.

1. Select Format>Materials.
2. In the Materials dialog box, add, edit, or delete a color style.
    o   To add a material, click the 'New' button, enter the material name, and then set the material properties.
    o   To edit an existing material format, select it in the list and then set the material properties.
    o   To delete a material, select it in the list and then click the Delete button.
3. Click the Save button to save changes after adding or editing a material.
4. To select the material for a part, click the arrow next to the Part Material box and select the material from the list.

TIP: All Material Styles use metric units. The units are automatically converted for you when you are in a Standard (inches) part.

Sheet Metal Bend Tables

When you select Bend Table as the unfolding method in the Sheet Metal Settings dialog box, the flat pattern analyzer uses the bend table to create the flat pattern. A bend table contains the bend allowance for the specified material thickness at specific bend radii and bend angles. If the bend angle or bend radius is not in the table, the flat pattern analyzer interpolates to determine the correct value.

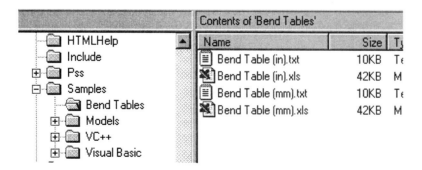

Autodesk Inventor provides a sample bend table in a spreadsheet. The sample bend tables are located in the Samples subdirectory under Inventor. You can use it to create a table for each material type and store multiple bend tables in one file.

To set up a bend table file

Using the sample bend table, you specify units of measure, and tolerances.

1. Browse to the sample bend table spreadsheet in the \Autodesk\Inventor\Samples directory and double-click to open.
2. Enter units of measure. Scroll to the line that starts with /U and enter units of measure. The default is cm.
3. Enter tolerances. Scroll to the lines that starts with /T and enter the following:
    o On line /T1, enter the +/- tolerance for sheet thickness.
    o On line /T2, enter the equal minimum and maximum bending radius.
    o On line /T3, enter the tolerance for equal minimum and maximum opening angle.

    Note: Tolerances 2 and 3 are used only under special conditions, as noted in the table.

4. Select File>Save A. Give the spreadsheet a new name, and click OK.

Use the bend table file with your units of measure and tolerances to create a bend table for each material thickness.

To begin, browse to the bend table file and double-click to open.

1. Enter sheet thickness. Scroll to the line that starts with /S and enter thickness.
2. Enter bend radii. Scroll to the line that starts with /R and enter radii.
3. Edit the equation used to calculate the bend allowance, as necessary.

    Note: All cells in the sample bend table use the same equation, but you can customize the equation for individual cells.

4. Highlight the table, and then press Ctrl+C to copy. Scroll down to an empty area of the spreadsheet and then press Ctrl+V to paste.
5. Rename the table and reset the material thickness, as needed.
6. Continue to copy and paste the table, renaming it and setting a new material thickness, as desired.
7. Select File>Save As. Select *.txt file type, and then click OK.

TIP: It is important to save the spreadsheet in a text (.txt) file type. The text format is used by the analyzer to calculate bends.

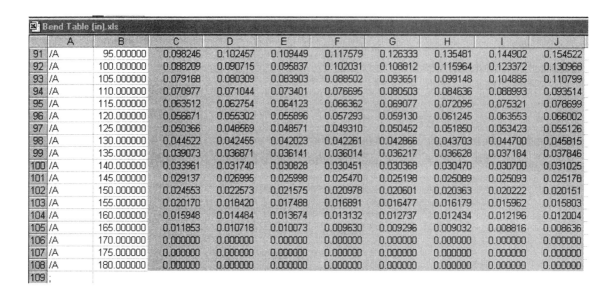

TIP: You don't have to maintain a link between the part file and the bend table.

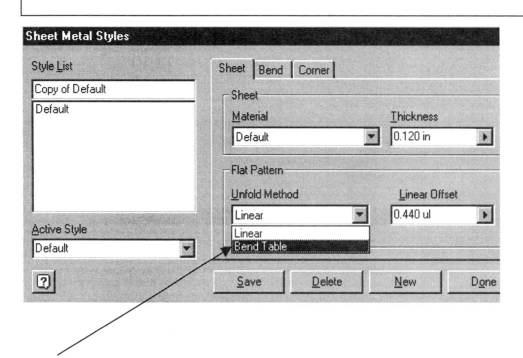

To select a Bend Table, select 'Bend Table' under the Unfold Method in the Sheet Metal Styles dialog box.

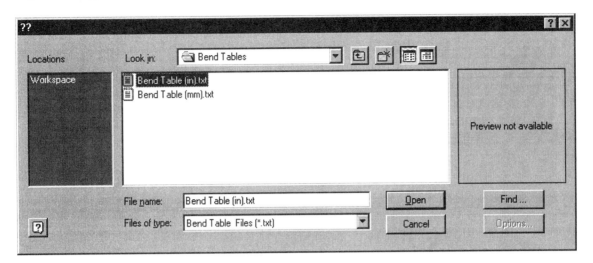

Locate the Bend Table.txt file you want.
Press 'Open'.

The Bend Table settings in the text file are now available to you.

Exercise 9-1:
Importing Materials

Drawing Name: Start a new part using Standard (inches)
Download ceramics.zip from www.schroff1.com/inventor.
Extract the ceramics.ipt file

Estimated time: 30 minutes

Start a new part file.

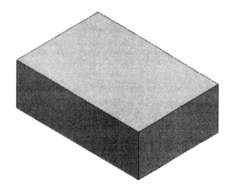

Create a basic block piece 4 x 6 x 2.

Go to Format->Organizer.

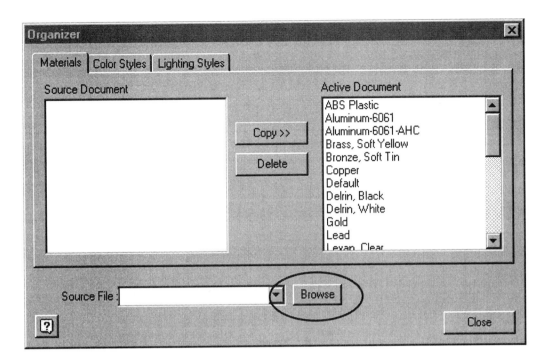

Press the Browse button.

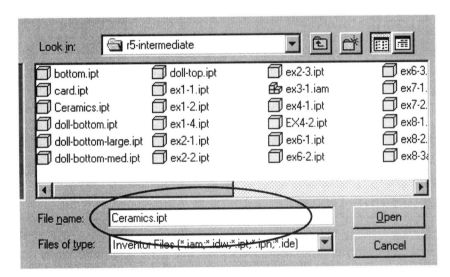

Locate the ceramics.ipt file.

Press 'Open'.

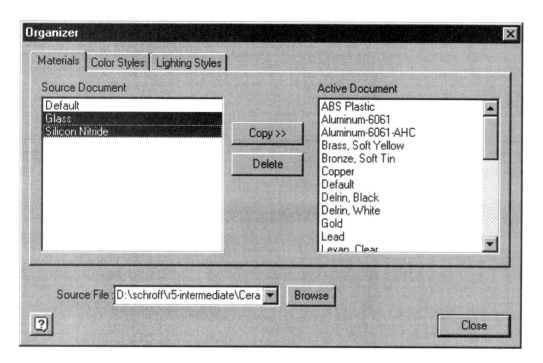

There are two materials in the ceramics.ipt file that are not in the active document.
They are Glass and Silicon Nitride.
Highlight both materials and select 'Copy'.
Press 'Close'.

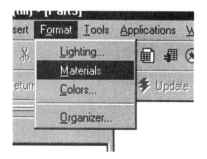

Select Format->Materials.

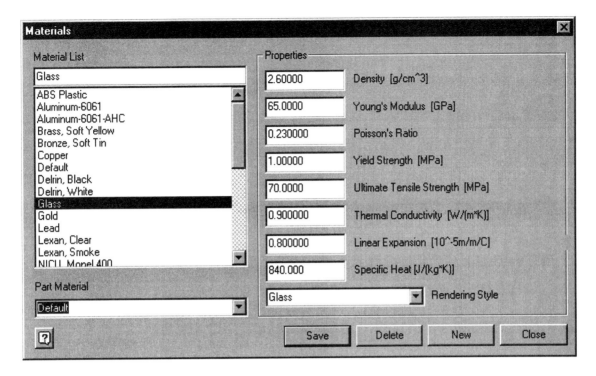

See how the Glass Properties were set up from the ceramics.ipt file.

Apply the Glass material to the block you created.

Save the file as Ex9-1.ipt.

Exercise 9-2:
Creating Materials

Drawing Name: Start a new part using Standard (inches)
Estimated time: 10 minutes

TIP: A good source for material information is http://www.matls.com/

We'll create a material definition for AISI 4130 Steel.

Open a new part file.

Go to Format->Materials.

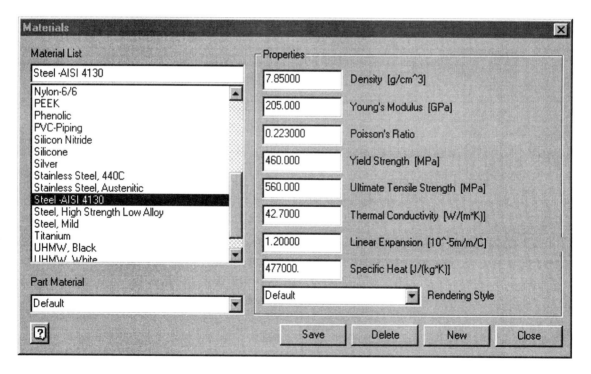

Press 'New'.
In the Material List, type over where it says Copy Of and enter Steel-AISI 4130.
Enter in the properties as shown in the dialog.
Press 'Save'.

Color Styles

To create a new color, use Format->Colors.

The Colors dialog creates color styles and specifies the color attributes of each style. Color styles interact with lighting styles to control the online display of color in part and assembly files.

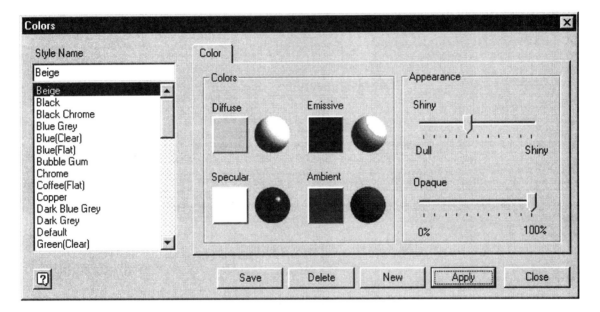

Style Name lists the color styles in the active part or assembly model file or template file. To edit a style, select it in the list and change its attributes. To add a new style, click the 'New' button and enter the name of the new style in the box.

Colors sets the color effect for the four reflective qualities of a face. To set the color used to render a reflective quality, click its color pad and select the color from the dialog box. To eliminate the effect of any of the reflective qualities, set its color to black.	
Diffuse	Controls the color of a face in response to directed light.
Emissive	Sets overall color, as it would appear if the part contained the light source. The result is similar to that of placing a light bulb inside the part to glow through the color. Emissive color does not interact with lighting styles.
Specular	Sets the color of the reflection from an external light source. To control the reflective intensity of the specular effect, set the Shiny quality.
Ambient	Sets overall color as it would appear with an even, indirect light source. The visible surface has a matte finish with no reflective effect. Controls the darkness of the unlighted sides of parts.
Appearance sets surface characteristics that interact with color.	
Shiny	Sets the level of reflective effect for the specified specular color.
Opaque	Sets the level of opacity for the color style. Move the slider toward 0% for more translucence or 100% for greater opacity.

Exercise 9-3:
Creating a Color

Drawing Name: Start a new part using Standard (inches)
Estimated time: 10 minutes

Go to Format->Colors

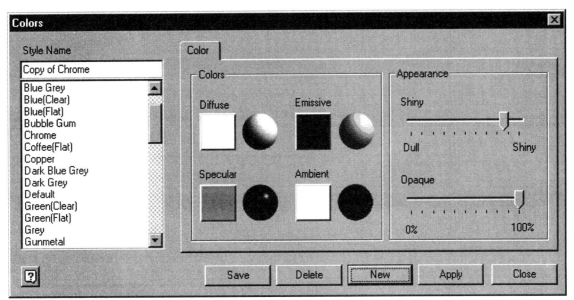

Highlight the Chrome color and press the New button.

Change the Style Name to Steel Chrome

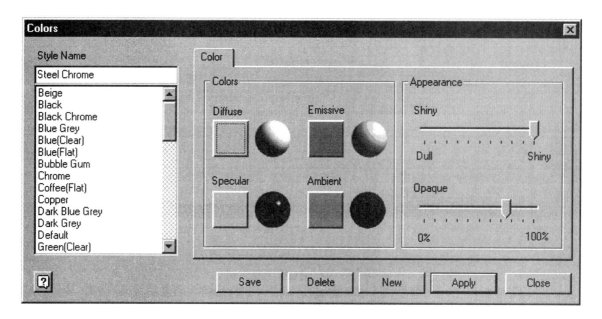

Experiment with different settings on Colors and Appearance.
Press 'Apply', 'Save', and 'Close'.

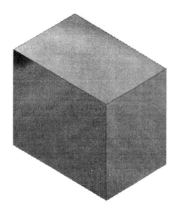

Create a block object to test the color.

To adjust the color, return to Format->Colors. Select the Steel Chrome and modify.

Save the file as Ex9-3.ipt.

Quiz 3

T F 1.   The order iMates are placed is also the order in which constraint can be applied.

T F 2.   You can control the visibility of iMate Symbols.

T F 3.   Once you place an iMate, you cannot delete it.

4.   Bend tables must be saved in the following file type:

    A.   *.xls
    B.   *.doc
    C.   *.cdf
    D.   *.txt

5.   Select the method of matching iMates that is NOT valid.

    A.   Use the Place Constraint tool to match constraint symbols
    B.   Hold down the Control key, select the mating features, right click and select iMate from the menu
    C.   Drag the selected iMate symbol over the corresponding symbol and drop in position.
    D.   Use the Use Interface option on the Place Constraint dialog to automatically detect and match iMates.

T F 6.   Material Styles can be defined using metric or standard units.

T F 7.   To change the brightness of a single light setting, change it's color.

8.   To create a new color, use this menu:

    A.   Create->Colors
    B.   Format->Colors
    C.   Tools->Colors
    D.   View->Colors

9.   The menu header to select to define new lighting is:

    A.   View
    B.   Format
    C.   Modify
    D.   Edit

T F 10.   The Style Organizer allows the user to copy color, lighting styles, and materials from one part file to another part file.

T F 11.   When using iMates, constraint names must match on the placed component and the unconsumed iMate in the assembly.

T F 12.   Material Styles can only be created inside presentation files.

13.   Identify the tool:

    A.   Create iMate
    B.   Create Interface
    C.   Create iPart
    D.   Rotate

T F 14.   When you place an iMate on a part, an iMate symbol will appear on the part indicating the type of assembly constraint added.

T F 15.   iMates can be combined to form composite assembly mates.

T F 16.   Composite iMates can only be accessed using the 'Drag and Drop' assembly method.

ANSWERS:
1) T; 2) F; 3) F; 4) D; 5) B; 6) F; 7) T; 8) B; 9) B; 10) T; 11) T; 12) F; 13) B; 14) T; 15) T; 16) F

Lesson 10
Engineer's Notebook

The Engineer's Notebook gives you the ability to create notes and store them as part of a model. A note can be attached to an edge, sketch, feature, part, or other selection in the model. Each note consists of a comment box and a view of the model.

When you add the first note to a model, a notebook is created. You can add comment boxes or additional views to a note or add more notes to the notebook.

The Engineer's Notebook can be used to save the history of development or to provide reminders for project designers. Notes might include design strategy, reason for a design decision, manufacturing instructions, or information from a test or FEA calculation. Notes can contain links to external files, such as spreadsheets, word processing documents, graphics, or audio files.

In the Engineer's Notebook browser, each note is assigned a name and listed in the order in which it was created. You can organize the notes as follows:

- Rename notes to provide a more meaningful label.
- Change the sort order of the notes to sort by name, author, date, or text.
- Drag individual notes to change the order.
- Create additional folders and move notes into them. You can also specify a folder as the destination for all new notes.

If you are using the Engineer's Notebook to maintain the history of a design, you can use several options to assure an accurate record.

Ordinarily, a note is deleted when the geometry to which it is attached is deleted. To maintain an accurate history, set the option to keep notes attached to deleted geometry

When you create a note, the note view captures the current state of the model. As you make changes to the model, the view in the note updates automatically. To keep it from updating, you can freeze a view in the note. The view and its comment then serve as a historical record.

TIP: If you remove the Freeze designation from a note view, it updates to reflect the current model.

As you add notes to a part model, each note is listed in the part browser under the item to which it is attached. For example, if the note is attached to a feature, it is nested under that feature in the browser. Notes attached to edges or other items that are not listed in the part browser are listed at the end of the part.

When an existing component is added to an assembly, any notes that are part of the component are listed in the assembly browser under the components to which they are attached. You can also add notes to the assembly.

- If you add a note to an assembly, or add a note to an assembly component in the assembly environment, the note is stored in the assembly file, and does not display in the part browser or the Engineer's Notebook when the part file is open.
- If you add a note to an assembly component that is activated in place in the assembly, the note is stored in the component file and displays in the part browser and the Engineer's Notebook when the component file is open, as well as in the assembly file.
- When you add a note at the assembly level, a folder is created in the Engineer's Notebook browser for each component in the assembly. Any note that was attached when a component was added is listed in the folder for that component in the Engineer's Notebook browser. Notes added to the assembly are listed in the main folder. If you double-click a note in a component folder, the Engineer's Notebook for that component opens.

Notes in assemblies can be organized in the same ways as notes in parts; however, you cannot move a note in a component folder out of its folder.

When the Engineer's Notebook for a part or assembly is active, the Engineer's Notebook toolbars are available.

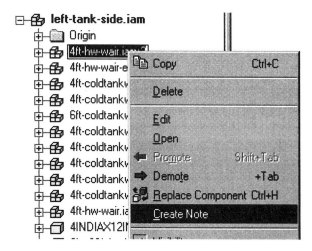

To add a note to a part in an assembly, highlight the part, right click and select 'Create Note'.

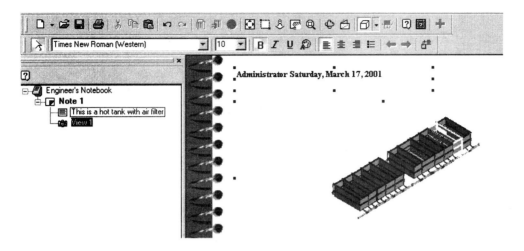

The Notebook will open. A screen capture will automatically be included with the note.

Enter the note in the comment box on the notebook page.

You can change the layout of a note in the Engineer's Notebook, add comments, views, or arrows to the note, format the text in a comment box, or change the view in a view box.

- To move a comment box or view box, drag it to the desired location.
- To change the size of a comment box or view box without changing the shape, drag a corner of the box to create the desired size.
- To change the shape of a comment box or view box, drag one side of the box to create the desired shape.

TIP: When you change the size of a comment box, the text adjusts to the width of the box. You cannot change the height of a comment box to be less than that needed to display the text. When you change the size of a view box, the view is scaled to fit in the box.

You can add comment boxes, view boxes, or arrows to a note. To add an element to a note, right-click on the notebook page (not in a comment box or view box) and select the desired element from the menu.

- To add a comment box, select Insert Comment from the menu. Click to place the top left and bottom right corners of the box.
- To add a view box, select Insert View from the menu. Click to place the top left and bottom right corners of the box.
- To add an arrow, select Insert Arrow from the menu. Click to place the points for the arrowhead and leader line. Right-click and select 'Done' to complete the operation.

To apply formatting to text in a comment box, select the desired text and use the options on the Text toolbar to change the font or color of the text or to apply bold, italics, or underlining.

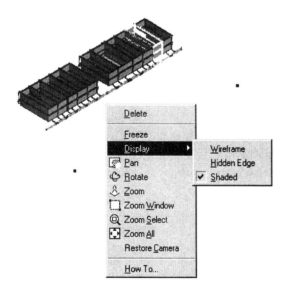

You can change size, orientation, or display style of any view in a note.

1. Right-click in the view box and select one of the view tools from the menu.
2. Manipulate the image until the desired view is displayed.
3. Click the corresponding view button on the toolbar to close the view tool.

If you select 'Freeze' from the view menu, the view will no longer update when you change the model. To update the view, clear the Freeze check mark.

As you add notes, each one is assigned a name and listed in the Engineer's Notebook browser in the order in which it was created.

Adding an Arrow to Notes

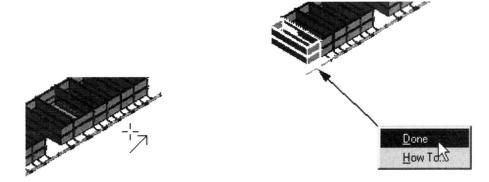

To add an arrow, you can use either Insert->Arrow from the menu or the Arrow tool from the Notebook toolbar.

Select the start point of the arrow and then select the end point.
Right click and select 'Done'.

Rename a Note

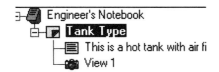

1. Click the note name in the browser to select it.
2. Click the name again to activate the edit box.
3. Enter the new name.

You can also change the name of a folder, comment, or view.

Arrange Notes

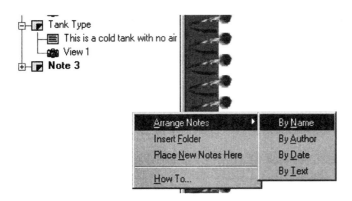

1. Click in the open area of the browser to cancel any selections.
2. Right-click and select Arrange Notes from the menu.
3. Select the sort method (by Name, Author, Date, or Text).

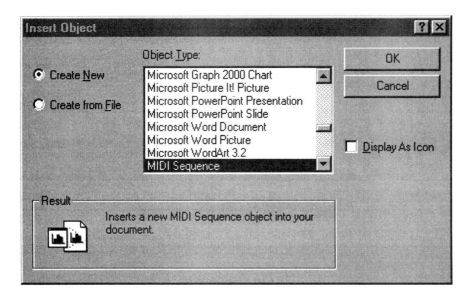

Insert Object into Notebook

You can insert a midi file or any other object into your notebook by select Insert->Object under the menu. Select the object type and then 'OK'.

TIP: A midi file allows you to record a voice memo and then play it back. You must have a microphone, speaker and sound card for this to work properly.

The Notebook Toolbar

![Select icon]	Select	
Times New Roman (Western) ▼	Font Drop-Down	
10 ▼	Font Height Drop-Down	
B	Bold text	
I	Italic text	
U	Underline text	
(color icon)	Text Color	
(icon)	Left Justify	
(icon)	Center Justify	
(icon)	Right Justify	
(icon)	Bullets	
⇐	Go to Previous Note	
⇒	Go to Next Note	
(icon)	Add an arrow to a note	

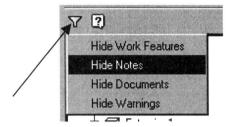

If you select the Filter button over the Browser, you can elect to Hide Notes.

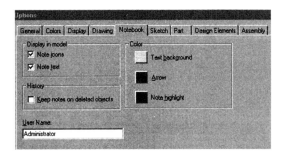

The Notebook tab under the Options dialog controls the colors of Notebook and how they are displayed. Access the Options dialog under the Tools menu.

Display in Model sets the display of note indicators in the model.	
Note Icons	Displays note icons in the model. Select the check box to display design note to display icons in the graphics window. Clear the check box to suppress the display of an icon. Note: If you attach multiple notes to a single item, only the first note displays a symbol.
Note Text	Displays note text in pop-up windows in the model. Select the check box to display the text of a design note when the cursor pauses over a note symbol. Clear the check box to suppress the display of note text.

Sets archival options for design notes.	
Keep Notes On Deleted Objects	Retains notes attached to deleted geometry. Select the check box to save notes attached to geometry that is deleted. Clear the check box to delete notes when associated geometry is deleted.

Color sets the colors of elements in design notes. The color pad next to each item shows the current color setting. To change the color for an item, click the color pad to open the color dialog box and select the color.	
Text Background	Sets the background color for the comment boxes in design notes.
Arrow	Sets the color for arrows in design notes.
Note Highlight	Sets the color for the highlighted component in note views.

User Name sets the default information that is included in a design note.	
Name	Sets the name to include in design note comments. Enter the name. Note: Changing the user name affects only those notes created after the change is made. You cannot change a name on an existing note.

Exercise 10-1

Creating an Engineering Note

File: ex6-2.ipt
Estimated Time: 30 minutes

Open the file ex6-2.ipt created in Lesson 6.

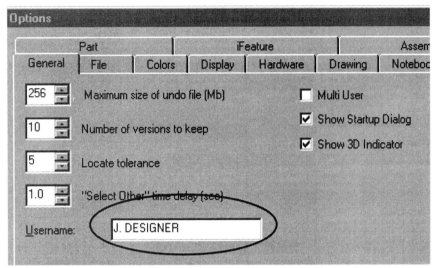

Go to Tools->Application Options.
Go to the General Tab.
Change the User Name to your name. Press 'Apply' and OK.

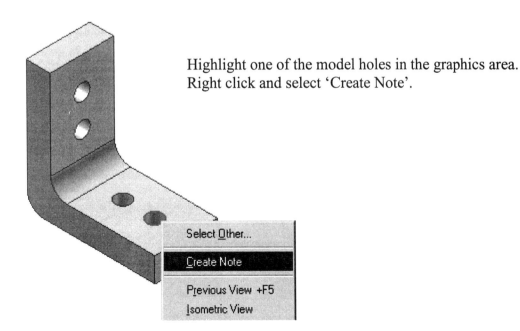

Highlight one of the model holes in the graphics area.
Right click and select 'Create Note'.

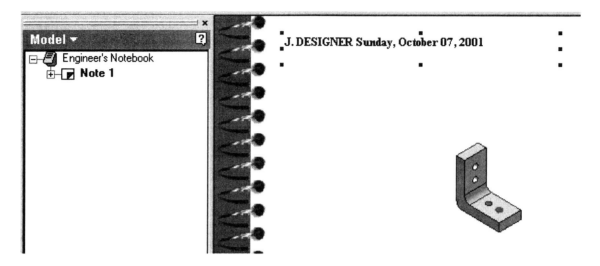

The Engineer's Notebook is launched.
Note that the User Name you just input is reflected in the header.

 Select the Arrow tool.

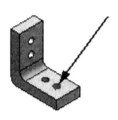

Draw the arrow.
The arrowhead is located at the first point selected.
Right click and select 'Done'.

J. DESIGNER Sunday, October 07, 2001
These holes should be replaced by a single slot.

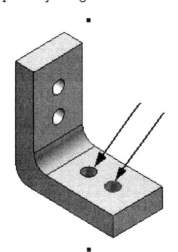

Place your mouse in the comment box.
Add the comment.

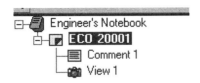

In the browser, change the name of the note to ECO 20001.

Close the notebook.

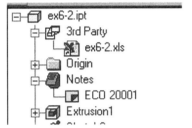

In the browser, we see the Notes we have added.

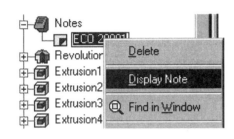

Highlight the line that says ECO 20001.
Right click and select 'Display Note'.
The Engineer's Notebook will re-open.

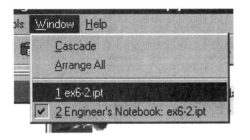

Go to Window and see that we can switch our graphics window between the part file and the Engineer's Notebook.
Switch back to the part file.

Change the model view to wire frame.

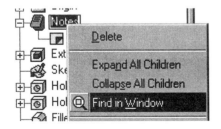

Highlight the Notebook comment in the browser.
Right click and select 'Find in Window'.
Your screen will zoom in to locate the note.

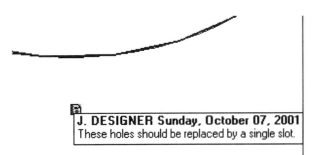

Mouse over the Note icon.
You will then see the note created.

Save the file as ex10-1 it will be used in Lesson 11.

Lesson 11
Design Assistant

Design Assistant is a tool that can help you find, track, and maintain your Autodesk Inventor files and related word processing, spreadsheet, or text files. You can perform searches based on the relationships between files, create file reports, and work with the links between Autodesk Inventor files.

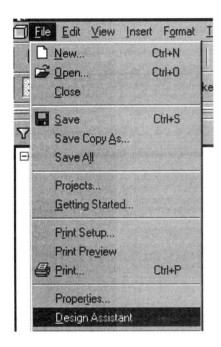

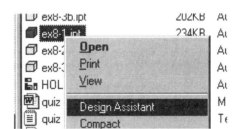

You can open Design Assistant from Autodesk Inventor or from Microsoft ® Windows Explorer.

Using Design Assistant Inside an Inventor file

Open Design Assistant from Autodesk Inventor to work with the properties of files that are currently open in Autodesk Inventor. You cannot work with linkage relationships between files.

Design Assistant opens with the active file and its referenced files displayed in the Properties mode browser. You cannot work with files other than those you used to open Design Assistant.

When you make changes to properties of a file that is open in Autodesk Inventor, you must save the file to incorporate the changes into the file.

Using Design Assistant from Explorer

Microsoft ® Windows Explorer gives the user the ability to work with many different files or groups of files, or to work with the links between files. You can work with the displayed files, and then use the available options to locate and work with other groups of files.

Design Assistant opens with the selected files displayed in the browser of the active mode.

- Use the Properties mode to work with the properties of the selected files. When you make changes to properties, they are saved automatically.

  Use the Manage mode to work with linkage relationships between Autodesk Inventor files. Changes to links between files are not saved until you click the Save button.

TIP: If you open Design Assistant from Microsoft ® Windows Explorer and change the properties of a file that is open in Autodesk Inventor, there is a risk that you will lose unsaved changes to properties. Always save an open Autodesk Inventor file before using Design Assistant to change its properties.

Every Autodesk Inventor file contains a set of design properties that you can use in a variety of ways. Some properties, such as author and creation date, are set automatically when a file is created. You must specifically set other properties, such as cost center, manager, or status.

Some Design Assistant search options use design properties to find files. You can also use Design Assistant to set design properties and copy design properties from one file to another.

Using Design Assistant to Copy Design Properties

You can use Design Assistant to copy specified design properties from one file to another file or group of files. The available options are determined by the method used to open Design Assistant.

Copy Design Properties is an excellent tool when you have several drawings affected by the same ECO or several drawings rolling to the same revision level (such as when a design package is being released).

Set the properties of one file with the ECO Number or Revision Level and then Use Copy Design Properties to update all the files.

Exercise 11-1:

Copy Design Properties

File:	New using Standard
	Ex6-1.ipt
Estimated Time:	10 minutes

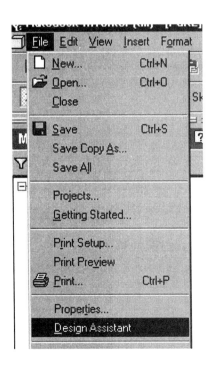

Open a new part file.
Exit the Sketch mode.
Open ex6-1.ipt.
Make ex6-1.ipt your current drawing.

Go to File->Design Assistant.

Go to Tools->Copy Design Properties

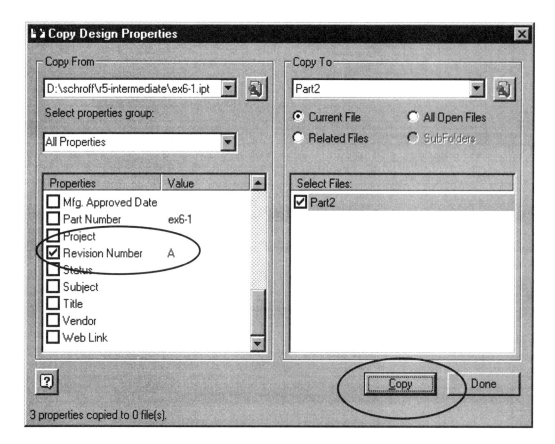

Set Copy From to ex6-1.ipt.
Set Copy to Part 2
Put a Check Mark next to the Revision Number under Properties.
Place a Check Mark next to Part2 under Select Files
Press Copy.

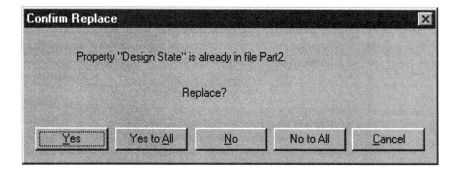

The next dialog box appears. Press 'Yes To All'.

Then press 'Done'.

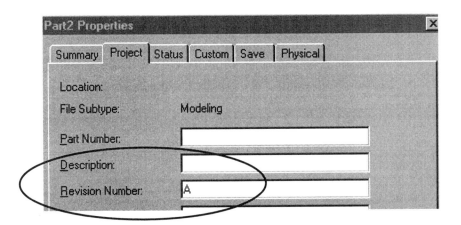

Switch to Part2.
Go to File->Properties.
Select the Project tab.

Note that the Revision
Number was
automatically copied
over.

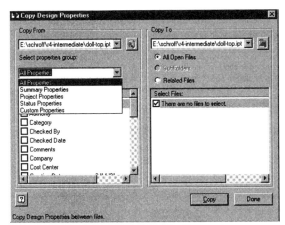    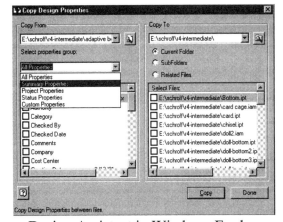

Design Assistant in Inventor   Design Assistant in Windows Explorer

Copy From specifies the source file for the properties.	
<ul><li>If you opened Design Assistant from Autodesk Inventor, the box contains the active file, and its properties are shown in the Properties list.</li><li>If you opened Design Assistant from Windows Explorer, click the arrow and select from the list of files in the active folder or click the Browse button to find the file.</li></ul>	
Select Properties Group	Specifies the group of properties to display in the Properties list. Click the arrow and select from the list.
Properties	Specifies the property values to copy. Select a check box to add a property to the set of properties to copy; clear a check box to remove the property from the set. The properties in the list are determined by the entry in the Select Properties Group box.
Copy To selects the destination folder or file.	
<ul><li>If you opened Design Assistant from Autodesk Inventor, click the arrow and select from the list of active files.</li></ul>	

	• If you opened Design Assistant from Microsoft ® Windows Explorer, click the Browse button to search for the folder or file.

All Open Files	Copies the specified properties to all of the files currently displayed in the Design Assistant window. Available only if Design Assistant was opened from an Autodesk Inventor session.
Current Folder	Copies the specified properties to all of the files in the destination folder. Available only if Design Assistant was opened from Windows Explorer.
Subfolders	Adds the files in the current folder and its subfolders to the Select Files list. Available only if Design Assistant was opened from Windows Explorer.
Related Files	Copies the specified properties to the files that are referenced in the destination file.
Select Files	Selects specific files as destination files. If the selection in Copy To is a folder, the list includes the files in the folder. If the selection in Copy To is a file, the files in the list are the files that it references. Select a check box to include a file in the destination files; clear a check box to exclude a file.

The Design Assistant Properties mode helps find, track, maintain, and report on your Autodesk Inventor files, using design properties as the key to the files. You can also work with other files, such as word processing or spreadsheet documents, that are referenced by Autodesk Inventor files.

The Properties mode browser contains two sections:

The left section of the Properties mode browser shows the folders and files available to the active Design Assistant session. If you initiated the session from within Autodesk Inventor, you cannot work with other files. If you initiated the session from Microsoft ® Windows Explorer, you can select File>Open from the menu to load other folders or files.

- When you select a folder in the list, the files within the folder are displayed in the right section of the browser.
- When you select a file in the list, all referenced files are displayed in the right section of the browser. For example, if the file is an assembly, all the component files are listed.

The right section of the Properties mode browser shows the files with which you are working and the specified properties for each file.

- To change the properties that display in the browser or print on reports, select View>Customize.
- To create a report, select Tools>Reports and choose the report type.
- To copy properties from a file to another file or group of files, select Tools>Copy Design Properties.
- To Find files, select Tools>Find and choose the search method.

Modes in Design Assistant

There are two modes in Design Assistant: Properties and Manage.

Left click on the Properties tool.

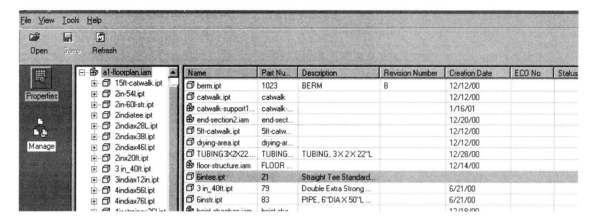

You will see a view of all the files in the assembly selected and their properties.

Now, select the Manage tool.

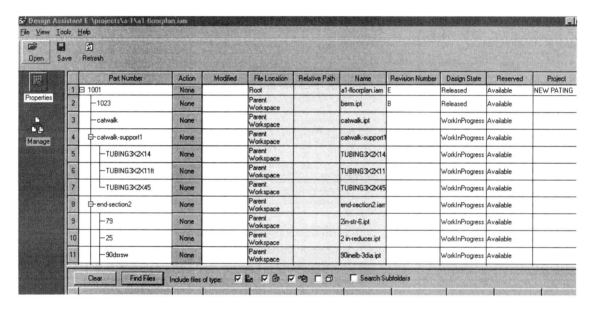

Now you get a Drawing Tree view of the assembly.

Reports from Design Assistant

Design Assistant gives the user the ability to create two reports:
- Hierarchy
- Properties

Hierarchy Reports

A Hierarchy Report creates a report that shows the hierarchy within the selected folder or assembly. If the selected item is a folder, the report shows the subfolders that it contains. If the selected item is an assembly file, the report shows the paths for the files referenced by the assembly.	
Expand Hierarchy to Level	Specifies the number of levels that the report will show. Click the arrow and select from the list.
Next	Opens the Report Location dialog box so that you can specify the path and file name for the report.

A hierarchy report is an excellent way to get the information needed to create a drawing tree or "where-used" list.

Exercise 11- 2:
Hierarchy Reports

File:	engine.iam (this is a sample file that is included with Inventor R5 from Autodesk.)
Estimated Time:	10 minutes

Go to Windows Explorer.

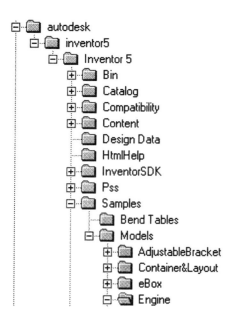

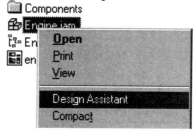

Locate the file engine.iam.
The file is located under the path:
Inventor 5/Samples/Models/Engine.

Right click and select 'Design Assistant'.

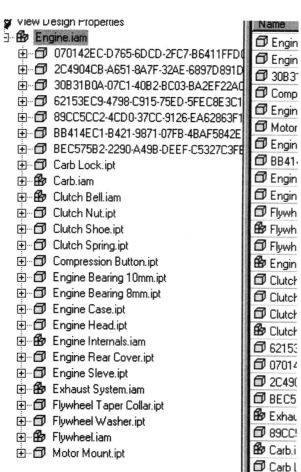

If you expand the assembly in the Design Assistant you can see there are a lot of sub-assemblies and components.

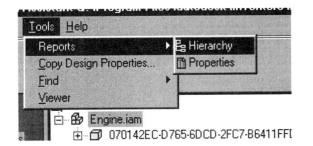

Select Tools->Reports->Hierarchy from the menu.

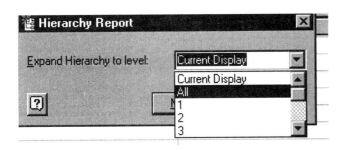

To get a report of all files referenced by the assembly, select 'All' from the drop-down list.
Press 'Next'.

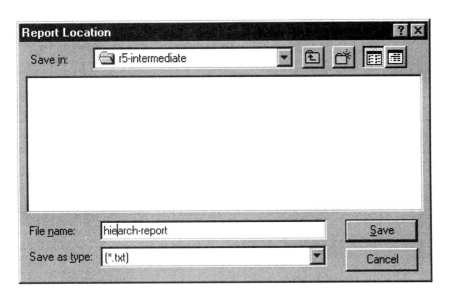

Locate where you wish your hierarchy report stored.
Type in a name for your report under File Name.
Press' Save'.

TIP: If your assembly file references a lot of part and sub-assembly files, it may take a little time to create your report. Be patient.

Locate the report you just created in Windows Explorer.

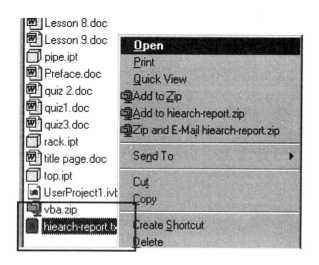

Highlight hiearch-report.txt.
Right click and select 'Open'.

```
Design Assistant Hierarchy Report
File: G:\Program Files\autodesk\inventor5\Inventor 5\Samples\Models\Engine\Engine.iam
Expand to Level: All
Sunday, October 07, 2001 5:35 PM

    G:\Program Files\autodesk\inventor5\Inventor 5\Samples\Models\Engine\Engine.iam
        G:\Program Files\autodesk\inventor5\Inventor 5\Samples\Models\Engine\Components\Engin
        G:\Program Files\autodesk\inventor5\Inventor 5\Samples\Models\Engine\Components\Engin
        G:\Program Files\autodesk\inventor5\Inventor 5\Samples\Models\Engine\Components\30B31
        G:\Program Files\autodesk\inventor5\Inventor 5\Samples\Models\Engine\Components\Compr
        G:\Program Files\autodesk\inventor5\Inventor 5\Samples\Models\Engine\Components\Engin
        G:\Program Files\autodesk\inventor5\Inventor 5\Samples\Models\Engine\Components\Motor
        G:\Program Files\autodesk\inventor5\Inventor 5\Samples\Models\Engine\Components\Engin
        G:\Program Files\autodesk\inventor5\Inventor 5\Samples\Models\Engine\Components\BB414
        G:\Program Files\autodesk\inventor5\Inventor 5\Samples\Models\Engine\Components\Engin
        G:\Program Files\autodesk\inventor5\Inventor 5\Samples\Models\Engine\Components\Engin
```

Note how the report uses indents to demarcate the level of each part file.

Design Property Reports

Design Property Report creates a report that shows values of the specified properties for the files in the selected file or group of files. If the selected item is a folder, the report shows the files that it contains. If the selected item is an assembly file, the report shows the files referenced by the assembly.	
Expand Hierarchy to Level	Specifies the number of levels that the report will show. Click the arrow and select from the list.
Next	Opens the Report Location dialog box so that you can specify the path and file name for the report.

TIP: To change the properties included in a Design Properties report, select Tools>customize and select the properties before running the report.

The Design Property report is an excellent tool to create an Item Master. You can extract the part number, revision, description, where-used, release date, last eco, etc. The properties you can extract are based on your work habits.

    1)   Have you been updating your properties and managing your files so that the properties reflect revision level, etc.?

    2)   Have you added the desired custom fields, such as ECO No?

Let's see how well the engine assembly has been managed.

Exercise 11-3
Design Property Reports

File: engine.iam
Estimated Time: 10 minutes

Locate the engine.iam file under Inventor R5/Samples/Models/Engine.

Highlight, Right click and select Design Assistant.

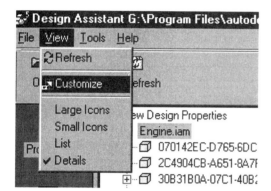

Use View->Customize under the menu to select which properties you wish to extract.

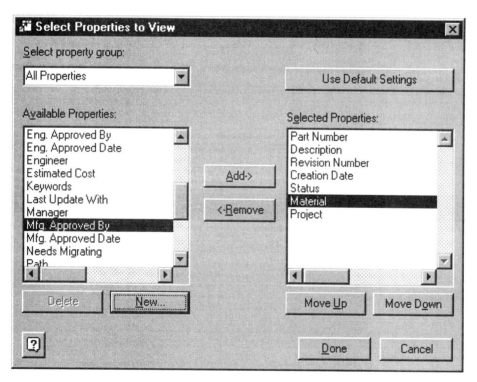

Add Description and Material to the list of selected Properties. Use the Move Up and Move Down buttons to set the order as shown.

You can select the fields to be included in the report.
You can control the order in which the fields are printed using the Move Up and Move Down buttons.

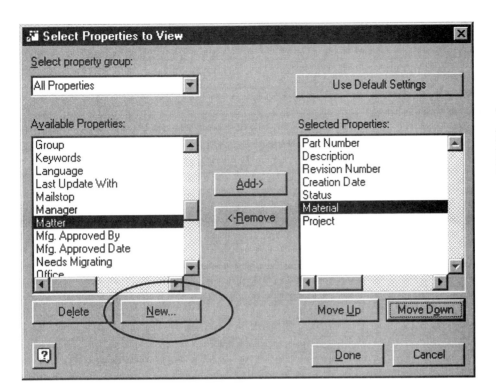

To add a property name, press the 'New' button.

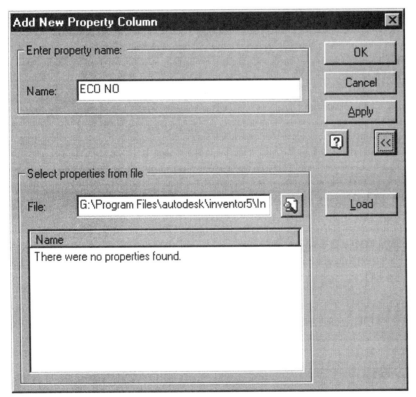

Under Name, type ECO NO.
Press 'Apply' and 'OK'.

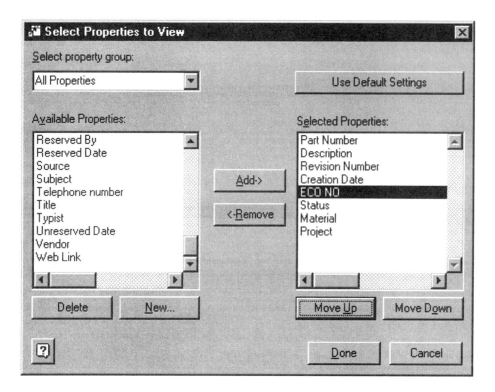

Move ECO NO so it is above Status in the properties list.
Press 'Done'.

Once you have selected the properties you wish to include in your report,
go to Tools->Reports->Properties.

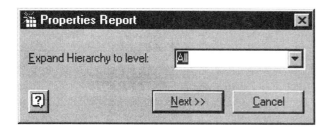

You can expand the hierarchy to include all the drawings referenced by the drawing
selected.

Press "Next'.

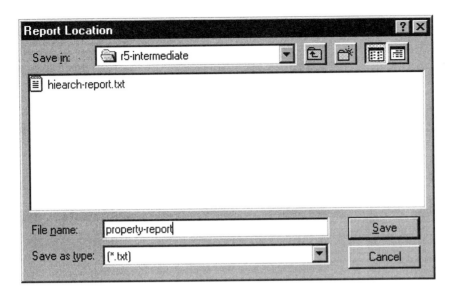

Locate where you want the file to be stored, name it and press 'Save'.

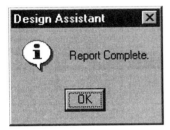

After a few seconds, the Report Complete dialog should appear.
Press 'OK'.
Locate the property-report using Explorer.
Right click and select 'Open'.

```
Design Assistant Properties Report
File: G:\Program Files\autodesk\inventor5\Inventor 5\Samples\Models\Engine\Engine.iam
Expand to Level: All
Sunday, October 07, 2001 5:58 PM


G:\Program Files\autodesk\inventor5\Inventor 5\Samples\Models\Engine\Engine.iam
Name                                          Part Number              Description              Revision
-----------------------------------------------------------------------------------------------------------
Engine Case.ipt                               Engine Case
Engine Sleve.ipt                              Engine Sleve                                      -
30B31B0A-07C1-40B2-BC03-BA2EF22AC956.ipt DIN 912 - M2.5 x 12      Cylinder Head Cap Screw
Compression Button.ipt                        Compression Button                               -
Engine Head.ipt                               Engine Head                                      -
Motor Mount.ipt                               Motor Mount                                      -
Engine Rear Cover.ipt                         Engine Rear Cover                                -
BB414EC1-B421-9871-07FB-4BAF5842E411.ipt DIN 912 - M2.5 x 5       Cylinder Head Cap Screw
Engine Bearing 8mm.ipt                        Engine Bearing 8mm                               -
Engine Bearing 10mm.ipt                       Engine Bearing                                   -
Flywheel Washer.ipt                           Flywheel Washer
Fluwheel.iam                                  Fluwheel
```

Your report as it will appear in NotePad.

Because a txt file is created, it is very easy to import into Excel.

Open EXCEL.

Set the Files of type to Text Files.

Locate the property report text file created. Select 'Open'.

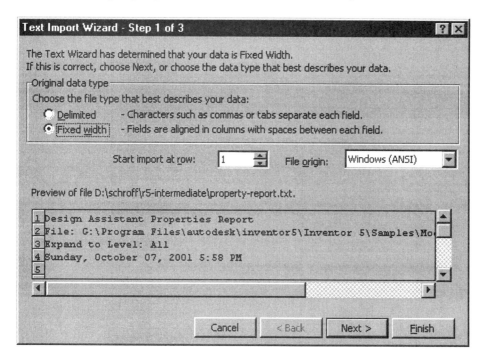

Press 'Next'.

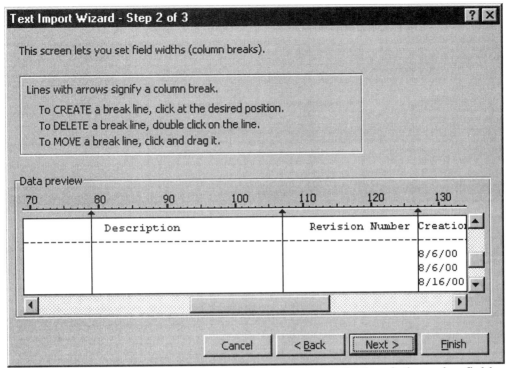

Double Click on the lines you need to delete because the break through a field.
Single click to place new lines to demarcate the start of a new field.
Press 'Next'.

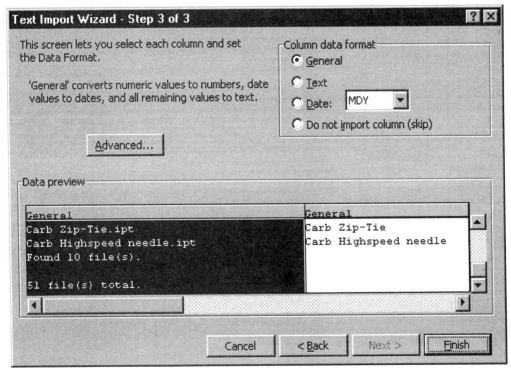

Press 'Finish'.

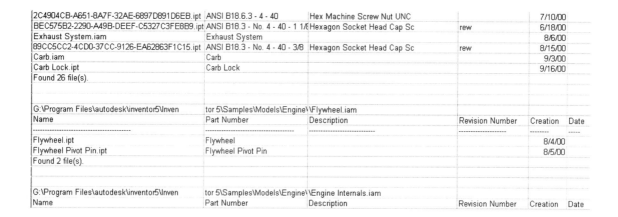

Name	Part Number	Description	Revision Number	Creation	Date
2C4904CB-A651-8A7F-32AE-6897D891D6EB.ipt	ANSI B18.6.3 - 4 - 40	Hex Machine Screw Nut UNC		7/10/00	
BEC575B2-2290-A49B-DEEF-C5327C3FE8B9.ipt	ANSI B18.3 - No. 4 - 40 - 1 1/8	Hexagon Socket Head Cap Sc	rew	6/18/00	
Exhaust System.iam	Exhaust System			8/6/00	
89CC5CC2-4CD0-37CC-9126-EA62863F1C15.ipt	ANSI B18.3 - No. 4 - 40 - 3/8	Hexagon Socket Head Cap Sc	rew	8/15/00	
Carb.iam	Carb			9/3/00	
Carb Lock.ipt	Carb Lock			9/16/00	
Found 26 file(s).					
G:\Program Files\autodesk\inventor5\Inven	tor 5\Samples\Models\Engine\\Flywheel.iam				
Name	Part Number	Description	Revision Number	Creation	Date
--	--	--	--------------------	--------	-----
Flywheel.ipt	Flywheel			8/4/00	
Flywheel Pivot Pin.ipt	Flywheel Pivot Pin			8/5/00	
Found 2 file(s).					
G:\Program Files\autodesk\inventor5\Inven	tor 5\Samples\Models\Engine\\Engine Internals.iam				
Name	Part Number	Description	Revision Number	Creation	Date

Your Excel file can now be edited and used to create an Item Master.

Engineering Change Control

Status Properties define the status of the selected part, assembly, drawing, or template file. You can use status properties to classify and manage your Autodesk Inventor files, search for files, create reports, and automatically update title blocks and parts lists in drawings and bills of materials in assemblies. Enter the desired information in the boxes.

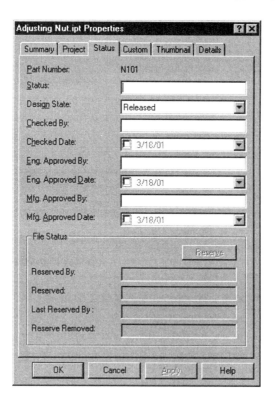

Status Properties is the perfect tool for Engineering Change Control.

Part Number	Displays the Part Number that is set on the Project tab.
Status	Sets the status for the file. You can enter any status classification.
Checked By	Names the person who checked the file.
Checked Date	Shows the date that the file was checked. To change the date, click the arrow and select a date.
Eng Approved By	Names the person who approved the file for Engineering.
Eng Approved Date	Shows the date that the file was approved in Engineering. To change the date, click the arrow and select a date.
Mfg Approved By	Names the person who approved the file for Manufacturing.
Mfg Approved Date	Shows the date that the file was approved for Manufacturing. To change the date, click the arrow and select a date.
File Status	Shows the reservation status of the file for collaborative projects. You can also set the reservation status. To use the reservation option, you must first select the Multi-user option in Autodesk Inventor. Select Tools>Options>General tab and then select the Multi-user check box. Reserve/Unreserve Sets the file status. When you change the status to Reserved, your name and the current date are entered in the appropriate boxes. Click the button to switch the status. Reserved By If the file is currently reserved; shows the name of the person who reserved it. Reserved If the file is currently reserved, shows the date that it was reserved. Last Reserved By Shows the user name of the last person to reserve the file if the file is not currently reserved. Reserve Removed Shows the date that the reserve status was removed from the file if the file is not currently reserved.

Exercise 11-4:
ECOs With Design Assistant

Drawing Name: ex6-1ipt
Estimated Time: 30 minutes

You receive the following ENGINEERING CHANGE ORDER.

ECO NUMBER	20001			
ORIGINATOR	**DATE**	**DOCUMENT NO**	**DESCRIPTION OF CHANGE**	**CURRENT REV**
J. DESIGNER	2001/03/01	B106	SEE BELOW	A
REASON FOR CHANGE: BETTER FIT				
MATERIAL DISPOSITION: USE UP EXISTING STOCK				
WHERE USED:				
APPROVALS:				

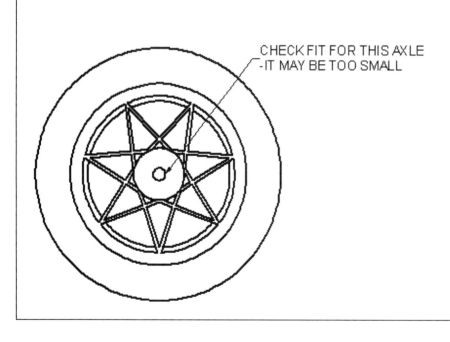

CHECK FIT FOR THIS AXLE
-IT MAY BE TOO SMALL

Your first task is to mark the file as having a change pending.

Locating a File with Design Assistant

We must locate the file with part number B106.
In some companies, the files are saved under the part number, but in this case, the file is not saved with the part number, because we had a temp in who used his own numbering system.

Open a blank part file.
Close any other active files.
Go to File->Design Assistant.

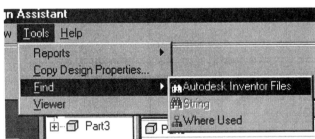

Go to Tools->Find->Autodesk Inventor Files.

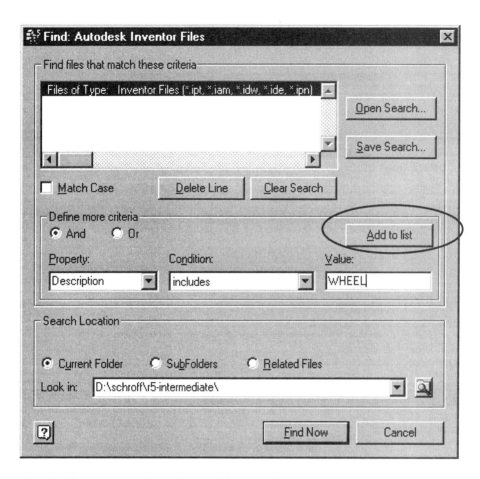

Set the Property to Description Value to Wheel.
Set your search location depending on where you have stored your files.
Press 'Add to List'.

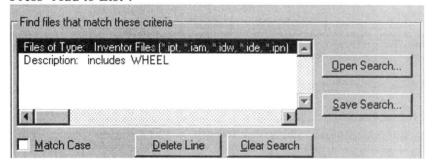

Our search criteria appears in the upper box.
Press 'Find Now'.

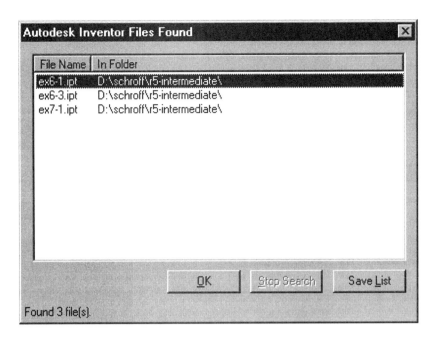

We see three files listed. We want the ex6-1.ipt file
Locate the ex6-1.ipt file in Windows Explorer.

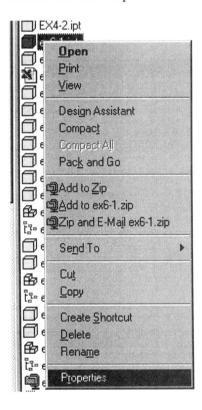

Highlight the file.
Right click and select 'Properties'.

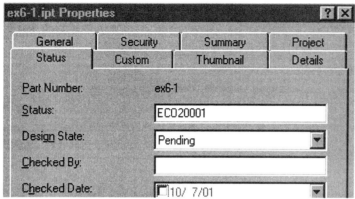

Select the Status tab.
Under Status, enter the ECO Number: ECO 20001
Change the Design State to Pending.

Now anyone looking at this file will see there is an ECO Pending.

Select the Summary tab.
In the Comments section, we can add a remark about the pending ECO.

Press 'Apply'.
Press 'OK'.

Highlight the file in Explorer.
Right click and select Design Assistant.

In the Design Assistant, we see that the various fields are updated.

Name	Part N...	Status	Revision Number	Creation Date	Project
ex6-1.ipt	ex6-1	ECO20001	A	10/5/01	

Go to View->Customize.

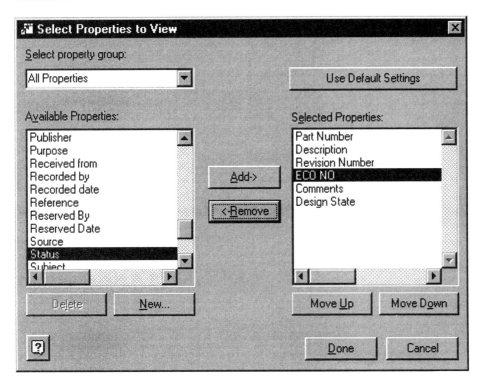

Modify the Selected Properties to this list:

- Part Number
- Description
- Revision Number
- ECO NO
- Comments
- Design State

Press 'Done'.

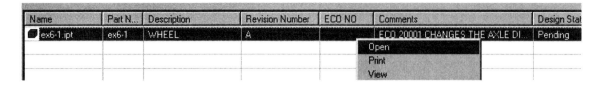

Design Assistant updates with the new property list.
If we highlight the part name and right click, we have the option to Open, Print, or View the file.

If we highlight the part name, a preview of the part appears in the lower left corner of the screen.

Lesson 12
Collaboration

In a collaborative environment, you edit a part while others are referencing it as they work on other parts in an assembly. What happens when you save the part?

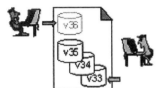 Each time you save changes, a version of the model is created in the file. Other designers who are referencing the file continue to see the earlier version of the file and do not see the changes until they refresh their view of the assembly.

Note: You can set the number of versions that are retained in files. The setting is on the General tab of the Tools>Application Options dialog box.

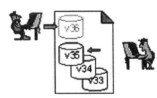 If you are working in a shared or semi-isolated environment, you can select View>Refresh to update files that are referenced from the server. If you are working in an isolated environment, you must copy the latest files from the server to see the latest changes.

You can open any of the saved versions of a file. When you open a file, click the Options button on the dialog box to see a list of versions.

Reserving Files

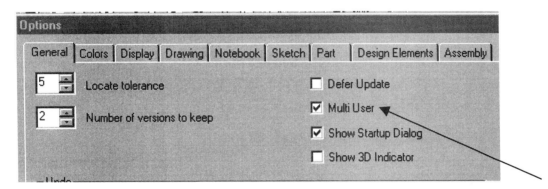

When you are working in a collaborative environment, you set the Multi-user option on the General tab of the Options dialog box. When this option is set, Autodesk Inventor displays warning messages about the reservation status of files as you work with them.

You use Design Manager to reserve groups of files before working on them in a network location or moving them from network locations to your personal workspace. You reserve the files by changing their status property to reserved.

If you try to edit a file reserved by someone else, a warning message is displayed. If necessary, you can still edit the reserved file and save changes. For example, if the person who reserved a file is out of the office, someone else can still access and make changes to the file to work on a high priority project. However, if the person who reserved the file did not save changes prior to you opening the file, you will replace those changes.

If you do not reserve a file before working on it, you are prompted to reserve a file the first time you edit it. When you close the file, you are prompted to preserve or release the reservation. If you continue to reserve the file, the reservation will stay in effect even if you close and reopen Autodesk Inventor.

NetMeeting

Using Windows NetMeeting, you can collaborate with other designers in an Autodesk Inventor session. Meeting participants can each take control of the session to work on the design, including opening, viewing and editing multiple files. You can use collaboration tools in a chat setting and on a graphics white board.

You can also use NetMeeting to hold on-line training sessions.

Video and Audio Conferencing
NetMeeting's audio and video conferencing features let you communicate with anyone on the Internet.

Whiteboard
The whiteboard lets you collaborate in real time with others via graphic information.

Chat
Chat lets you conduct real-time conversations via text, with as many people as you like.

Internet Directory
The Microsoft Internet Directory is a Web site provided and maintained by Microsoft to locate people to call on the Internet.

File Transfer
File transfer lets you send one or more files in the background during a NetMeeting conference.

Program Sharing
NetMeeting's Program Sharing feature lets you flexibly share multiple programs during a conference and retain greater control over the way they're used.

Remote Desktop Sharing
Remote Desktop Sharing lets you operate a computer from a remote location.

Security
NetMeeting uses three types of security measures to protect your privacy.

Advanced Calling
This feature gives you the flexibility to send a mail message to a NetMeeting user or initiate a NetMeeting call directly from your mail address book.

Using Windows NetMeeting, you can share Autodesk Inventor with other designers across a network or the Internet. You use collaboration tools to exchange ideas in a chat setting and on an electronic white board.

Individuals participating in the meeting can each take control of Autodesk Inventor to:

- Modify existing part or assembly designs by adding, editing or deleting part features or assembly constraints.
- Collaborate on a new design.
- Use a senior engineer, designer, or draft person's expertise to assist junior members of the design team.

As you work on an assembly with Autodesk Inventor, you use Windows NetMeeting in situations such as:

- Two designers at separate sites work together on a collaborative design to follow up after visits by engineering staff to resolve missed details.
- A designer works with a manufacturer's representative and a sales engineer to resolve fine points of an assembly design.
- An R&D team which is state-side can review design changes with their manufacturing plant in the Pacific Rim

In addition to working with designers in remote sites, you can use Windows NetMeeting in your own workplace to facilitate resolution of design problems.

You must have an active Autodesk Inventor session and one or more Autodesk Inventor files open. You also need to have an active NetMeeting session and have set the host security options.

1. From the Autodesk Inventor menu, select Tools > Online Collaboration > Meet Now.
2. In the Place a Call dialog box, enter the following actions:
   o Enter the name of the participant's computer (on which Windows NetMeeting is running).
   o Click the arrow and select the connection type (Automatic, Directory or Network).
3. Click Call. A message displays while waiting for the participant to respond.
4. After the first participant responds, call the next participant. Continue until all participants are ready.

As the host, you have control of the Autodesk Inventor session when the meeting begins. When a participant signals that he or she wants to operate Autodesk Inventor, you can relinquish control. The participant can operate normally.

You can forward control of the session to a meeting participant. At the top of the session window, select Control>Forward Control. The participant clicks to Accept or Reject control.

In a chat or white board setting, the host can regain control of the session by clicking the mouse or typing on the keyboard.

Usually, participants collaborate in a session similar to this:

- The host is working in an assembly and notifies participants that a meeting is needed.
- The host starts a Windows NetMeeting session and sets up the host security options.
- Participants start Windows NetMeeting on their own computers.
- The host selects Tools>Online Collaboration>Meet Now, then enters information about the participant's computer.
- On the participant's computer, a message signals the start of the meeting.
- A window opens on each participant's computer, showing a working session of Autodesk Inventor.

At the start of the meeting, the host has control of the Autodesk Inventor session. To operate Autodesk Inventor, double-click in the graphics window. On the host's computer, a window displays the request. When the host accepts, you gain control of the session and can operate Autodesk Inventor normally. Other meeting participants follow the same sequence when they want to operate Autodesk Inventor.

Any participant can start a chat or white board session, but only the host can change control of Autodesk Inventor.

You must have Windows NetMeeting running, but Autodesk Inventor does not need to be installed on the meeting computer. When the host calls the meeting:

1. Wait for a message on your screen to indicate the host is calling your computer.
2. Click to accept the call and join the meeting. A window opens, showing a working session of Autodesk Inventor.
3. As the meeting continues, you can choose one or more of the following actions:
    o Double-click in the graphics window to signal the host that you want to operate Autodesk Inventor.
    o On the Collaboration toolbar, click the Chat tool to initiate a chat session, and then enter text.
    o On the Collaboration toolbar, click the Whiteboard tool to initiate a white board session, and then use graphics tools to sketch shapes.

When another participant signals the host that he or she wants to operate Autodesk Inventor, the host retakes control of the design session, and then gives control to the new participant.

The host can retake control of a chat or white board session by typing on the keyboard or clicking the mouse.

You can download the latest version of NetMeeting for free from Microsoft's website at www.microsoft.com/windows/netmeeting/download/.

You can also locate any service packs and updates on the Microsoft website.

NetMeeting System Requirements

The following are the minimum system requirements to install and run Microsoft NetMeeting.

- 90 megahertz (MHz) Pentium processor
- 16 megabytes (MB) of RAM for Microsoft Windows 95, Windows 98, Windows Me
- 24 megabytes (MB) of RAM for Microsoft Windows NT version 4.0 (Microsoft Windows NT 4.0 Service Pack 3 or later is required to enable sharing programs on Windows NT.)
- Microsoft Internet Explorer version 4.01 or later
- 28,800 bps or faster modem, integrated services digital network (ISDN), or local area network (LAN) connection (a fast Internet connection works best).
- 4 MB of free hard disk space (an additional 10 MB is needed during installation only to accommodate the initial setup files).
- Sound card with microphone and speakers (required for audio support).

To use the data, audio, and video features of NetMeeting, your computer must meet the following hardware requirements:

- For Windows 95, Windows 98, or Windows Me, a Pentium 90 processor with 16 MB of RAM (a Pentium 133 processor or better with at least 16 MB of RAM is recommended).
- For Windows NT, a Pentium 90 processor with 24 MB of RAM (a Pentium 133 processor or better with at least 32 MB of RAM is recommended).
- 4 MB of free hard disk space (an additional 10 MB is needed during installation only to accommodate the initial setup files).
- 56,000 bps or faster modem, ISDN, or LAN connection.
- Sound card with microphone and speakers (sound card required for both audio and video support).
- Video capture card or camera that provides a Video for Windows capture driver (required for video support).

NetMeeting Troubleshooting

Unable to hear the other participant(s) in the NetMeeting on the speakers/headphone

SYMPTOMS

When you participate in a NetMeeting conference using audio, you may be able to hear the other person, but he or she may be unable to hear you (or vice-versa).

CAUSE

This behavior can occur if any of the following conditions exists:

- The microphone is not working or is not properly connected to the sound card.

- The volume is turned off or set very low, or the speakers are not properly connected to the sound card.

- Both participants are not using full duplex.

- You are using a Slirp dial-up connection or another emulated Transmission Control Protocol/Internet Protocol (TCP/IP) connection.

- You or your Internet service provider (ISP) are using a proxy server to connect to the Internet, and the ports used to send audio are closed (ports 1720 and 1731).

- Audio is disabled by a system policy.

- There are already two or more people participating in the meeting. NetMeeting provides audio for 1 to 1 connection. The third person in the conference does not have audio capabilities. In order to have audio available for more than two participants at a time you must use an MCU server. For more information about MCUs please see the NetMeeting resource kit online.

- You or your Internet service provider (ISP) is using a Network Address Translator (NAT) that either does not support the H.323 protocol or is not configured to allow H.323 through. H.323 is the protocol used by NetMeeting to transport audio and video.

RESOLUTION

To resolve this behavior, follow the steps in the appropriate section:

Microphone Is Not Working

If the other person cannot hear you, determine whether your microphone works by using the Sound Recorder tool. To do so, follow these steps:

Click **Start**, point to **Programs**, point to **Accessories**, point to **Multimedia**, and then click **Sound Recorder**. In Windows 98, click **Start**, point to **Programs**, point to **Accessories**, point to **Entertainment**, and then click **Sound Recorder**.

NOTE: If Sound Recorder is not installed, install it using the **Add/Remove Programs** tool in **Control Panel**.

Click **Record**, and then speak into the microphone.

If you cannot record a .wav file, verify that the microphone is properly connected to the sound card and that the microphone settings are correct. To do so, double-click the Speaker icon on the taskbar, and then verify that the Microphone slider is at the top and the **Mute** check box is not selected.

NOTE: If there is no Speaker icon on the taskbar, follow these steps:

1. Click **Start**, point to **Settings**, click **Control Panel**, and then double-click **Multimedia**.

2. Click the **Show volume control on the taskbar** check box to select it, and then click **OK**.

If you still cannot record a .wav file, use another microphone.

Volume Is Turned Off or Is Very Low

If you cannot hear the other person, verify that you can hear .wav files by using the Sound Recorder tool. To do so, follow these steps:

Click **Start**, point to **Programs**, point to **Accessories**, point to **Multimedia**, and then click **Sound Recorder**. In Windows 98, click **Start**, point **Programs**, point to **Accessories**, point to **Entertainment**, and then click **Sound Recorder**.

NOTE: If Sound Recorder is not installed, install it using the **Add/Remove Programs** tool in **Control Panel**.

On the **File** menu, click **Open**.

1. Locate and click a .wav file, and then click **Open**.

2. Click **Play**.

If you cannot hear the .wav file, verify that the volume settings are correct. To do so, double-click the Speaker icon on the taskbar, and then verify that the Volume Control slider is at the top and the **Mute** check box is not selected.

NOTE: If there is no Speaker icon on the taskbar, follow these steps:

1. Click **Start**, point to **Settings**, click **Control Panel**, and then double-click **Multimedia**.

2. Click the **Show volume control on the taskbar** check box to select it, and then click **OK**.

If you are using amplified speakers, verify that they are properly connected to the sound card, and that they are turned on and the volume control is turned up.

Full-Duplex Is Not Being Used By Both Participants

With full-duplex audio, you and the other person can speak (and hear) simultaneously.

With half-duplex audio, you and the other person must take turns speaking.

If you are using half-duplex sound card drivers and have a sensitive microphone, you may be the only person who can speak because you are continuously sending data.

NetMeeting 2.1 supports DirectSound. If your sound card supports full duplex audio and you are using half-duplex DirectSound drivers contact your hardware vendor to inquire about the availability of updated drivers for your sound card or disable DirectSound support in NetMeeting.

A Slirp Connection Is Being Used

Slirp is a TCP/IP emulator that enables you to create a serial line Internet protocol (SLIP) or Point-to-Point protocol (PPP) connection when you are logged on to a UNIX server.

Audio Ports Are Closed On the Proxy Server

If the audio ports are closed on the proxy server, contact your network administrator or ISP.

System Policies Are Enabled

To verify whether audio is disabled by a system policy, click the **Tools** menu in NetMeeting. If the **Audio Tuning Wizard** command is unavailable and there is a sound card in your computer, audio may be disabled by a system policy. If this is the case, contact your network administrator.

Unable to Share the Inventor Program

SYMPTOMS

Only three participants in a NetMeeting conference may be able to share programs.

CAUSE

This behavior can occur if any of the conference participants uses NetMeeting 2.0 or earlier.

RESOLUTION

To resolve this issue, upgrade to the most current version of NetMeeting from the following Microsoft Web site:

http://www.microsoft.com/netmeeting

MORE INFORMATION

With NetMeeting 2.1, up to 32 computers can share programs. The total number of participants who can share a program is dependent on the host computer's resources and network bandwidth. When more than three participants share programs in a conference, a computer with NetMeeting 2.0 or earlier cannot share a program.

The Colors In Inventor Don't Look Right

SYMPTOMS

When you use a shared program in a NetMeeting conference, the shared program may appear discolored.

CAUSE

This behavior can occur when the computers participating in the NetMeeting conference are using a color palette of more than 256 colors. NetMeeting supports sending only up to 256 colors across a network connection.

RESOLUTION

To work around this behavior, change the Color Palette setting to High Color (16 Bit) or lower on the computers participating in the conference. To change the Color Palette setting:

1. Click **Start**, point to **Settings**, click **Control Panel**, and then double-click **Display**.

2. Click the **Settings** tab.

3. In the **Color Palette** box, click **High Color (16 Bit)** or a lower setting.

4. Click **OK**.

5. Restart your computer when you are prompted.

Unable to see Video in the My Video Window

SYMPTOMS

You may see a black screen when you view the My Video window in Microsoft NetMeeting, or you may be unable to view live video from a video capture card.

CAUSE

This behavior can be caused by any of the following conditions:

- The video capture card is configured to use an unsupported video format.

- The video capture card is using video overlay mode. (Video overlay mode is not supported by Microsoft NetMeeting).

- The video capture card does not support Microsoft Video 1.0 for Windows.

- If you are running NetMeeting 2.0 you may have multiple video capture devices; if you are running NetMeeting 2.1 or later, you may have the wrong video capture device selected.

RESOLUTION

To resolve this issue, use the appropriate method:

Configure Video Format

Configure the video capture card to one of the video formats supported by Microsoft NetMeeting, and confirm that the video capture card supports Microsoft Video 1.0 for Windows. Currently, Microsoft NetMeeting supports the following video formats: RGB4, RGB8, RGB16, RGB24, and YVU9.

Remove Extra Video Capture Device

To verify that only one video capture device is installed on your system, double-click **Multimedia** in Control Panel. On the Advanced tab (Devices in Windows NT), double-click **Video Capture Devices**. If there are two devices listed, click the device no longer installed in your computer, click **Properties**, click **Remove**, and then click **OK**.

Verify Video Capture Device

If you use NetMeeting 2.0, verify that only one video capture device is installed on your computer. To do so, follow these steps:

1. In Control Panel double-click **Multimedia**.

2. On the **Devices** tab (**Advanced** tab in Windows 95), double-click **Video Capture Devices**. If there is more than one device listed, click the device that is no longer installed in your computer.

3. Click **Properties**, click **Remove**, and then click **OK**.

NOTE: If you do have multiple video capture devices, you may have to remove the device that you are not using in NetMeeting.

If you use NetMeeting 2.1 or later, verify that the device you want to use is currently selected. To do so, follow these steps:

1. In NetMeeting, disconnect from any conferences that are running.

2. On the **Tools** menu, click **Options**.

3. On the **Video** tab, click the device you want to use in the **The video capture device I wish to use is** box, and then click **OK**.

MORE INFORMATION

Video overlay mode enables a video capture card to send video directly to the memory on the video capture card, bypassing the central processing unit (CPU) and reducing the processor overhead. Microsoft NetMeeting does not capture video from a video capture card in video overlay mode.

To determine if your video capture card supports preview mode or overlay mode, refer to the documentation that came with your video capture card or contact the manufacturer of your video capture device. For information about general video issues with Microsoft NetMeeting, refer to the Netmeet.txt file or the Netmeet.htm file in the NetMeeting folder.

TIP: If you don't find your problem listed here, there is more information on troubleshooting NetMeeting on Microsoft's website.

Exercise 12-1

Hosting a NetMeeting

Estimated time: 120 minutes

 TIP: You must have an active Internet connection in order to participate in or host a NetMeeting.

We start by launching Microsoft NetMeeting.

NetMeeting can be launched from the Start Menu or you may have placed a shortcut icon on your desktop.

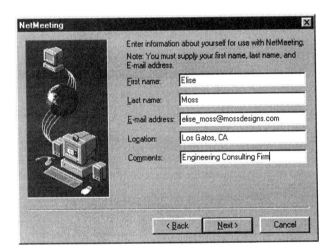

Press the 'Next' button.

 TIP: You must supply a first name, last name and email address. Location and Comments are optional.

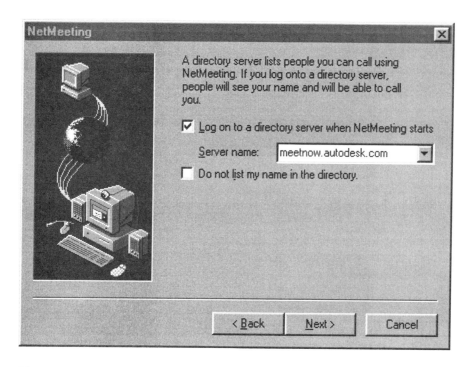

You can select a server to use for your Net Meeting or use Autodesk's server.

Press 'Next'.

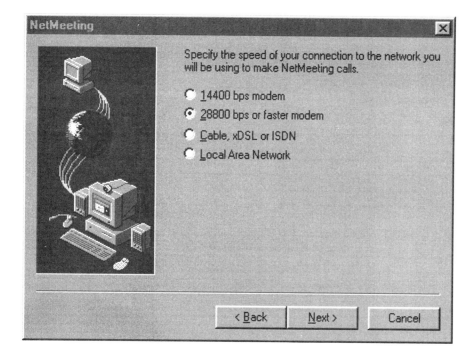

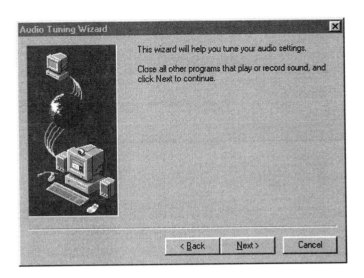

The software will adjust your audio settings, so you can use a microphone in your NetMeeting.

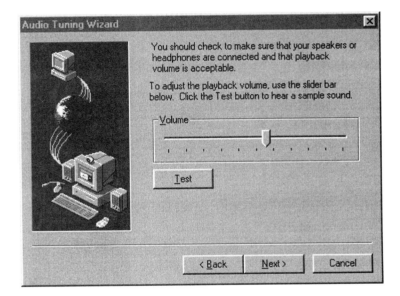

Pressing the Test button will play a series of tones. You can then adjust the volume on your headset, on your speakers, on your computer or on the dialog box to set it to a comfortable level.

Press 'Stop' when your volume is set properly to stop the tones from playing.
Then Press 'Next'.

TIP: I use headphones so I do not disturb the other people working around me. It is a courteous thing to do. Any standard set of headphones that plug into a Walkman™ should be able to plug into your laptop or workstation.

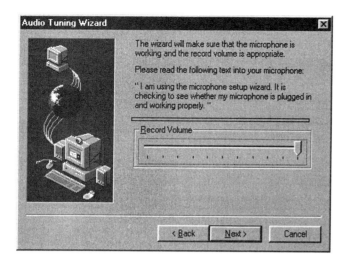

The NetMeeting will then test your microphone set up.
If the Wizard does not detect a microphone, verify that you have it plugged into the correct port.

If you do not plan to use a microphone, you can select 'Next'.

TIP: I highly recommend using a microphone for NetMeeting. It allows you to use your hands for drawing in Inventor or manipulating the meeting.

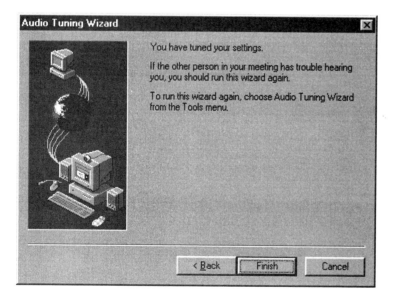

Press 'Finish'.

Once the Wizard is completed, you will see the NetMeeting dialog box.

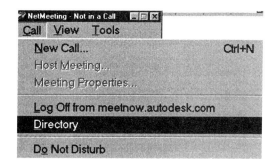

Pressing Call->Directory will allow you to access the parties you wish to invite to your NetMeeting. You can also access the directory by pressing the Directory button on the right side of the NetMeeting dialog box.

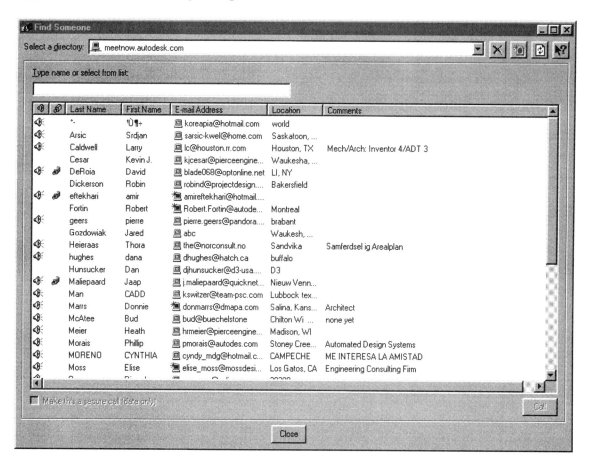

In the directory, you will find all the users who currently are logged onto NetMeeting. If you have set up your NetMeeting with your correspondents, they should be logged in and waiting for your call.

Refresh button in Directory

The Refresh button located in the upper right of the Directory window will refresh the list of people currently logged on.

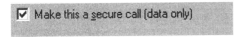

At the bottom of the Directory window, you can elect to have your NetMeeting be a secure call.

You can see whether or not you are in a secure NetMeeting at the bottom of the NetMeeting dialog box. You will see the words 'In a secure call' and a lock.

If you are in a secure call, there is no audio or video.

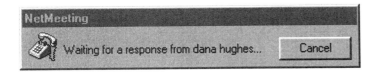

Highlight the person's name on the list you wish to call and press the 'Call' button located in the lower right corner of the directory.

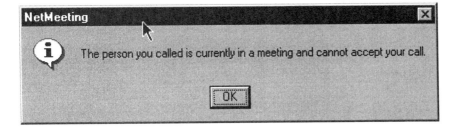

If the person you are calling is already in a meeting, you will see this dialog box.

If someone is calling you, you will see the dialog box that says 'Incoming Call'. To join the NetMeeting, press the 'Accept' button. To decline, press the 'Ignore' button.

Once you have all the participants in your NetMeeting on-line, you can start the session inside of Inventor.

TIP: You must have elected to install NetMeeting when you installed Inventor to host or participate in a NetMeeting. If you did not install the NetMeeting software, you can download it for free from the Microsoft website.

The participants are listed in the NetMeeting during an active meeting.

During the meeting, you can review any documents or share a program; Chat, share a white board, or transfer files.

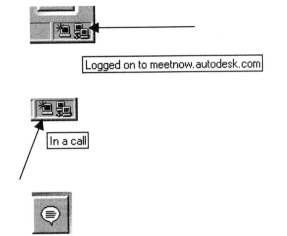

In the lower right corner of the NetMeeting dialog, you will see two icons. The icon with two computers indicates the server where the meeting is taking place.

The icon with one computer and a red asterisk indicates an active call is taking place.

Chat

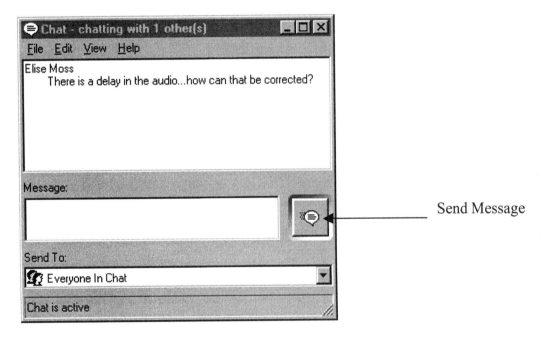

Send Message

If you do not have a broadband connection, the audio will have a slight delay.
It is similar experience to talking over a short wave radio.

The Chat board works similar to any chat room. You type your message in the message area. Press Return to send or press the Send Message button.
The top area of the Chat window shows incoming messages and tracks the conversation.

You can print your chat conversation at the end of the NetMeeting to have a log of the meeting.

The Whiteboard

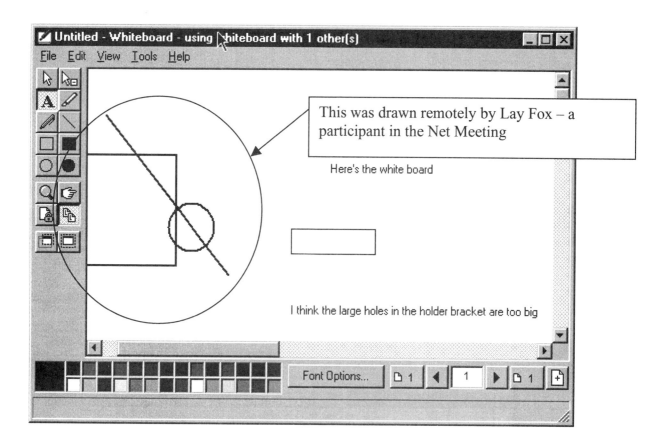

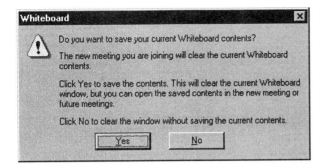

You can save the contents of the whiteboard in a file for reference later.

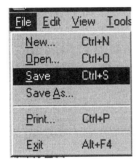

Go to File->Save.

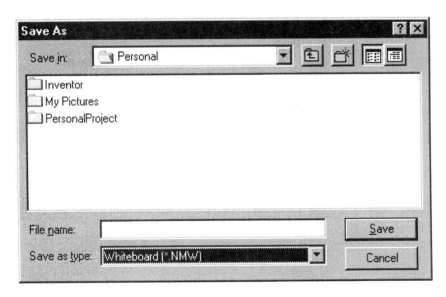

Whiteboard files are saved using *.nmw files.

TIP: You do not have to be in an active NetMeeting to use the White Board. You can create a quick sketch, save it and email it to someone or use it for the next NetMeeting.

Sharing a Program

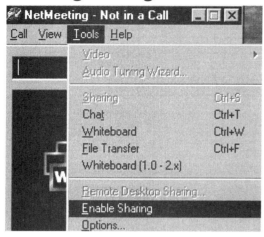

To allow others to see the Inventor Program, go to Tools->Enable Sharing in the NetMeeting menu or press the Share Program button.

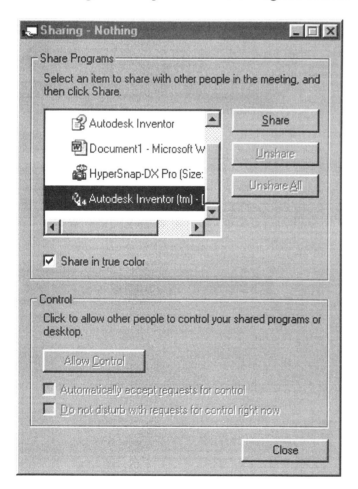

Selecting the Share Program tool will allow the other callers to see Inventor.

Locate Inventor in the Browser, highlight and select the Share button.

It will automatically be placed in bold.
You can also allow other users to control your software remotely from their workstations by pressing the Allow Control button.

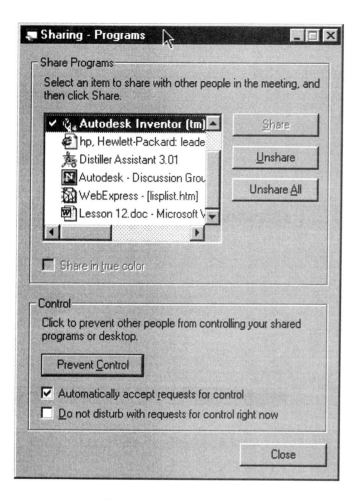

Pressing the Allow Control brings up two options the user can enable/disable to set up control of Inventor.

If you wish the other user to be able to control your software you should enable 'Automatically accept requests for control'. Otherwise, you will see a dialog box whenever a participant in the Net Meeting wants control of the program.

Press 'Close'.

TIP: I do not recommend shared control of Inventor unless all parties are on a DSL connection. It is extremely slow otherwise.

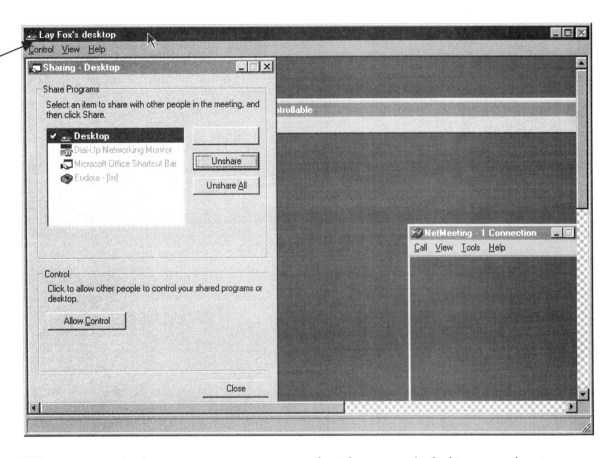

When you are sharing a program, you can see the other person's desktop as an inset on your monitor.

In the upper left corner, you will see whose desktop you are observing.

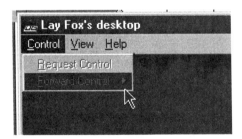

If you wish control of the other person's desktop, you go to the upper left corner and select 'Control'.

If the other person has not enabled Sharing of his desktop, the Request Control and Forward Control will be grayed out.

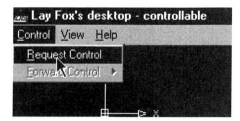

Once Sharing is enabled, you will be able to Request Control.

If the other participant has control of the program, his/her initials will appear next to the mouse in the program.

File Transfer

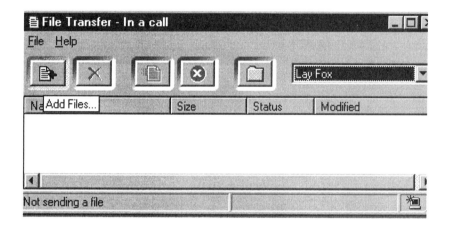

To send a file to one of the participants in the NetMeeting, activate File Transfer. Select the 'Add Files' button.

You can only use File Transfer if you are in an active Net Meeting session.

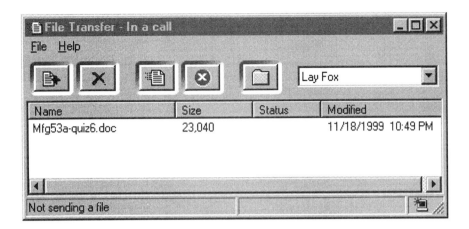

Locate the file and it will be added in the list area.
Press the File Transfer button to send.

The recipient will see a dialog box indicating a file is being sent.

They can opt to open it immediately or close the dialog box and open the file later.

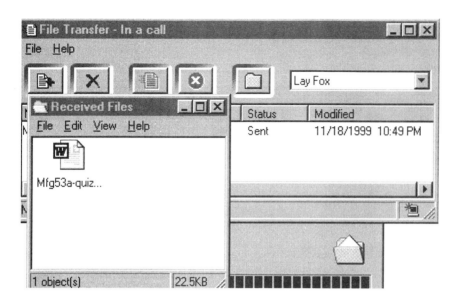

Pressing the End Call terminates the Net Meeting.

Using Pack and Go

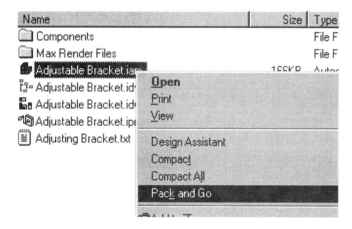

Pack and Go is available for Inventor assemblies and drawings.

It can only be accessed through Windows Explorer.
Launch Explorer and locate the desired drawing file.
Highlight, right click and select 'Pack and Go'.

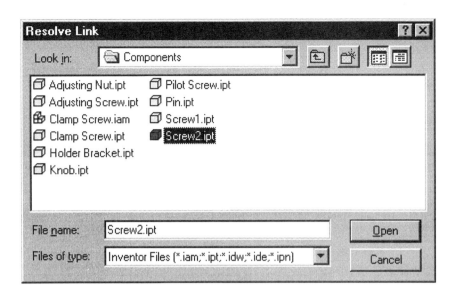

If some of the parts of an assembly are not in the same path, you will be asked to locate the part file(s). The Resolve Link dialog box will appear. Locate the required file and select 'Open'.

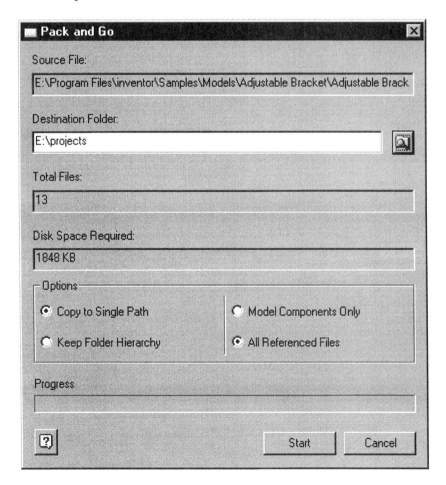

Select the destination directory for your files.

The dialog box will show how many files are referenced.

The dialog box will tell you how much space the files will take up. This saves the user problems if the files are too large for a floppy diskette.

You can elect to retain the path hierarchy or store the files in a single path.

Press 'Start' to create the Pack and Go.

The files will be copied to the Destination Folder.

Using Compact

The Compact tool acts similar to a Purge in AutoCAD removing any unused reference data inside a file.

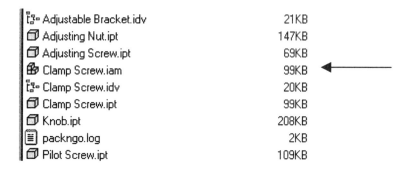

Locate the Clamp Screw.iam in the Explorer.
It should be located under /Samples/Models/Adjustable Bracket/Components.
Note the file size.

Right click and Select 'Compact'.

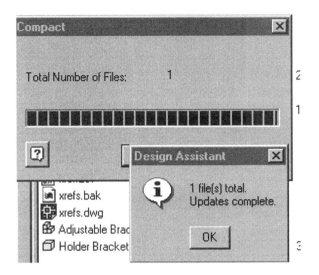

Press 'Start'.

The file will be purged. Press 'OK'.

Note the new file size.

Using Compact All

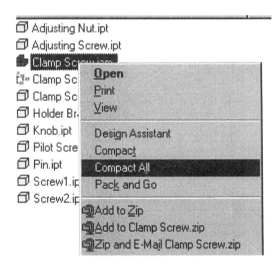

If you wish to purge all the parts used in an assembly, select the assembly file.
Right click and select Compact All.
All files referenced by the assembly file will be purged.

Zip and Email files

In the Explorer, select the file you wish to email to someone. Right click and select Zip and Email.

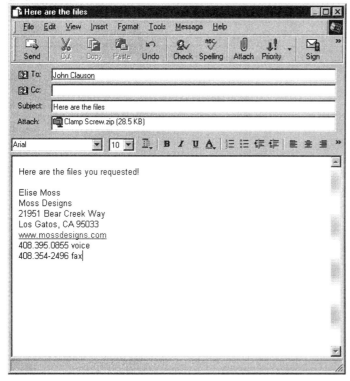

The system will automatically compress the file(s) into a Zip file and bring up Outlook Express.

TIP: In order for this to work properly, you should have WinZip and Outlook Express installed on your system.

You can download WinZip for free from www.winzip.com.

Outlook Express can be downloaded free from Microsoft's website.

Using Send To

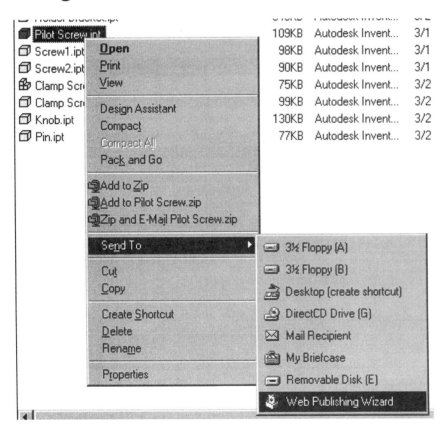

You can use Send To in the Explorer to send a file either through email or to another directory.

Send to Mail Recipient

The Send to Mail Recipient automatically launches Outlook Express with the highlighted file as an attachment.

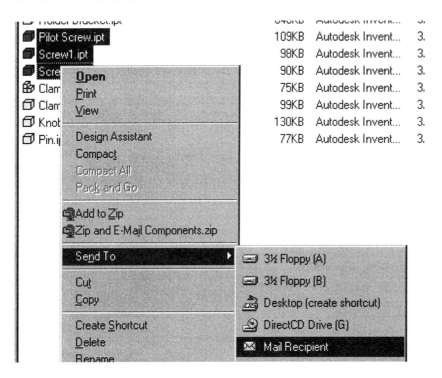

You can email more than one file at a time by holding down the control key to highlight the selected files, then right click and select Send to->Mail Recipient.

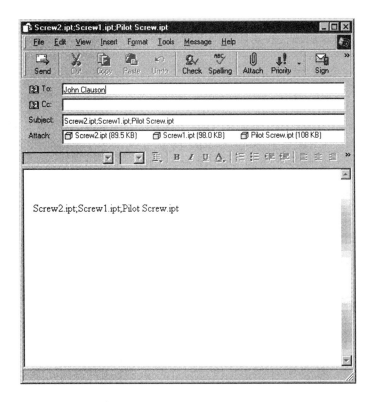

Send To Web Publishing Wizard

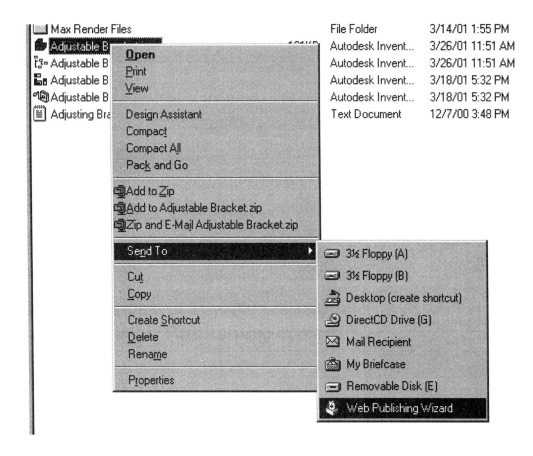

You can also publish your Inventor files to the Web. Highlight the file to be published in Explorer. Right click and select Send To->Web Publishing Wizard.

TIP: In order for this to work properly, you should have Web Publishing Wizard installed on your system. This is a Microsoft application that can be downloaded for free from the Microsoft website at: www.microsoft.com/windows/.

Be sure to download the correct version for your operating system.

You also need to have access to your company's website and be able to upload files.

Press 'Next'.

Press 'Next'.

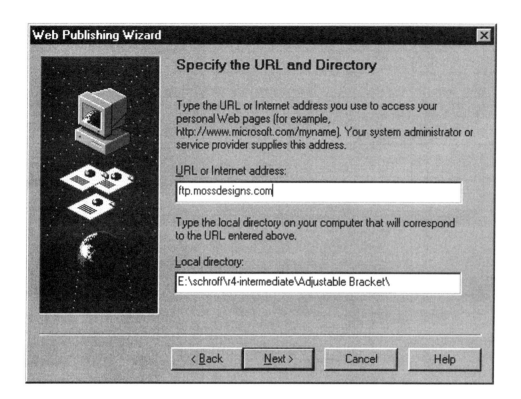

Under URL, enter the Internet address of your website.

Press 'Next'.

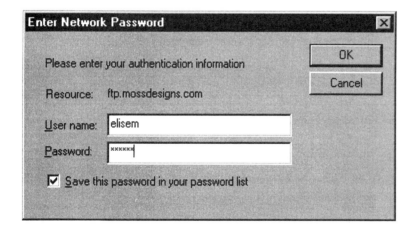

Enter your user name and password.

Press 'OK'.

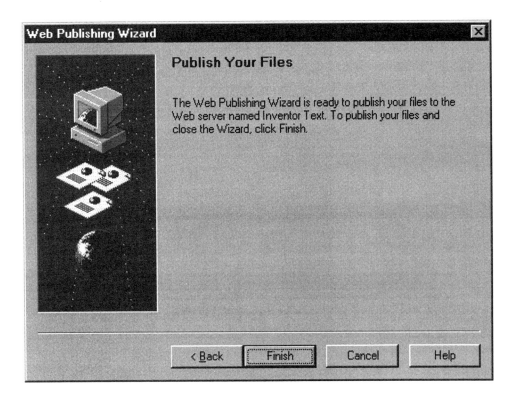

Press 'Finish'.

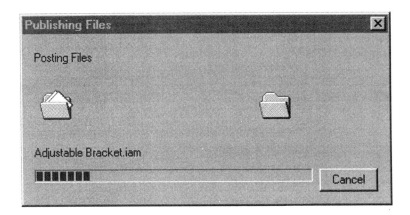

Your files will then be copied over to your website.

TIP: All this process does is upload the selected files to your web server. The files can then be downloaded and used by someone else as long as they have Inventor installed.

i-drop

i-drop is Autodesk's XML-based framework for publishing design objects within Web pages. You can easily exchange Autodesk design data with part suppliers across the World Wide Web, a company-wide intranet, or local intranet. For example, with i-drop technology, you can drag an .ipt file or SAT file from a supplier's Web site directly into an assembly file opened within Autodesk Inventor.

Use your Web browser to locate an .ipt file or SAT file, and then drag that file into your assembly document. The cursor turns to an eyedropper when you pause the cursor over a file that has been enabled by i-drop. A copy of the part is created in a target directory as specified by the publisher of the iPart. If the target directory or directory structure doesn't exist, Autodesk Inventor displays a message giving you the option of creating the part copy in your local workspace. The target directory or directory structure should be noted on the iPart publisher's Web site. If desired, you can then recreate that directory or directory structure on your local drive or server. Autodesk Inventor .ipt files and SAT files are the supported file formats.

The following list includes some of the possible applications of i-drop technology:

- Retrieve standard or custom-made parts from an outside vendor.
- Help ensure that consistent design data is used across an entire organization.
- Facilitate direct access to standard part libraries.
- Facilitate direct access to a one-off, multiple-use part.
- Visually preview a bitmap image of the file before dragging it.

You cannot view i-drop content in a Netscape browser. To view content, your web browser must be Microsoft Internet Explorer 5.x or above.

TIP: You can learn more about idrop technology at http://idrop.autodesk.com/

Here is a listing of current applications that can use i-drop:

- 3D Studio VIZ® Release 3i
- AutoCAD® 2002
- AutoCAD® 2000i
- AutoCAD Architectural Desktop 3.3
- AutoCAD Architectural Desktop 3.0
- AutoCAD Architectural Desktop 2i
- Autodesk® CAD Overlay® 2002
- Autodesk® CAD Overlay® 2000i
- Land Desktop 3
- AutoCAD® Land Development Desktop Release 2i
- AutoCAD LT 2002
- AutoCAD LT 2000i
- AutoCAD Map® 5
- AutoCAD Map® 2000i
- AutoCAD® Mechanical 6
- AutoCAD® Mechanical 2000i
- Mechanical Desktop® Release 6
- Mechanical Desktop® Release 5
- Autodesk Inventor™ 5
- Autodesk Inventor™ 4

For each (ipt) object you intend on publishing on an HTML page, you must have the following:

- The **DWG, SAT, or IPT file** you want to have transferred
- **JPG/GIF Image file** that shows your customer a picture of the DWG file
- **XML Object File** describing the embedded object
- **idrop-schema.xml**
- **htm file**
- **background.jpg**

This is the only XML code needed:

```
<?xml version="1.0"?>
  <package xmlns="x-schema: idrop.xdr">
  <proxy defaultsrc="background.jpg"></proxy>
  <dataset defaultsrc="[filename].ipt"></dataset>
  </package>
```

Let's go through each line of the code and describe what's going on.

```
<?xml version="1.0"?>
```

-This tells the browser what version of XML we are coding with.

<package xmlns="x-schema: idrop.xdr">

-This defines the legend or key that describes the tags you are using in XML.

Developer's Notes about this:

1.When the xmlns="x-schema: idrop.xdr" string is used as part of the package value, the XML parser is required to validate the package XML file (and only the package file). If the package XML file does not conform to the schema, an error appears in the browser. Validating the XML file is a performance hit but is extremely helpful as a debugging tool when you are building your site.

Rule of Thumb: It is fine to use the x-schema specification when the package files are being developed, but we advise that it should be removed when your files are published. Once your satisfied that your web page works with i-drop, you can remove this tag and effectively cease the error checking. If you consider that a single page may have more than one i-drop instance on the page, leaving it in could show a noticeable performance hit. Factor in the time it may take to retrieve the schema from some other site, and the page may display quite slowly.

2. If you prefer to keep this error-checking on all of the time, remember that if the schema file can not be found, the i-drop control will not display. So a web site developer has two options:

(a) Copy the schema file to your server, and reference it there (Notice this is a relative specification):

Example: <package xmlns="x-schema:..\schemas\idrop.xdr">

This has the advantage of always being around - but you have to make an effort to check back here for updates. Or:

(b) Probably the most preferable approach for an externally available web page, is this:

Example: <package xmlns="http:\\idrop.autodesk.com\idrop.xdr">

Point the namespace to the schema on Autodesk's web site. This works, but will increase performance hit to display each i-drop control on the HTML page. Also, this will *not* work if you are developing i-drop using this link on an Intra-net with no external access.

<proxy defaultsrc="background.**jpg**"></proxy>

-This is a transparent image file that is used as a 'skin' or frame around the wheel.jpg file. You will need to add this file to the same location as your i-drop content. You can download this file from the publisher's website at www.schroff1.com/inventor/.

<dataset defaultsrc="[filename].**ipt**"></dataset>

-This is the link to the object you are using.

</package>

        -This tag closes the object file.

That's all there is for the object file! All you would typically need to do to get started is change to your appropriate filenames and you have finished your object file.

To create the graphic file, you can use a screen capture program.

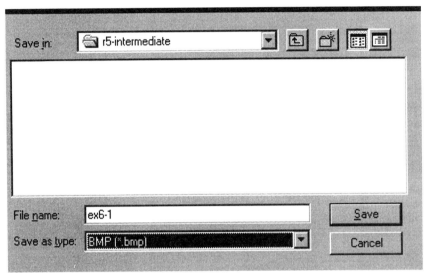

Or you can do a File->Save Copy As->bmp.

Bitmap files can also be used, but they are not as good quality as a jpeg file.

At this point, we have two of the six items on our required list:

    ✓ The part file   ex6-1.ipt
    ✓ The bmp/jpeg file

Now, we have to create the xml object code.
Open Notepad.

```
ex12-2.xml - Notepad
File  Edit  Search  Help
<?xml version = "1.0" encoding = "UTF-8"?>
<package xmlns = "x-schema:InventorSchema.xdr">
</proxy>
<proxy defaultsrc="background.jpg">
<caption>Drag and drop to insert ipart into your Inventor part or assembly file</caption>
</proxy>
<dataset defaultsrc = "ex6-1.ipt">
<datasrc clipformat = "CF_IDROP.INV">
<datafile src = "ex6-1.ipt"/>
<metadatafile>
<srcinfo type = "iam">
<software majorversion = "5" minorversion = "0"/>
<document majorversion = "5" minorversion = "0"/>
</srcinfo>
<destination pathtype ="workspace" pathname = ""/>
</metadatafile>
</datasrc>
</dataset>
</package>
```

Type in the code as shown.

```
<?xml version = "1.0" encoding = "UTF-8"?>
<package xmlns = "x-schema:InventorSchema.xdr">
</proxy>
<proxy defaultsrc="background.jpg">
<caption>Drag and drop to insert ipart into your Inventor part or assembly file</caption>
</proxy>
<dataset defaultsrc = "ex6-1.ipt">
<datasrc clipformat = "CF_IDROP.INV">
<datafile src = "ex6-1.ipt"/>
<metadatafile>
<srcinfo type = "iam">
<software majorversion = "5" minorversion = "0"/>
<document majorversion = "5" minorversion = "0"/>
</srcinfo>
<destination pathtype ="workspace" pathname = ""/>
</metadatafile>
</datasrc>
</dataset>
</package>
```

I have added a caption line under the background.jpg file that instructs viewers on how idrop works.

We now have three of the six items in our list.

✓ The **DWG, SAT, or IPT file** you want to have transferred
✓ **JPG/GIF Image file** that shows your customer a picture of the DWG file
✓ **XML Object File** describing the embedded object

You also need the xml schema. This can be downloaded for free from Autodesk's website.
You can also copy the code below into a notepad file. Save as 'idrop-schema.xml'.

```
<?xml version="1.0"?>

<!--
********************************************************************
-->
<!-- i-drop package schema
-->
<!--
-->
<!-- The i-drop package is a description of a high-level "object" that
can  -->
<!-- be dropped into an i-drop aware application. The package lists
native  -->
<!-- file formats and web page proxy representations.
-->
<!-- The full information about i-drop can be found at:
-->
<!-- http://vizdevel.autodesk.com/idrop
-->
<!--
-->
<!-- Author: Michael Pittman (michael.pittman@autodesk.com)
-->
<!--
********************************************************************
-->

<Schema name="idrop-13mar2000"
        xmlns="urn:schemas-microsoft-com:xml-data"
        xmlns:dt="urn:schemas-microsoft-com:datatypes">

<!--
********************************************************************
-->
<!-- Attributes -->

<AttributeType name="src" dt:type="uri" required="no">
        <description>URL of a source file</description>
</AttributeType>

<AttributeType name="defaultsrc" dt:type="uri" required="no">
        <description>URL of a default source file</description>
</AttributeType>
```

```
<AttributeType name="clipformat" dt:type="string" required="no">
      <description>Custom defined clipboard format</description>
</AttributeType>

<AttributeType name="clsid" dt:type="uuid" required="no">
      <description>Class ID of an ActiveX control</description>
</AttributeType>

<AttributeType name="codebase" dt:type="uri" required="no">
      <description>URL to an ActiveX control distribution (ala object
tag in HTML)</description>
</AttributeType>

<AttributeType name="name" dt:type="string" required="no">
      <description>Name of a parameter (ala object tag in
HTML)</description>
</AttributeType>

<AttributeType name="value" dt:type="string" required="no">
      <description>Value of a parameter (ala object tag in
HTML)</description>
</AttributeType>

<!--
********************************************************************
-->
<!-- Elements -->

<ElementType name="package">
      <description>i-Drop XML package file</description>
      <element type="proxy" minOccurs="1" maxOccurs="1"/>
      <element type="dataset" minOccurs="1" maxOccurs="1"/>
</ElementType>

<ElementType name="proxy">
      <description>Stand-in for the dataset</description>
      <attribute type="defaultsrc" required="yes"/>
      <element type="caption" minOccurs="0" maxOccurs="1"/>
      <element type="img" minOccurs="0" maxOccurs="*"/>
      <element type="activex" minOccurs="0" maxOccurs="*"/>
</ElementType>

<ElementType name="caption">
      <description>Caption to display with the proxy</description>
</ElementType>

<ElementType name="img">
      <description>Bitmap image file</description>
      <attribute type="src" required="yes"/>
</ElementType>

<ElementType name="activex">
      <description>HTML-like definition of an ActiveX
control</description>
      <attribute type="clsid" required="yes"/>
      <attribute type="codebase" required="no"/>
      <element type="param" minOccurs="0" maxOccurs="*"/>
```

```
</ElementType>

<ElementType name="param">
      <description>Parameter to an ActiveX control</description>
      <attribute type="name" required="yes"/>
      <attribute type="value" required="yes"/>
</ElementType>

<ElementType name="dataset">
      <description>Collection of data files to choose
from</description>
      <attribute type="defaultsrc" required="yes"/>
      <element type="datasrc" minOccurs="0" maxOccurs="*"/>
</ElementType>

<ElementType name="datasrc">
      <description>Collection of data files to treat as
one</description>
      <attribute type="clipformat" required="no"/>
      <element type="datafile" minOccurs="1" maxOccurs="1"/>
      <element type="xreffile" minOccurs="0" maxOccurs="*"/>
</ElementType>

<ElementType name="datafile">
      <description>Single data file (may have
dependencies)</description>
      <attribute type="src" required="yes"/>
</ElementType>

<ElementType name="xreffile">
      <description>Externally referenced file</description>
      <attribute type="src" required="yes"/>
</ElementType>

</Schema>
```

We now have four of the six items in our list.

- ✓ The **DWG, SAT, or IPT file** you want to have transferred
- ✓ **JPG/GIF Image file** that shows your customer a picture of the DWG file
- ✓ **XML Object File** describing the embedded object
- ✓ **idrop-schema.xml**

The next item on our list is the html file.

Again we open Notepad and type in the following code:

```
<HTML>
<TITLE><B>idrop example <B> </TITLE>
<BODY>

<object classid="clsid:21E0CB95-1198-4945-A3D2-4BF804295F78" id="IDrop1" width="300" height="275" border="0">
<param name="package" value="ex12-2.xml"/>
<param name="background" value="background.jpg">
<param name="proxyrect" value="0,0, 240,236">
<param name="griprect" value="0, 0, 240, 236">
<param name="validate" value="1">
</object>
</BODY>
</HTML>
```

<HTML>…</HTML>

Defines the beginning and end of the HTML document. This is the very first thing and very last thing in the file.

<TITLE> <B> idrop example <B> </TITLE>

Defines the title for the page. <B> formats the title to use bold font.

<BODY> </BODY>

Marks the beginning and end of the body of the webpage.

<object classid="clsid:21E0CB95-1198-4945-A3D2-4BF804295F78" id="IDrop1" width="300" height="275" border="0">

The next line identifies the idrop code to use with the web page.

```
<param name="package" value="ex12-2.xml"/>
<param name="background" value="background.jpg">
<param name="proxyrect" value="0,0, 240,236">
<param name="griprect" value="0, 0, 240, 236">
<param name="validate" value="1">
</object>
</BODY>
</HTML>
```

The remainder of the html code is listed above.

We now have five of the six items in our list.

- ✓ The **DWG, SAT, or IPT file** you want to have transferred
- ✓ **JPG/GIF Image file** that shows your customer a picture of the DWG file
- ✓ **XML Object File** describing the embedded object
- ✓ **idrop-schema.xml**
- ✓ **htm file**

All that remains is the

- **background.jpg**

This can be downloaded from the publisher's website at www.schroff1.com/inventor/.

idrop is still relatively new technology and it has not been fully documented.
I hope to create a full tutorial on how to create idrop content once Autodesk makes that information available to me. The tutorial will be posted on my website at www.mossdesigns.com, so keep checking for it.

TIP ON TRANSCRIPTING

The Transcript feature has been removed in Inventor R5 and is no longer supported. A transcript is a script similar to VBA (but not VBA) that contains instructions to play operations multiple times. This feature will record all your actions inside Inventor and can be replayed later. You cannot activate this feature from the user interface (as it is removed) and you need to work in the registry.

You have to edit registry keys directly (using regedit or a similar interface) to turn transcripting on. Without Inventor running, you should set the registry key:

HKEY_CURRENT_USER\Software\Autodesk\Inventor\RegistryVersion5.1\System\Preferences\
Transcript\TranscriptingOn
to 1

Then you should set the following if you wish to have an user interface to play the file:

HKEY_CURRENT_USER\Software\Autodesk\Inventor\RegistryVersion5.1\System\Preferences\
Transcript\AllowReplay
to 1.

Then launch Inventor and create your drawing. This creates a transcript file (*.tf) in the location specified in the registry key two keys above the one specifying TranscriptingOn. By default, this is the key:

\Autodesk\Inventor 5\Bin\Inventor.exe:TransDir

You can manually edit this *.tf file if you wish.

To run the macro, start Inventor with no document open, then
* drag and drop the macro (*.tf) file onto the Inventor window.
* or from the "Tools" pull down menu, choose "Replay Transcript".
 (You might want to edit the file to remove the last couple of lines, which actually close the drawing).

NOTE: Transcripting is no longer officially supported in Release 5 and may have unpredictable
        results.

QUIZ 4

T F 1. You can insert an Excel spreadsheet into the Engineer's Notebook.

T F 2. You must have an active Internet connection in order to host or participate in a NetMeeting.

3. To create an Engineering Note:

    A. Highlight the feature, sketch, part, or assembly name in the browser, right click and select 'Create Note'
    B. Select the feature, sketch, or part in the graphics area, right click and select 'Create Note'
    C. Select Tools->Create Note from the menu
    D. A or B, but not C

4. Design Assistant is a:

    A. Set of tutorials that help the user in creating designs
    B. set of dialogs to assist the user in fixing design problems
    C. allows the user to manage Inventor files and engineering documentation
    D. allows the user to collaborate over the internet

5. You can create two types of reports in Design Assistant:

    A. Hierarchy and Properties
    B. Where-Used and Properties
    C. History and Where_Used
    D. Item Master and Where-Used

6. Pack and Go can be used for Inventor files but it can only be accessed using:

    A. Inventor
    B. Windows Explorer
    C. NetMeeting
    D. Design Assistant

7.   To copy properties from one file to another, use:

       A.   Design Assistant
       B.   Windows Explorer
       C.   Engineer's Notebook
       D.   Parameters

8.   Pack and Go:

       A.   Compresses all the selected files and any referenced filesinto a zip file
       B.   Copies all the selected files and any referenced files into a directory
       C.   Emails all the selected files and any referenced files
       D.   All of the above

T F 9.   NetMeeting is an Autodesk application

10.   Engineering Notes can be sorted by:

       A.   Name
       B.   Date
       C.   Author
       D.   All of the above

T F 11.   If you set your NetMeeting to be secured, you can not use audio or video.

12.   You can access Design Assistant using:

       A.   Microsoft Word
       B.   Windows Explorer
       C.   Internet Explorer
       D.   Microsoft Excel

T F 13.   You can add an Engineer's Note to an edge, sketch, feature, or part.

14.   You can hide Notes in the Browser by:

       A.   Using the Browser Filter
       B.   Disabling the Show Notes in Browser in the Application Options
       C.   Highlight the Note in the browser, right click and disable Visible
       D.   All of the above

15.   Compact can be used to:

   A.   compress a file
   B.   purge a file of unreferenced data
   C.   reduce a file's size
   D.   all of the above

16.   To set the colors used by Engineer's Notebook, use:

   A.   Format->Colors
   B.   Format->Standards
   C.   Tools->Options->Notebook
   D.   Inside the Engineer's Notebook

17.   This tool, available in the Engineer's Notebook, does this:

   A.   Inserts a Comment
   B.   Inserts an arrow
   C.   Exports a Note
   D.   Imports a Note

T F 18.   You must configure your NetMeeting before you can use it.

19.   The toolbar shown is:

   A.   Notebook
   B.   Standard
   C.   Paint
   D.   WordArt

T F 20.   The Engineer's Notebook has it's own toolbar.

ANSWERS:
1) T; 2) T; 3) D; 4) C; 5) A; 6) B; 7) A; 8) B; 9) F; 10) D; 11) T; 12) B; 13) T; 14) A; 15) D; 16) C; 17) B; 18) T; 19) A; 20) T

Lesson 13
Simulating Motion

Driven Assembly Constraints simulate mechanical motion by driving a constraint through a sequence of steps. Specified increments and a distance reposition the component sequentially.

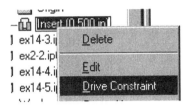

To Access: In the browser, right-click the assembly constraint and select Drive Constraint.

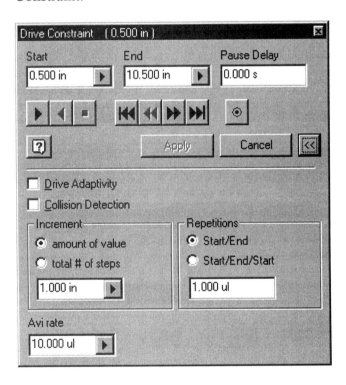

Set a precise amount of motion along a vector or about an axis. Use to simulate motion or test a range of motion for a constrained component. Click the More button to override default values for Increment and Repetitions.	
Start	Sets start position of the offset or angle. Value may be entered, measured, or set to dimensioned value. Default value is the defined offset or angle.
End	Sets end position of the offset or angle. Value may be entered, measured, or set to dimensioned value. Default is start value plus 10.
Pause Delay	Sets delay between steps in seconds. Default is 0.01.
Drive Adaptivity	Select check box to adapt components while maintaining the constraint relationship, if needed.
Collision Detection	Select check box to drive the constrained assembly until a collision is detected. When in interference is detected, it is displayed and its constraint value shown.
Increment	Amount of Value specifies that the increment will be the value specified in the edit box. Default is 1.0. Total # of Steps divides the drive sequence into a specified number of equal steps. Edit box sets the value of each increment or the number of steps. Value may be measured, entered, or as dimensioned.
Repetitions	Start/End drives the constraint from the start value to the end value and resets at the start value. Start/End/Start drives the constraint from the start value to the end value and then in reverse to the start value. Edit box sets the number of repetitions.
Avi rate	Specifies the increments at which a "snapshot" is taken for inclusion as a frame in a recorded animation.

TIP: Driven Constraints can only be defined in an assembly file.

	Advance and reverse the drive sequence. The dialog box remains open while the drive sequence plays. Values may be changed any time the sequence is paused or stopped.
▶	Forward drives the constraint forward. Not available unless both Start and End boxes have values. May resume forward play after a Stop.
◀	Reverse drives the constraint in reverse. Not available unless both Start and End boxes have values. May resume reverse play after a Stop.
■	Stop temporarily stops the constraint drive sequence. Allows values to be edited and forward or reverse play to be resumed, advanced a step at a time, or advanced to beginning or end.
⏮	Go to Start returns the constraint to the starting value and resets the constraint driver. Not available unless the constraint driver has been run.
⏪	Single Step Reverse reverses the constraint driver one step in the sequence. Not available unless the drive sequence has been stopped.
⏩	Single Step Forward advances the constraint driver one step in the sequence. Not available unless the drive sequence has been stopped.
⏭	Go to End advances the constraint sequence to the end value.
◉	Start recording begins capturing frames at the specified rate for inclusion in an animation.

Exercise 13-1

Moving a Ball

File: Ball.iam
Estimated Time: 15 Minutes

Download the ball and tube assembly
From the publisher's website:
www.schroff1.com/inventor

You can also create your own
Tube and Ball for this exercise.

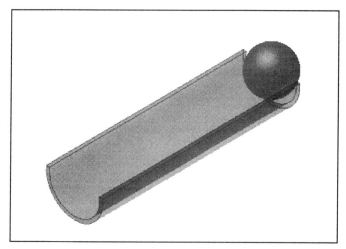

We want to simulate the motion of the ball moving down the tube.

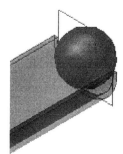

We start by turning on the visibility of the XY plane on the ball.

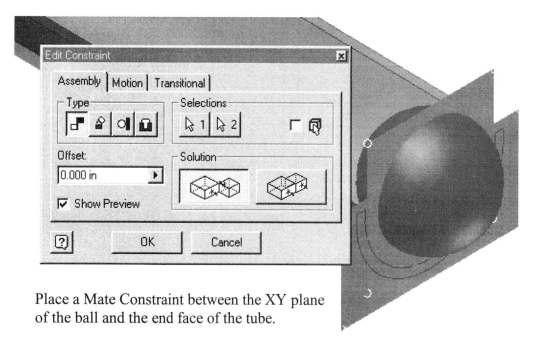

Place a Mate Constraint between the XY plane
of the ball and the end face of the tube.

Once you've placed the Mate constraint, you can turn off the visibility of the ball's XY plane.

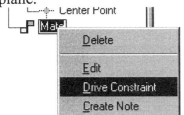

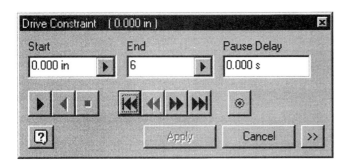

Highlight the Mate constraint in the Browser.
Right click and select 'Drive Constraint'.

Set the start to 0 and the end equal to the length of the tube.

Press the Forward button and you will see the ball move down the tube.

Exercise 13-2
Turning a Handle

File: Lever.iam
Estimated Time: 15 Minutes

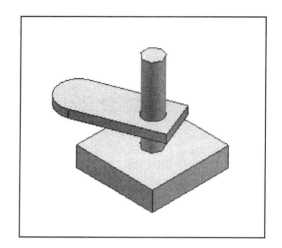

Download the lever assembly
From the publisher's website:
www.schroff1.com/inventor

You can also quickly create a base with
a cylinder and a small handle. Use an
insert constraint between the handle's
hole and the cylinder.

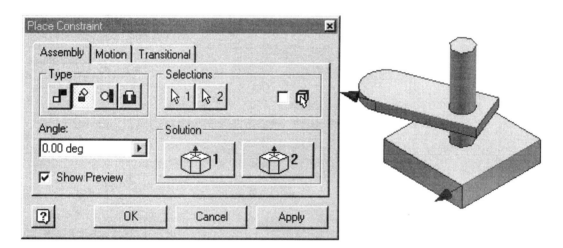

We add an angle constraint between one side of the handle and one side of the base.
Set the angle to 0 degrees.

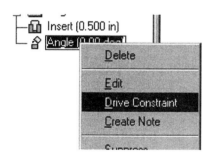

Locate the angle constraint in the browser.
Right click and select 'Drive Constraint'.

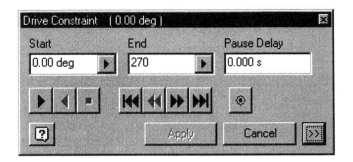

Set the Start at 0 degrees.
Set the End to 270 degrees.

Press the Forward button to
watch the handle turn.

Save the file as Ex13-2.iam.

Exercise 13-3
Compressing a Spring

File: spring.iam
Estimated Time: 15 Minutes

Download the spring assembly
from the publisher's website:
www.schroff1.com/inventor

One of the more difficult exercises is to
simulate a spring undergoing tension or
compression.

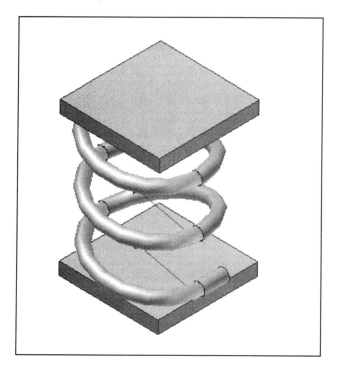

This is accomplished by creating and assembling spring segments instead of a single
spring helix.

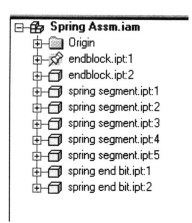

To simplify the process you can create a single
spring segment and a spring end part and then
use multiple instances to comprise your spring.

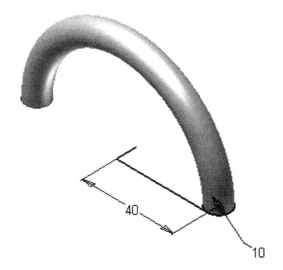

Each spring segment is defined by a spring diameter and a wire diameter.
A 180-degree revolution is performed around an axis.

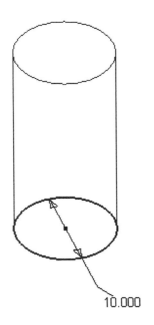

The spring end is a simple cylindrical extrusion. For a flattened end, you can chamfer one of the cylinder's ends.

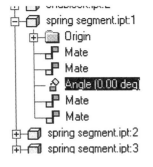

You assembly the spring segments using mate constraints. You control the spring compression with an Angle constraint.

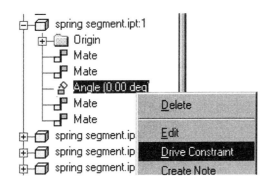

Highlight the Angle constraint.
Right click and select 'Drive Constraint'.

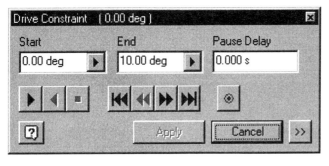

The Angle is set to go from 0 to
10 degrees. Press the Forward
button to watch the spring
compress.

The Angle and Drive Constraints must be applied to all spring segments in order for the
spring to look proper when it compresses.

Lesson 14
Additional Exercises

The project for this textbook is a scooter.
So far you have created the handle bar and wheel that will be used for the assembly.

Parts List for Scooter

Ex2-2	Handle Bar
Ex6-1	Wheel
Ex14-1	Frame
Ex14-2	Strut
Ex14-3	Foot Support
Ex14-4	Riser Bar
Ex14-5	Riser Clamp

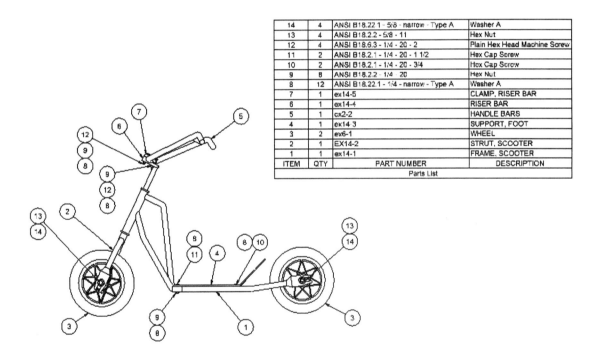

ITEM	QTY	PART NUMBER	DESCRIPTION
14	4	ANSI B18.22.1 - 5/8 - narrow - Type A	Washer A
13	4	ANSI B18.2.2 - 5/8 - 11	Hex Nut
12	4	ANSI B18.6.3 - 1/4 - 20 - 2	Plain Hex Head Machine Screw
11	2	ANSI B18.2.1 - 1/4 - 20 - 1 1/2	Hex Cap Screw
10	2	ANSI B18.2.1 - 1/4 - 20 - 3/4	Hex Cap Screw
9	8	ANSI B18.2.2 - 1/4 - 20	Hex Nut
8	12	ANSI B18.22.1 - 1/4 - narrow - Type A	Washer A
7	1	ex14-5	CLAMP, RISER BAR
6	1	ex14-4	RISER BAR
5	1	cx2-2	HANDLE BARS
4	1	ex14-3	SUPPORT, FOOT
3	2	ex6-1	WHEEL
2	1	EX14-2	STRUT, SCOOTER
1	1	ex14-1	FRAME, SCOOTER
			Parts List

You can use either the Fastener Library or the Standard Parts Library for the hardware. The Fastener Library is located on your Inventor CD. The Fastener Library must be installed separately in order to be utilized.

Fastener Library

In addition to the RedSpark Standard Parts, a Fastener Library is included on the Autodesk Inventor installation CD. Browse to the FastenerLibrary folder, and then double-click on Setup.exe to install fasteners.

1. Double-click the setup.exe file in the FastenerLibrary folder on the installation CD. The Autodesk Inventor Release 4 Fastener Library setup will run and will be completed after approximately 1 to 5 minutes.
2. Start Autodesk Inventor and close any open documents.
3. From the Tools menu, choose Fasteners > Fasteners Setup.
4. In the Fasteners Setup dialog box, choose Library Path to select the folder location to store the fasteners.

Note: When you select a folder in step 4, a new library search path is created in the active path file. The library path is created with the proper naming convention, for example:

[Library Search Paths]

_Inventor Fastener Library V1=E:\Inventor Files\Fastener Library

If no path file is defined, the search path is added to the Library Search Path section of the File Locations dialog box, which you can access by choosing Options from the Tools menu, then selecting the File Locations tab in the Options dialog box.

The Autodesk Inventor Fastener Library provides a set of the most commonly used fastening hardware in five international standards. It is a library of non-parametric, non-editable, standards based parts commonly used in machine design. It is an Autodesk Inventor add-in/bonus application.

The library parts can be inserted into Autodesk Inventor assembly models and appear in the assembly browser with their description as the name. The fasteners also contain bill of material (BOM) property information. Important information regarding the BOM properties is below.

The five standards included are ANSI (USA), JIS (Japanese), ISO (International), GB (Chinese), and DIN (German). The types of fastener components included in the library are screws, threaded bolts, nuts, washers, and pins.

TIP: The fasteners in the Inventor Fastener Library are non-parametric and non-editable. However, there are third-party developers who have created parametric fastener libraries for use with Inventor. A good source is Cad Management Group at http://www.cadmanagementgroup.com.

By default, a Bill of Materials or Parts List in Autodesk Inventor will display part description information. Examples of part description information are "Hexagon Socket Head Cap Screw" and "Hex-Head Bolt". Each of the Fastener Library parts contains this information. In addition to the basic description, each part also contains important standards information, which specifies the part and the international standard that it is based on. Examples of standards information are "ANSI B18.3 - 7/8 - 9 - 6 1/2" and "DIN 931-1 - M12 x 80". Together, the description and standards information fully specify the fastener.

You can configure the standards information in your BOMs on a per assembly basis. Alternatively, you can configure the default assembly template file that you use to include the standards information for all assemblies that you create based on that template. Detailed online help information is available in Autodesk Inventor to help you configure the information that is displayed in the BOM as well as how to setup and use templates.

If you are familiar with configuring the Bill of Materials, follow these instructions to include the standards information in your BOMs.

To display the "Standard" information of a fastener in the BOM:

Add the "Standard" property to the "Selected Properties" in the "Bill of Material Column Chooser".

To display the "Standard" property of a fastener in the Parts List:

Add the "Standard" property to the "Selected Properties" in the "Parts List Column Chooser".

To display the "Description" property of a fastener in the "Design Assistant":

Add the "Description" to the "Selected Properties" in the "Select Properties to View" dialog of the Design Assistant.

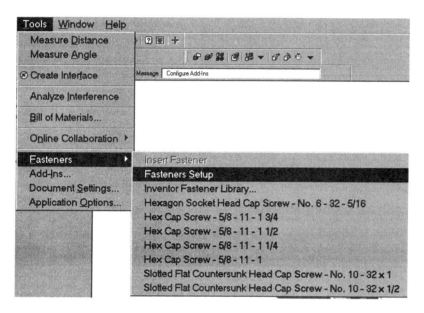

Go to Tools->Fasteners.
If you have just installed the fastener library, you need to do the Fasteners Setup.
To perform the Fasteners Setup, close all files.
Then go to Tools->Fasteners Setup.
Locate the path where you installed the Fasteners Library.
Press 'OK'.

Now open an assembly file and continue.

Insert Fastener

TIP: The Fastener Library can only be accessed inside an Assembly file. You will not be able to insert a fastener into a Part file.

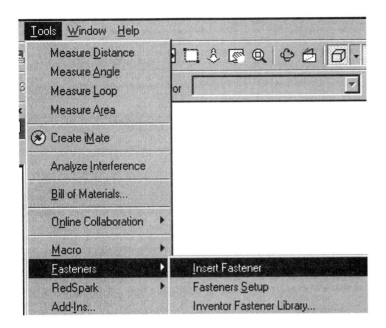

Go to Tools->Fasteners->Insert Fastener.

TIP: Inventor keeps track of your favorite fasteners in the menu. This saves time in selecting and placing fasteners. Use this short cut tool to quickly select a fastener.

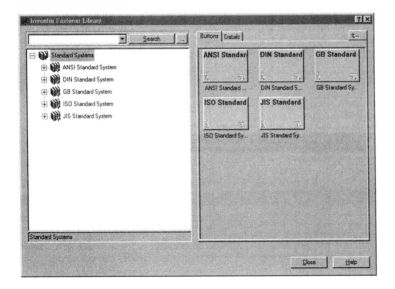

The Inventor Fastener Library dialog will appear.

We wish to insert a 10-32 countersunk screw.

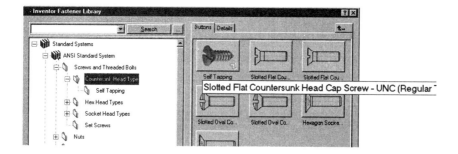

We can locate the desired screw by using the browser on the left. As we go down the browser tree, the buttons on the right update. Passing our mouse over each button provides a help tip about the parts located under that button.

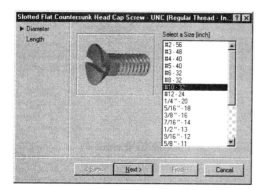

We select a Slotted Flat Countersunk Head Cap Screw- UNC. We highlight #10-32 and press 'Next'.

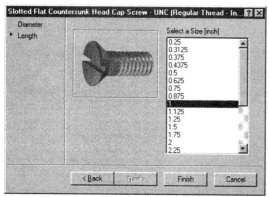

For a length, we select 1. Then we press 'Finish'.

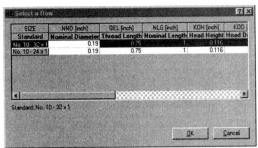

Inventor informs us there are two standard fasteners that meet our requirements. We select the 10-32 x 1.
Next, we press 'OK'.

We only need one screw so once one instance appears in the browser and in the drawing window, we pick to place the screw and then right click and select 'Done'.

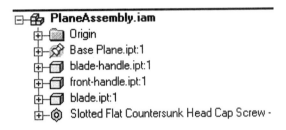

Notice how the Browser lists the fastener part.

Exercise 14-1:
Frame

File: Standard using Inches
Estimated Time: 60 minutes

This exercise reviews the following:

- Sweep
- Work Plane
- Work Axis
- Work Points
- 3D Sketches
- Extrude
- Loft
- Mirror Feature

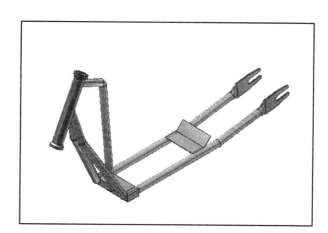

Start a New Part File using Standard.

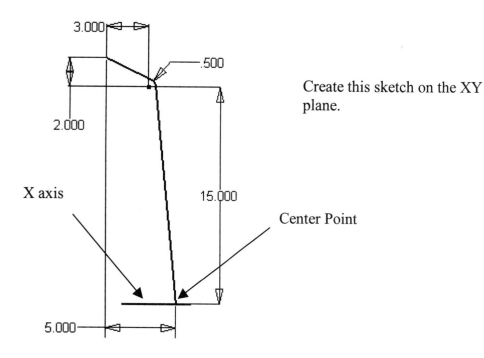

Create this sketch on the XY
plane.

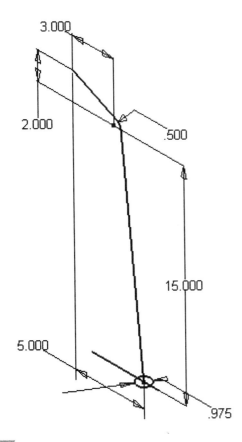

Place a .975 diameter circle on the XZ plane so it is coincident to the center point.

Perform a Sweep.

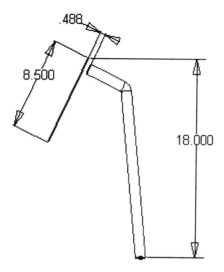

Draw a single line on the XY Plane. Use dimensions and constraints to locate it properly.

There is a parallel constraint between the line and edge of the pipe.

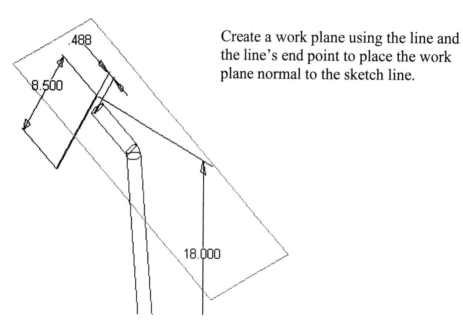

Create a work plane using the line and the line's end point to place the work plane normal to the sketch line.

Place a 1.35 diameter circle on the end of the sketch line.

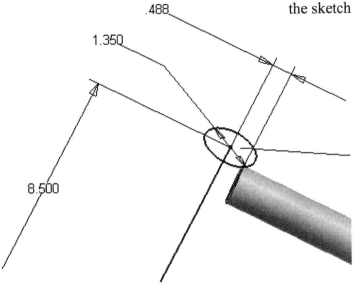

.488

1.350

8.500

Sweep the circle down the line.

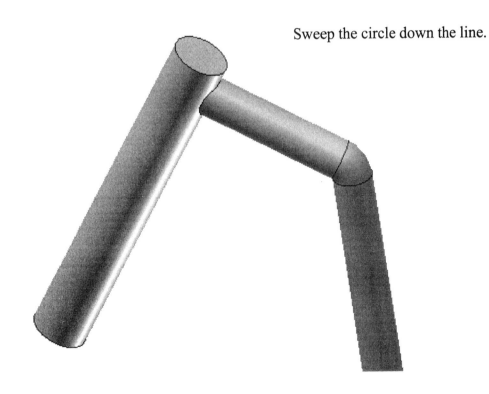

Select the top plane of the second sweep for a new sketch.

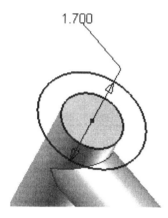

Draw a 1.7 diameter circle concentric to the cylinder.

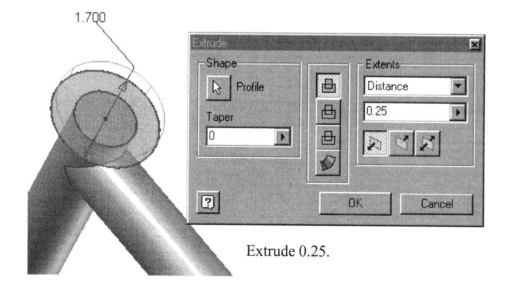

Extrude 0.25.

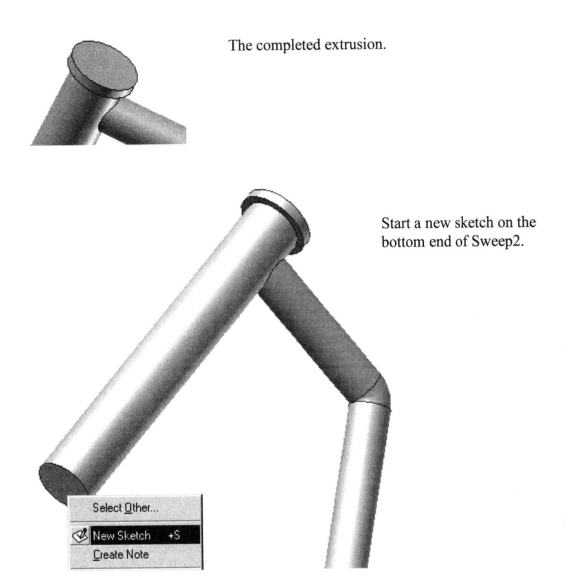

The completed extrusion.

Start a new sketch on the bottom end of Sweep2.

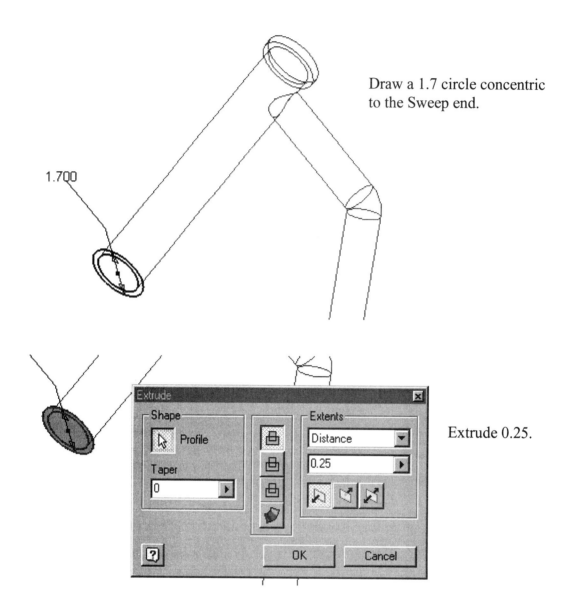

Draw a 1.7 circle concentric to the Sweep end.

1.700

Extrude 0.25.

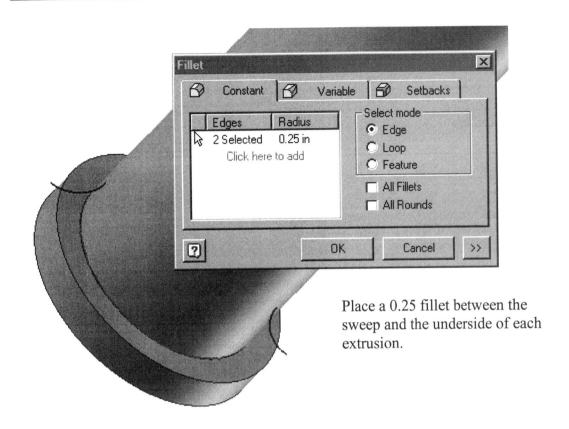

Place a 0.25 fillet between the sweep and the underside of each extrusion.

Create an Offset Work Plane a distance of -2.25 from the XY Work Plane.

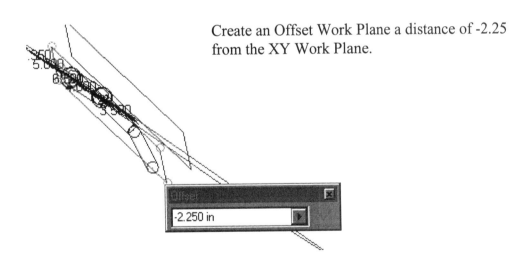

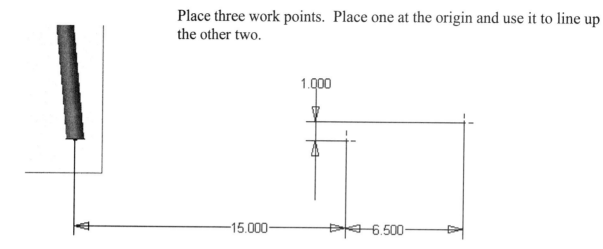

Place three work points. Place one at the origin and use it to line up the other two.

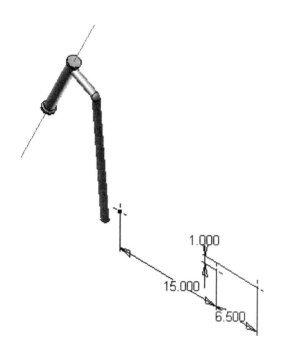

Place a work axis through Sweep2. Place an Angled Work Plane using the Work Axis and the XY plane at an angle of –10 degrees.

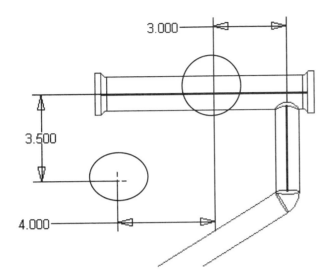

Place two points on the angled work plane.

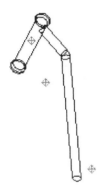

Place five work points – one at each point on the two sketches.

Enter 3D Sketch Mode.

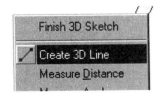

Right click in the graphics window and select 'Create 3D Line'.

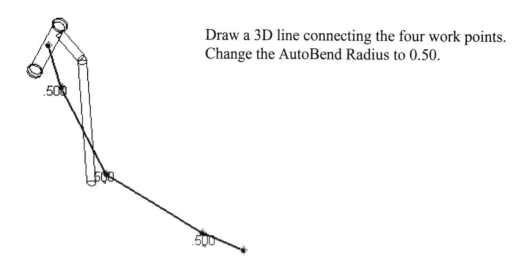

Draw a 3D line connecting the four work points.
Change the AutoBend Radius to 0.50.

Place a work plane on the end of the 3D sketch using the line and endpoint of the sketch.

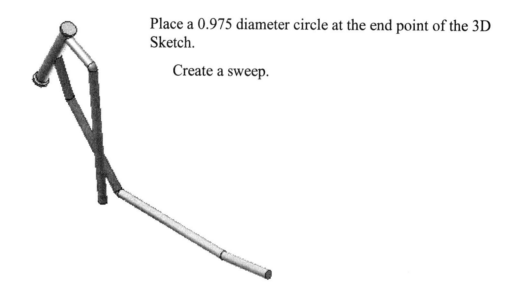

Place a 0.975 diameter circle at the end point of the 3D Sketch.

Create a sweep.

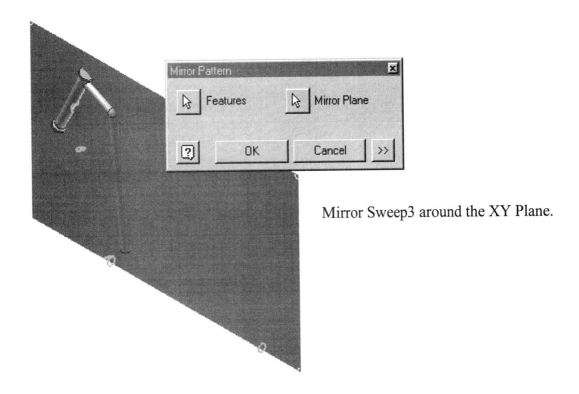

Mirror Sweep3 around the XY Plane.

Our model so far.

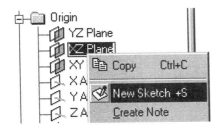

Start a New Sketch on the XZ Plane.

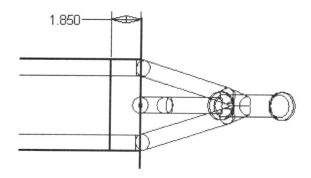

Draw a rectangle and constrain to the outer edges of the pipes in the vertical direction and the origin in the horizontal direction.

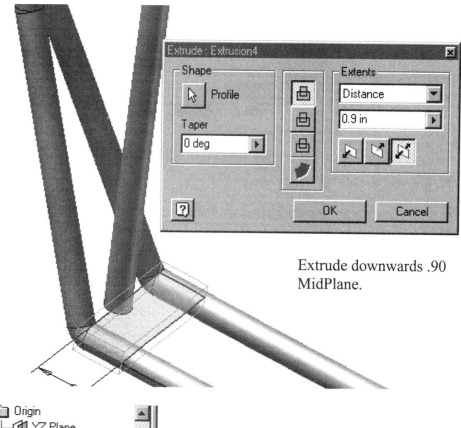

Extrude downwards .90 MidPlane.

Select the XY Plane for a New Sketch.

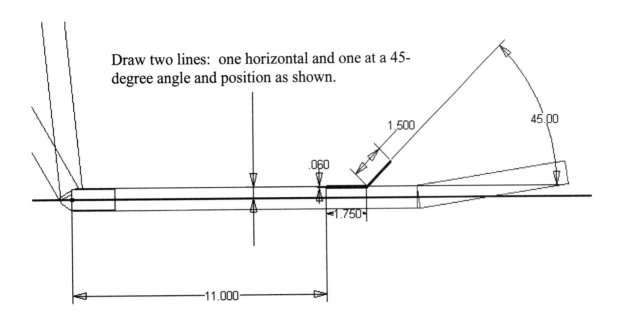

Draw two lines: one horizontal and one at a 45-degree angle and position as shown.

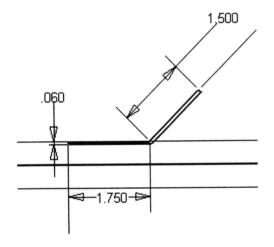

Offset the sketch and set the offset value as .060.

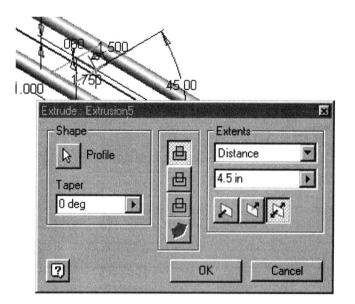

Extrude Mid-Plane a
Distance of 4.5.

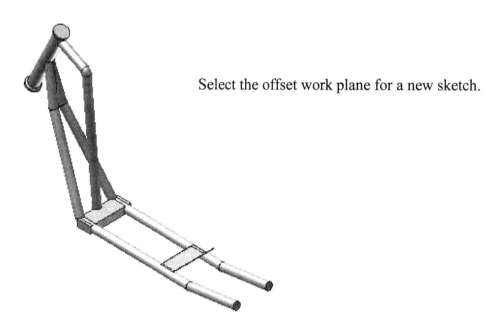

Select the offset work plane for a new sketch.

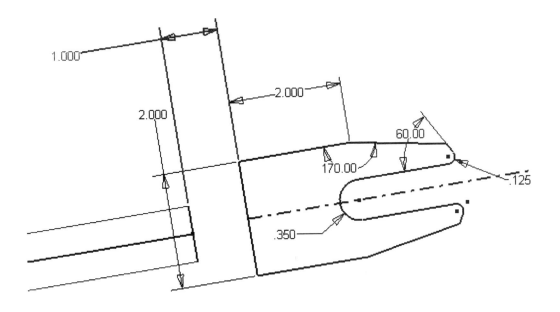

Create the following sketch.
If you mirror the geometry about the centerline, you only have to specify one side of the sketch.

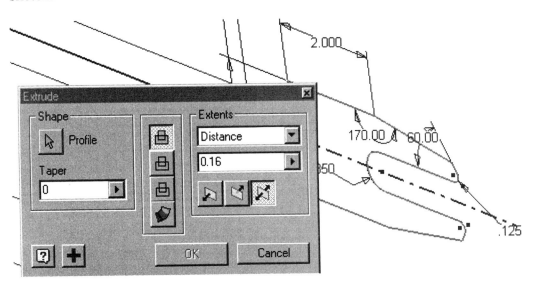

Extrude Mid-Plane a Distance of 0.16.

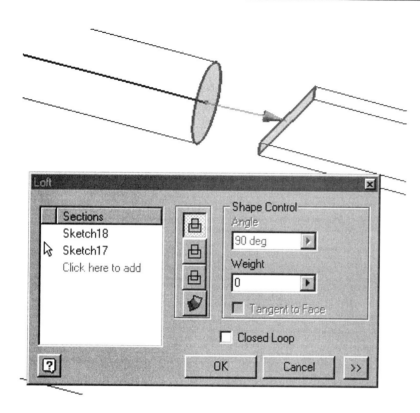

Create two sketches.
Project the end of
the rectangle for a
sketch.
Project the end of
the sweep for a
second sketch.
Create a loft between
the two sketches.

We've created a spade end to use for the axle.

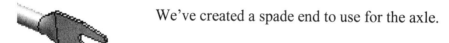

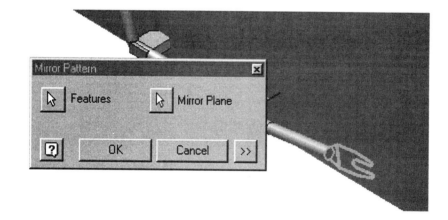

Mirror the Loft
and the Extrude
About the XY
plane.

Our model so far.

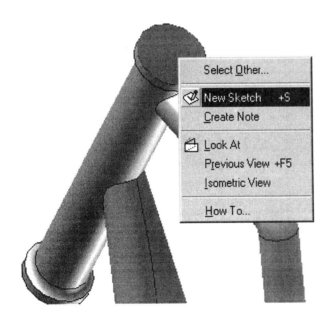

Select the top of the
cylinder for a New Sketch.

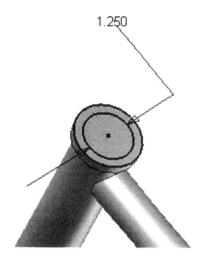

Draw a 1.25 diameter circle.

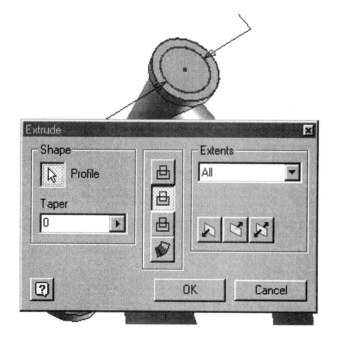

Extrude as a Cut
Through All.

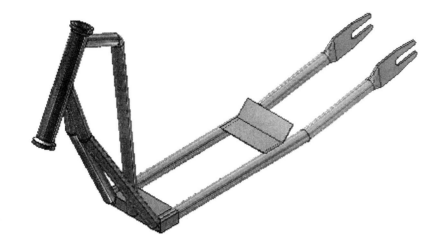

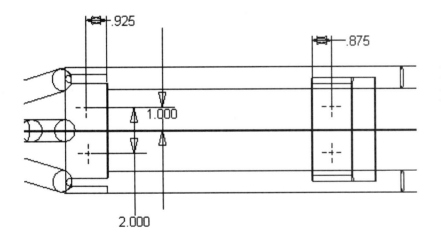

Place four hole points. Two points on the each platform.

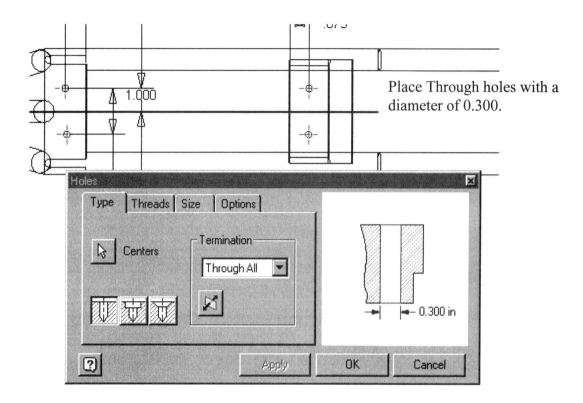

Place Through holes with a diameter of 0.300.

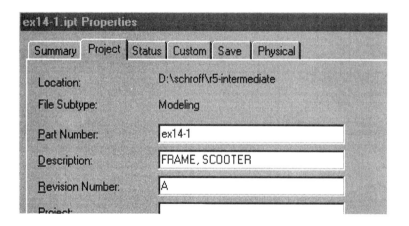

Assign a Description and Revision Number.

Save the file as Ex14-1.ipt.

Lesson 14-2
Strut

File: Standard using Inches
Estimated Time: 60 minutes

This exercise reviews the following:

- Sweep
- Work Plane
- Work Axis
- Work Points
- 3D Sketches
- Extrude
- Loft
- Mirror Feature

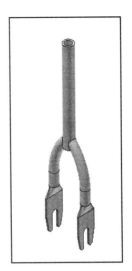

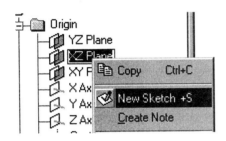

Create a sketch on the XZ Plane.

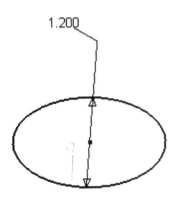

Draw a 1.2 circle with center point coincident to the origin.

Extrude 11 inches.

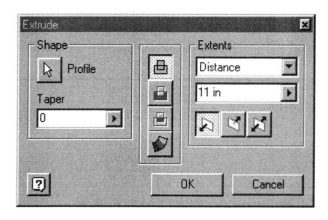

Create a New Sketch on the XY Plane.

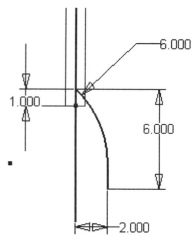

Create the sketch.

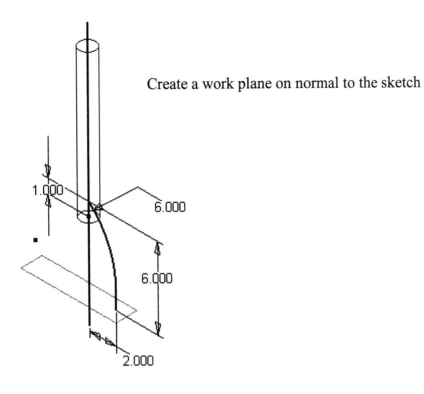

Create a work plane on normal to the sketch

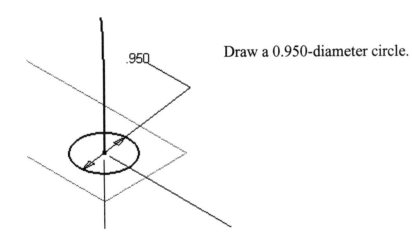

Draw a 0.950-diameter circle.

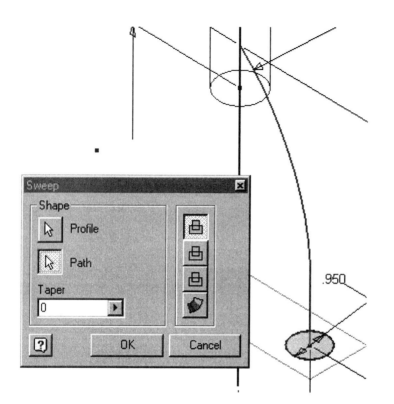

Sweep the circle up
the sketch path.

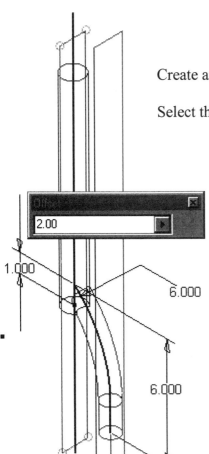

Create an Offset Work Plane 2.00 from the YZ Plane.

Select the Offset plane for a New Sketch.

You can either copy the spade sketch from ex14-1. ipt or redraw it. To copy it, open the ex14-1.ipt file. Locate the spade sketch. Right click, select 'Copy'. Switch to this file. Locate the offset work plane, select it, right click and select 'Paste'. Then rotate and move the sketch into the correct position.

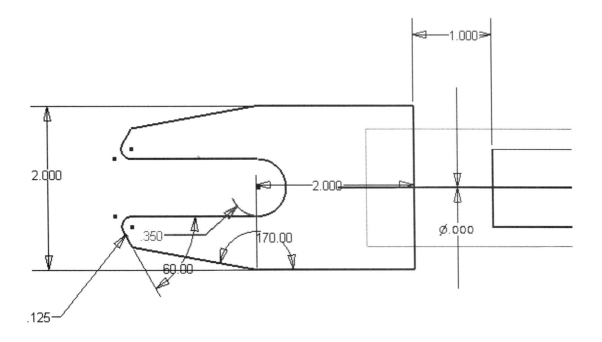

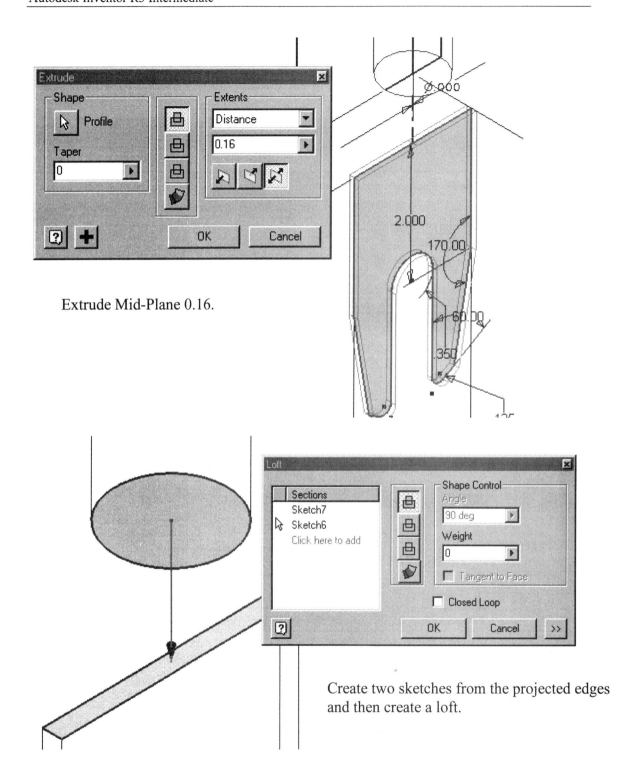

Extrude Mid-Plane 0.16.

Create two sketches from the projected edges and then create a loft.

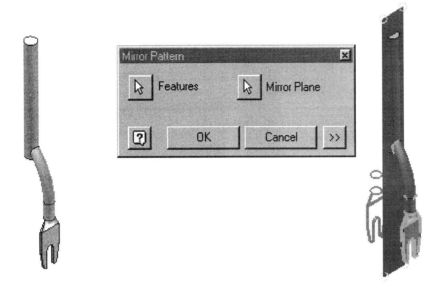

Mirror the Sweep, Extrude and Loft about the YZ Plane.

Select the top of the cylinder for a New Sketch.
Place a Point, Hole Center in the center of the cylinder top.

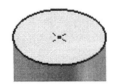

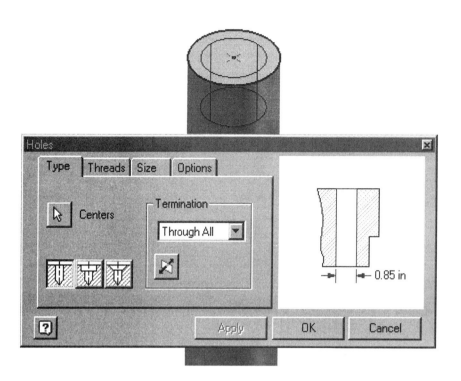

Place a 0.85-diameter hole Through All.

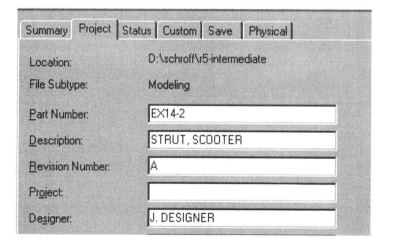

Fill in the Properties for this part.

Save the file as Ex14-2.ipt.

Exercise 14-3
Foot Support

File: New using Standard (inches)
Estimated Time: 30 minutes

This exercise reviews the following:

- Extrude
- Hole

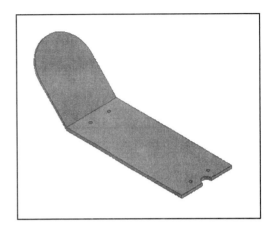

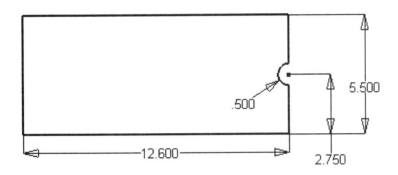

Create the sketch on the XZ (top) work plane.

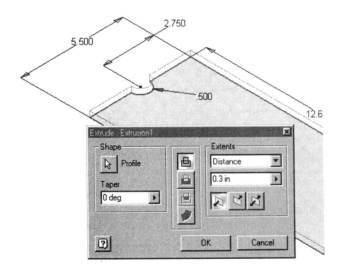

Extrude 0.3 in.

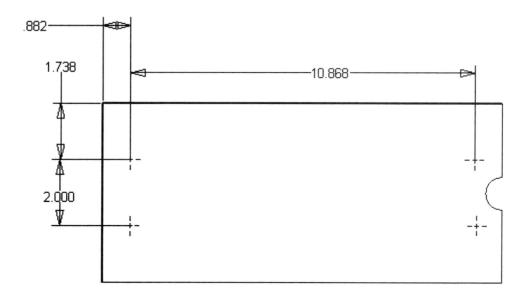

Place four hole points.

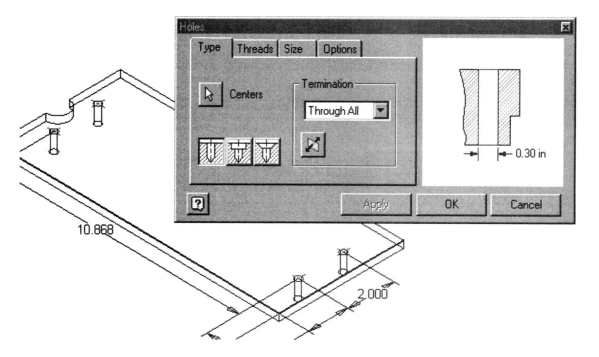

Place Through All holes with a diameter of 0.300.

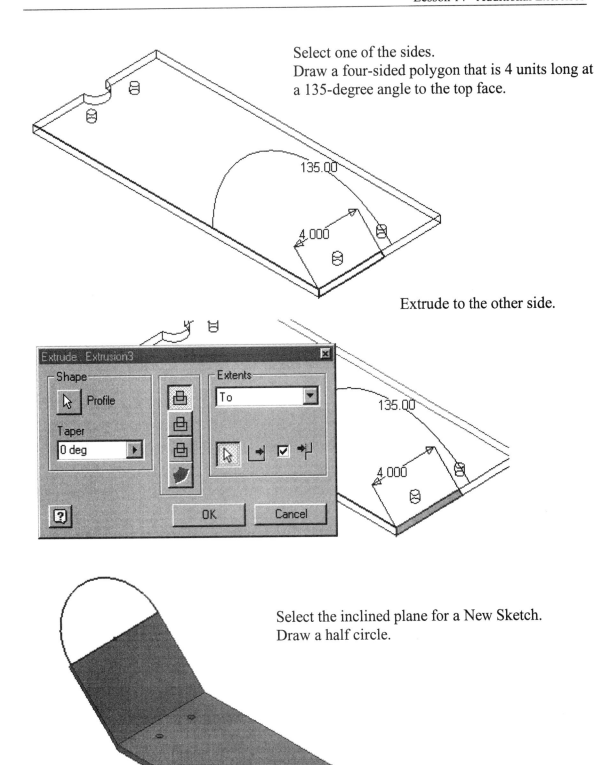

Select one of the sides.
Draw a four-sided polygon that is 4 units long at a 135-degree angle to the top face.

Extrude to the other side.

Select the inclined plane for a New Sketch.
Draw a half circle.

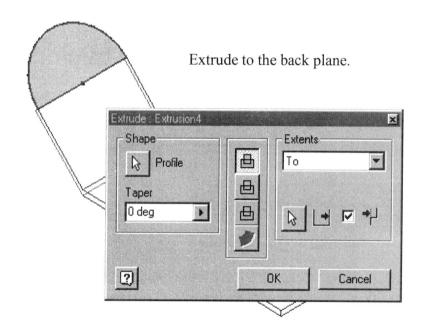

Extrude to the back plane.

Set the File Properties with a Description and Revision Number.
Save the file as ex14-3.ipt.

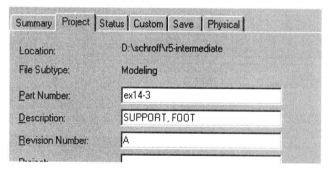

Exercise 14-4

Riser Bar

File: New using Standard (inches)
Estimated Time: 30 minutes

This exercise reviews the following:

- Extrude
- Hole

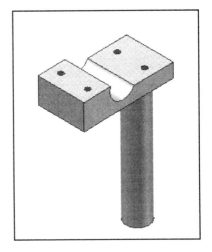

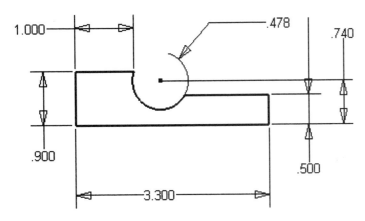

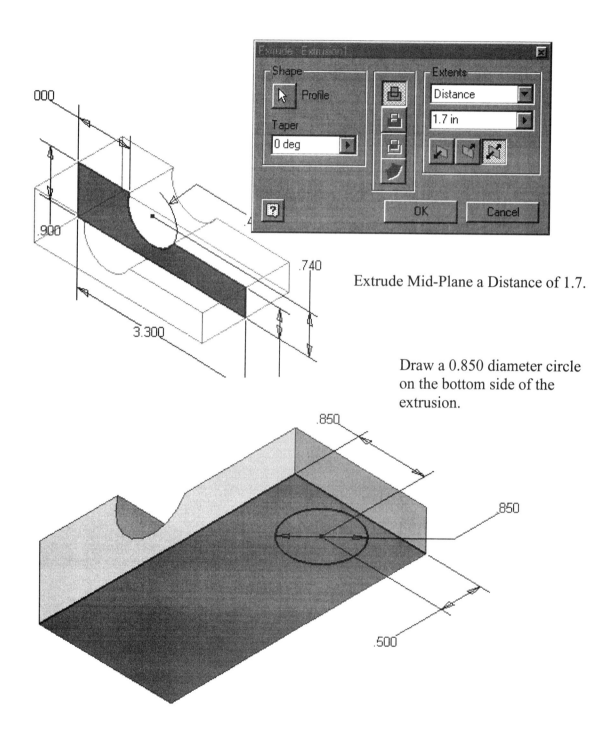

Extrude Mid-Plane a Distance of 1.7.

Draw a 0.850 diameter circle
on the bottom side of the
extrusion.

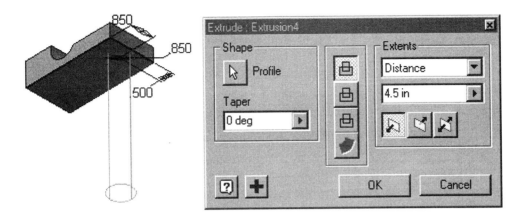

Extrude a distance of 4.5 in. down.

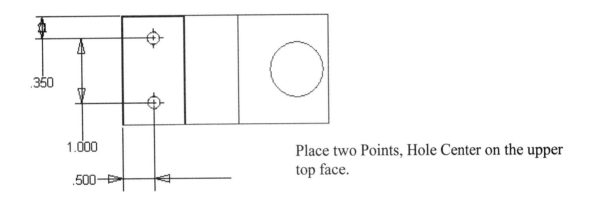

Place two Points, Hole Center on the upper top face.

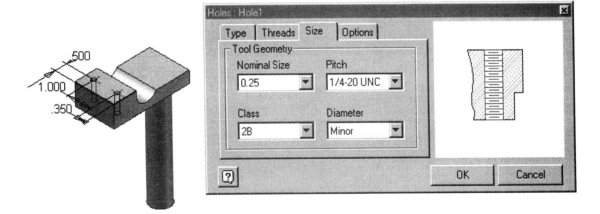

Place ¼-20 UNC-2B Through holes.

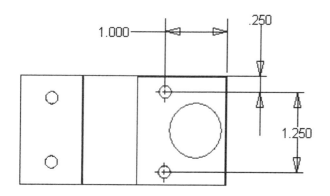

Place two Points, Hole Center on the lower upper face.

Place ¼-20 UNC-2B Through holes.

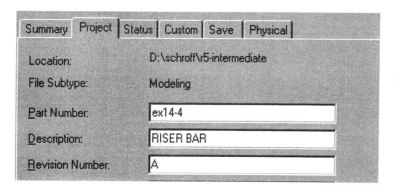

Save file as Ex14-4.ipt.

TIP: In R5, when in an idw file, do not hold down the shift key and pan. Doing so will rotate the sheet with no way to fix it other then to exit the drawing and reopen it. It does not do any damage to your drawing, but it will definitely panic a few people.

Exercise 14-5
Riser Bar Clamp

File: New using Standard (inches)
Estimated Time: 30 minutes

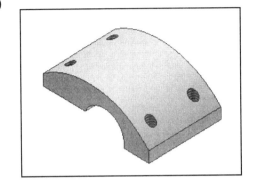

This exercise reviews the following:

- Extrude
- Hole

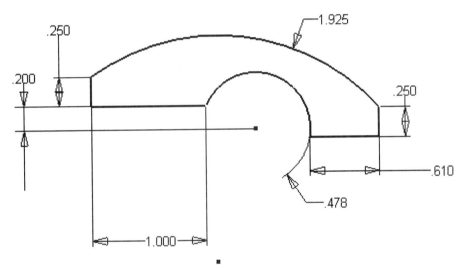

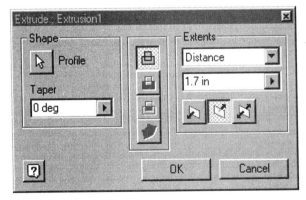
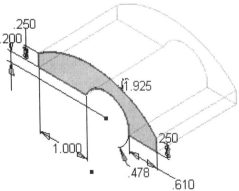

Extrude a distance of 1.7 in.

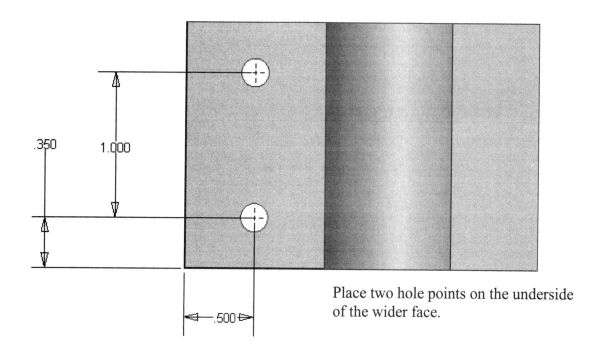

Place two hole points on the underside of the wider face.

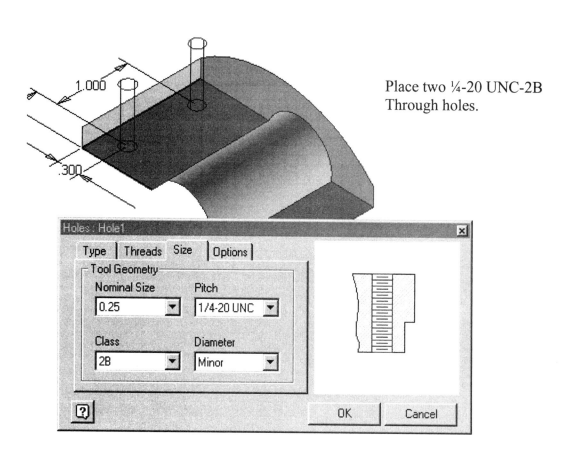

Place two ¼-20 UNC-2B Through holes.

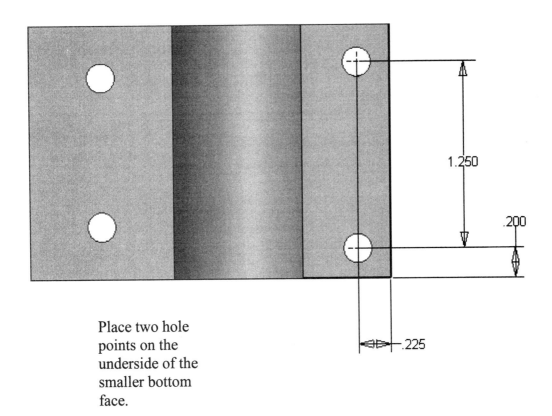

1.250

.200

Place two hole
points on the
underside of the
smaller bottom
face.

.225

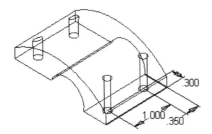

Place two ¼-20 UNC-2B Through holes.

.300

1.000   .350

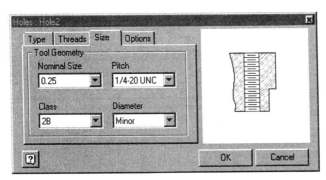

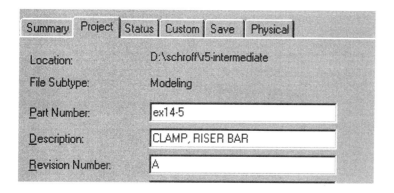

Save the file as Ex14-5.ipt.

Assemble your parts and add the appropriate hardware.

Additional Suggested Exercises:

Create an exploded view using Presentation.
Create an assembly drawing.
Create an animation.

TIP: In an assembly file, if you open one of the parts for modification in a separate window and then decide not to keep the modifications, you may opt to just close the window without saving. It will still appear with the unwanted changes in the assembly. The assembly is referencing the version of the part still stored in memory. To have the assembly use the part in the correct form, go to View > Refresh. This reloads the definitions of all parts in the assembly. This is the same as performing a Full Update.

Lesson 15
Visual Basic

Inventor Release 5 includes a Visual Basic Editor to allow users to customize Inventor. With VBA, you can create your own dialog boxes and interface tools. VBA does not create standalone applications, but always runs from inside Inventor.

You create IVB files by selecting Files->New Project. The advantage of an IVB file is that it's independent of the document.

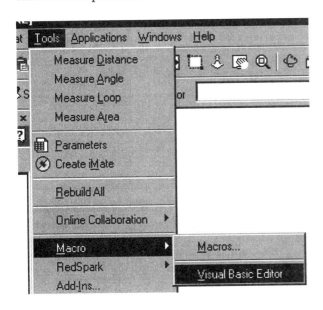

The Visual Basic Editor is accessed from
Tools->Macro->
Visual Basic Editor

TIP: If you plan to do a lot of customization, it is worthwhile to invest in a full copy of Visual Basic from Microsoft. That will give you access to a suite of tools. The Visual Basic Editor inside of Inventor is a scaled-down version of the full application.

The Internet is a great source for Visual Basic tutorials, ActiveX controls, and tools you can use for creating super applications.

TIP: It is a good idea to create a sketch of how you want your dialog box to appear before you start to help you with laying out your control tools.

Pipe Maker

Let's assume that you need to create pipes on a regular basis. You need a wide variety of pipe sizes. The interior diameter, wall thickness, and length can vary. You could handle this using Parameters or iParts, but the purpose of this exercise is to get familiar with the VBA tools.

Exercise 15-1
Dialog Box Layout

You do not need to have a file open to access the Visual Basic Editor. This project automatically will open a new part file and create the necessary geometry.

Estimated Time: 60 minutes

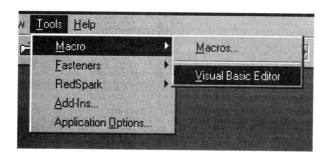

Start the Visual Basic Editor under the Tools Menu.

We see our project listed in the Browser.

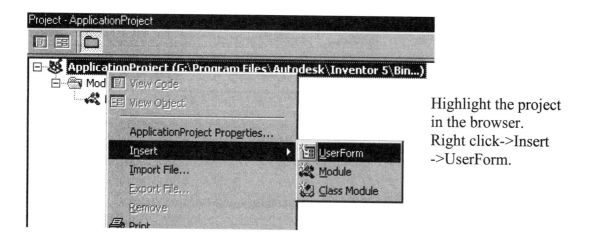

Highlight the project in the browser. Right click->Insert ->UserForm.

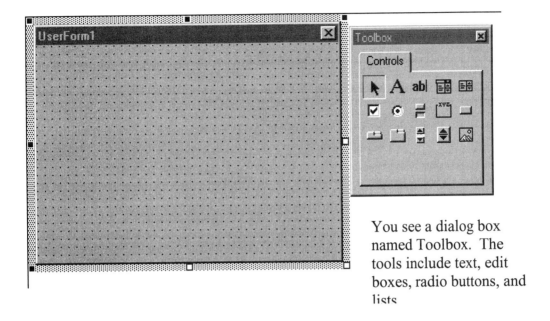

You see a dialog box named Toolbox. The tools include text, edit boxes, radio buttons, and lists

Your screen now has several items in it. The UserForm is a canvas for the dialog box you will create.

Toolbox

Icon	Name	Function
	Select	Select Objects is the only item in the **Toolbox** that doesn't draw a control. When you select it, you can only resize or move a control that has already been drawn on a form.
	Text	Allows you to have text that you do not want the user to change, such as a caption under a graphic.
	Text box	This is a box where the user can enter alphanumeric characters; also known as a data entry box.
	ComboBox	Allows you to draw a combination list box and text box. The user can either choose an item from the list or enter a value in the text box.
	ListBox	Use to display a list of items from which the user can choose. The list can be scrolled if it has more items than can be displayed at one time.
	CheckBox	Creates a box that the user can easily choose to indicate if something is true or false, or to display multiple choices when the user can choose more than one.
	OptionButton	Allows you to display multiple choices from which the user can choose only one.
	ToggleButton	Creates a button that toggles on and off.
	Frame	Allows you to create a graphical or functional grouping for controls. To group controls, draw the frame first, and then draw controls inside the frame.
	CommandButton	Creates a button the user can choose to carry out a command.
	TabStrip	Allows you to define multiple pages for the same area of a window or dialog box in your application.
	MultiPage	Presents multiple screens of information as a single set.
	ScrollBar	Provides a graphical tool for quickly navigating through a long list of items or a large amount of information, for indicating the current position on a scale, or as an input device or indicator of speed or quantity
	SpinButton	A spinner control you can use with another control to increment and decrement numbers. You can also use it to scroll back and forth through a range of values or a list of items.
	Image	Displays a graphical image from a bitmap, icon, or metafile on your form. Images displayed in an **Image** control can only be decorative and use fewer resources than a **PictureBox**.

We need to place three data entry variables: Pipe Inner Diameter, Pipe Outer Diameter, and Pipe Length.

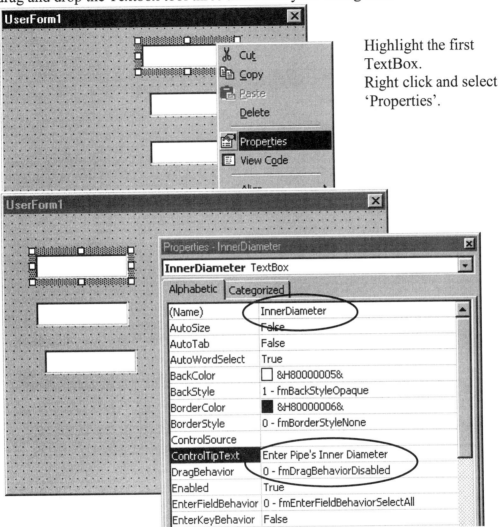

To place them, we use the Textbox tool. To insert the edit box onto your dialog box, just drag and drop the Textbox tool three times into your dialog box.

Highlight the first TextBox.
Right click and select 'Properties'.

In the Properties dialog, you can set how the textbox is defined.
Change the Name to InnerDiameter.
Add a ControlTipText to help users know what you want to be entered in the text box.
Close the Properties Dialog box.

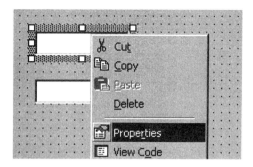

Select the second TextBox.
Right click and select 'Properties'.

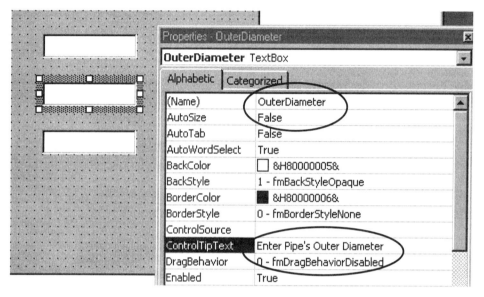

Set the Name of the TextBox as OuterDiameter.
Set the ControlTipText to 'Enter Pipe's Outer Diameter'.

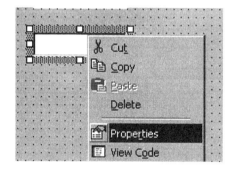

Select the third TextBox.
Right click and select 'Properties'.

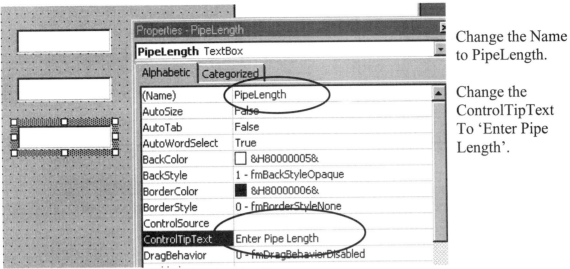

Change the Name to PipeLength.

Change the ControlTipText To 'Enter Pipe Length'.

Next we add three text labels for the TextBoxes.

Select the Text tool and drag it into the UserForm three times.

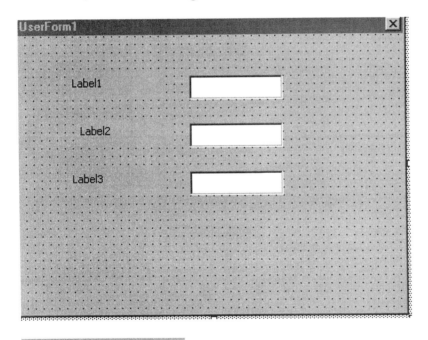

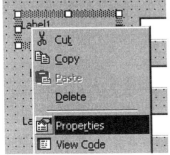

Select the first label.
Right click and select 'Properties'.

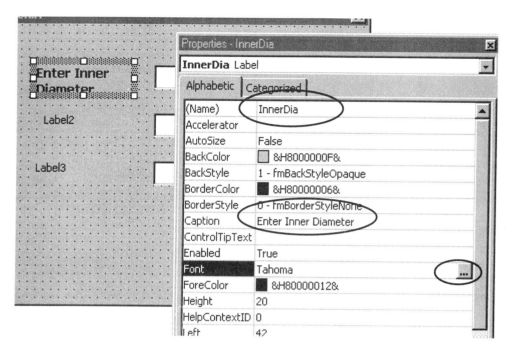

Set the Name to InnerDia.

The Caption is what the user will see when the dialog box is activated.

To change the appearance of the Font, select the ... button in the Font row.

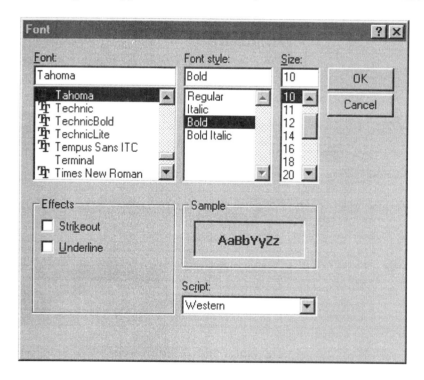

Set the Font to Tahoma, Bold, with a Size of 10.
Set OK.

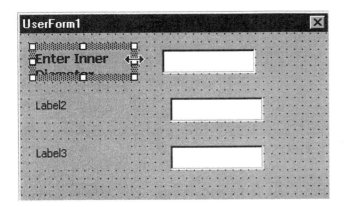

You can expand the label by using the grips when it is selected.

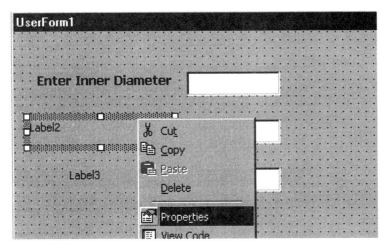

Select Label2.
Right click and select 'Properties'.

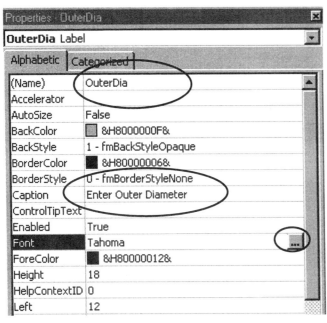

Set Name to OuterDia.
Set Caption to
Enter Outer Diameter.
Set the Font style to
Tahoma, Bold, Size 10.

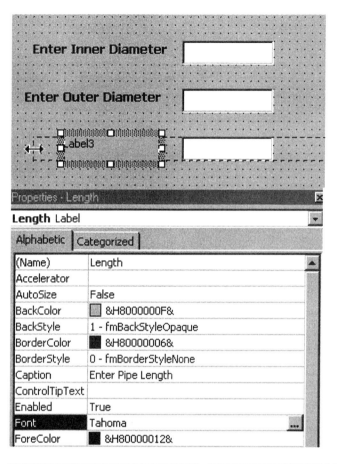

You can adjust the width, height, scale and location of the labels by selecting on the label and using your mouse to stretch and move it. Pay attention to the cursor cues – they tell you whether you are in MOVE mode or RESIZE mode.

Change the Properties of the Label3.
Set Name to Length.
Set Caption to
Enter Pipe Length.
Set the Font to
Tahoma, Bold, 10.

Our dialog box, so far.

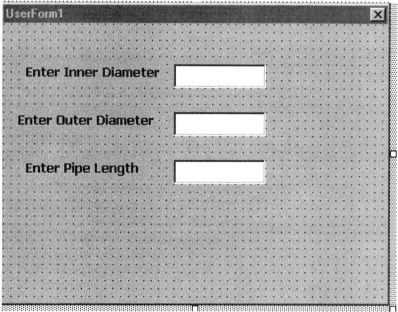

We need two command buttons. One will create the pipe and one will exit the dialog box.

Drag and drop two command buttons onto your dialog box.

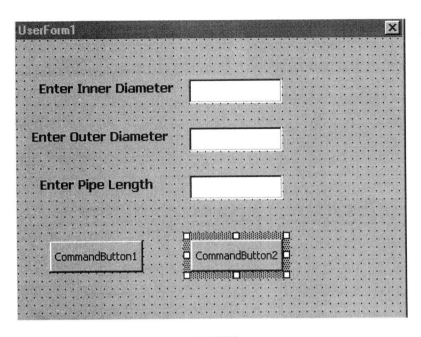

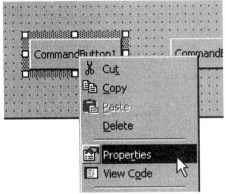

Select CommandButton1.
Right click and select Properties.

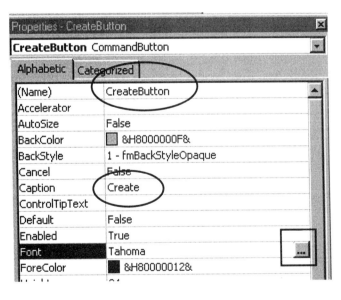

Change the Name to
CreateButton.
Change the Caption to
Create
Change the Font to
Tahoma, Bold, 10.

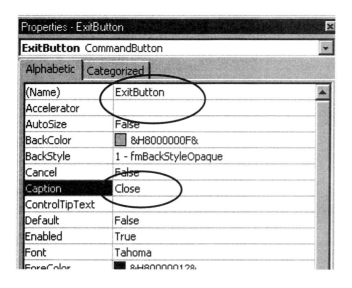

Change the Properties of the
CommandButton2.
Set the Name to
ExitButton.
Set the Caption to
Close.
Set the Font to
Tahoma, Bold, 10.

TIP: When defining the labels for your command buttons, use words and syntax similar to Inventor standard dialogs. That way your custom dialog box will work and look like an Inventor dialog box.

Select the entire dialog box by picking on one of its edges.
Press F4.
This brings up the Properties dialog box.

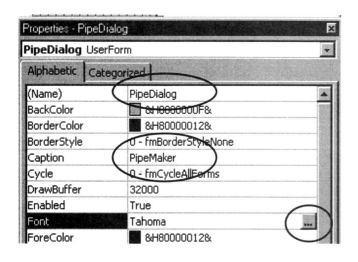

Change the Name to
PipeDialog.
Change the Caption to
PipeMaker.
Set the Font to
Tahoma, Bold, 10.

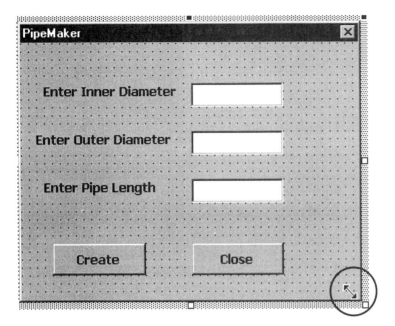

Our dialog box, so far.

We can resize the dialog so it doesn't have so much blank space by grabbing one of the corners and scaling.

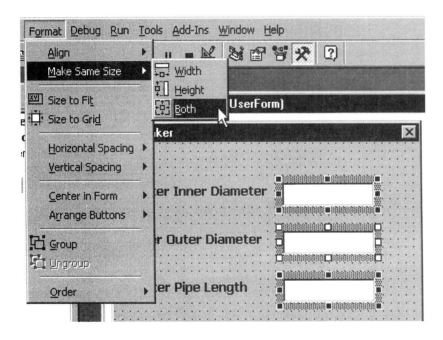

We can clean up the appearance of the dialog by going to the Format menu.
Select all three Edit boxes. You can select more than one edit box by holding down the Shift key.
Select Format-> Make Same Size-> Both.

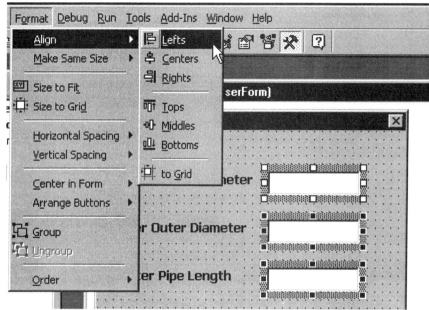

Next go to
Format->Align->
Lefts.
This will align the left
side of the edit boxes.

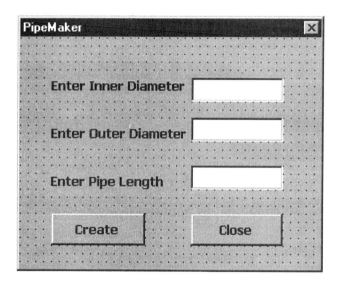

Our dialog box.

In the browser, we see the
dialog box we are building
under 'Forms'.

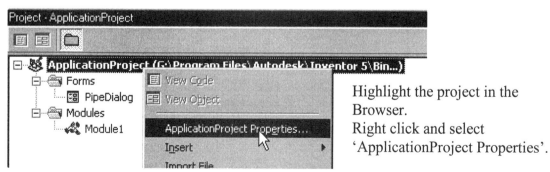

Highlight the project in the
Browser.
Right click and select
'ApplicationProject Properties'.

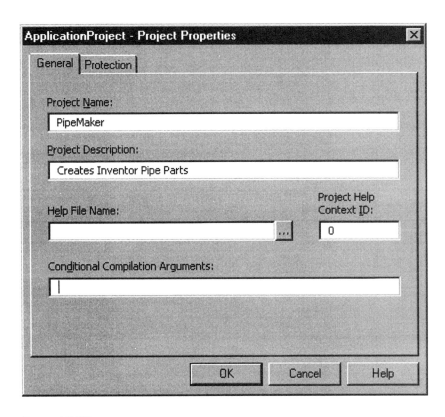

Fill in the Project Name As PipeMaker. Enter a Project Description. For advanced applications, you can create a *.hlp file and link it to the project. Creating help files is fairly easily done. Microsoft has a free download in their developer's area to allow you to do this.

Press 'OK'.

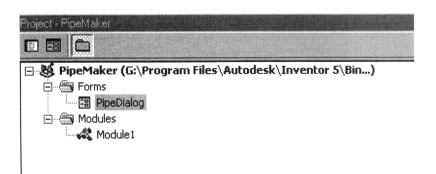

Our Browser updates with the new project name.

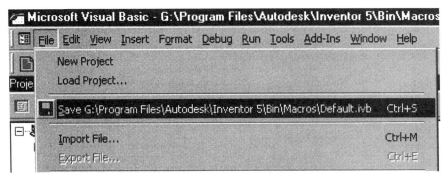

To save, go to File->Save or Ctrl-S.

Notice that the macro we are writing is being stored in the Macros subdirectory as 'default.ivb'.

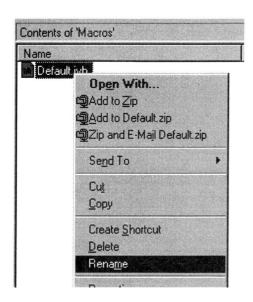

If you close Inventor, you can rename the default.ivb file to a name that is easier to remember.
Locate the default.ivb file in the Macros subdirectory using Windows Explorer.
Right click and select 'Rename'.
Rename the file to 'PipeMaker.ivb'.

Exercise 15-2
Assigning Subroutines

File Name: PipeMaker.ivb
Estimated Time: 60 minutes

Creating the dialog box was the easy part, we still need to make it work.
For our next exercise, we write the code.

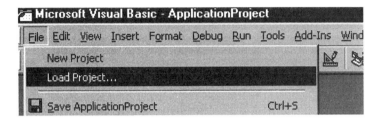

Start Inventor.
Go to Tools->Macros->Visual Basic Editor.
Under File->Load Project.

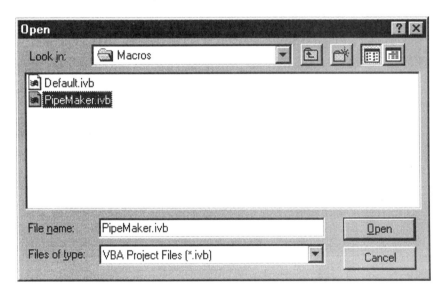

Locate the PipeMaker.ivb we created in the previous lesson.

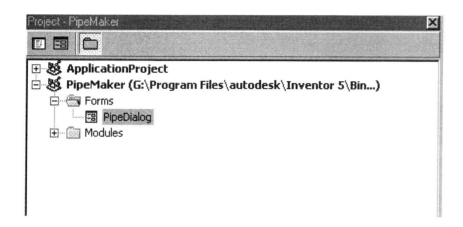

The project loads.

If you don't see the browser in your
window, go to
View->Project Explorer
Or
Control-R.

Double-click on the Close command button in your dialog box.

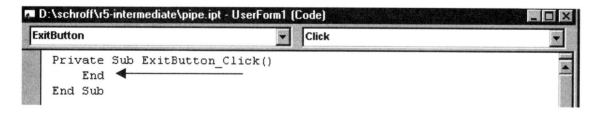

A new window pops up. This window controls the software code that runs the button.
Type the word End between the Private Sub and End Sub lines.
Close the window.

This means that when the user presses the Exit button, the program will automatically
end.

The Create Command button will initiate the key actions in this program; it will create the pipe.

Double-click on the Create button.

```
Private Sub CreateButton_Click()



End Sub

Private Sub ExitButton_Click()
     End
End Sub
```

We see the subroutine we already defined for the ExitButton.
Above that is the subroutine for the CreateButton.

```
Private Sub CreateButton_Click()

    'Define Variables
    Dim CenterRadiusO As Double
    Dim CenterRadiusI As Double
    Dim DistanceExtent As Double


End Sub

Private Sub ExitButton_Click()
     End
End Sub
```

To create a comment, place a ' before the line.

We start by defining our Variables.

We have three variables:

outer radius, called CenterRadiusO
inner radius, called CenterRadiusI
pipe length, called DistanceExtent

```
Private Sub CreateButton_Click()

    'Define Variables
    Dim CenterRadiusO As Double
    Dim CenterRadiusI As Double
    Dim DistanceExtent As |
```

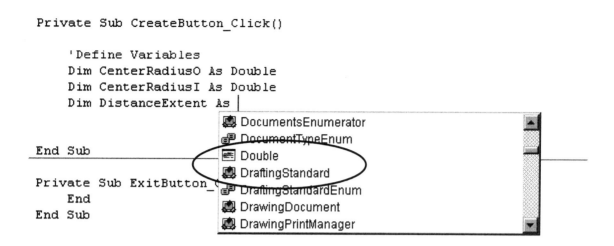

```
End Sub

Private Sub ExitButton_
    End
End Sub
```

As you type, Visual Basic will bring up a help box to provide you with the possible definitions available to you. Simply scroll down until you locate the desired definition. Double Left Pick to select.

Each Dim statement created a variable where we store information.

```
    'Define variables
    Dim CenterRadiusO As Double
    Dim CenterRadiusI As Double
    Dim DistanceExtent As Double

    'Set Variables from values in edit boxes
    CenterRadiusO = OuterDiameter / 2
    CenterRadiusI = InnerDiameter / 2
    DistanceExtent = PipeLength
```

Next, we define how we set the variables using the values from the edit boxes.

Be sure to set the variables so that you use the same variable names that you defined under the edit box property. If you use a different name or misspell a name, then the program will not work properly. This is one of the most common errors when programming.

```
'Set Variables from values in edit boxes
   CenterRadiusO = OuterDiameter / 2
   CenterRadiusI = InnerDiameter / 2
   DistanceExtent = PipeLength

 'error message if InnerDiameter is greater than OuterDiameter
 If InnerDiameter > OuterDiameter Then
    CreateButton.Enabled = False
    MsgBox ("Inner Diameter Must be a Smaller Value than Outer Diameter.")
    Exit Sub
 End If

End Sub
```

We do some error checking. We need to make sure the user enters a larger value for the outer diameter than the inner diameter.

CreateButton.Enabled = False means that the program will not create the part. Instead, we will see a message box with the message we see inside the parentheses.

Any If statement defined must be closed with an 'End If'.

```
 'error message if InnerDiameter is greater than OuterDiameter
 If InnerDiameter > OuterDiameter Then
    CreateButton.Enabled = False
    MsgBox ("Inner Diameter Must be a Smaller Value than Outer Diameter.")
    Exit Sub
 End If

 ' Create new part document
   Dim oDoc As PartDocument
   Set oDoc = ThisApplication.Documents.Add(kPartDocumentObject)

End Sub
```

If the inner diameter is less than the outer diameter, we proceed with the program.

Our first step is to open a new part file.

```
 ' Create new part document
   Dim oDoc As PartDocument
   Set oDoc = ThisApplication.Documents.Add(kPartDocumentObject)

   ' Get component definition from part document
   Dim oCompDef As ComponentDefinition
   Set oCompDef = oDoc.ComponentDefinition
```

Inventor internally handles the units in centimeters.

When executing the following line,
   Dim oDoc As PartDocument
   Set oDoc = ThisApplication.Documents.Add(kPartDocumentObject)
it automatically defaults to centimeters.

If you intend to have the units in either inches or mm, then you need to give it its full
path. The full path can also be accessed from 'TemplateDir' property of the 'Preferences'
object.

Next, we state our intention to create a component definition.

```
' Get component definition from part document
Dim oCompDef As ComponentDefinition
Set oCompDef = oDoc.ComponentDefinition

' Create a new sketch on the X-Y work plane.
Dim Sketch1 As PlanarSketch
Set Sketch1 = oCompDef.Sketches.Add(oCompDef.WorkPlanes.Item(3))
```

End Sub

Before we can place our geometry, we need to define which work plane to use.

```
' Create a new sketch on the X-Y work plane.
Dim Sketch1 As PlanarSketch
Set Sketch1 = oCompDef.Sketches.Add(oCompDef.WorkPlanes.Item(3))

' Set a reference to the transient geometry object.
Dim oTransGeom As TransientGeometry
Set oTransGeom = ThisApplication.TransientGeometry
```

End Sub

The number (3) in the WorkPlanes.Item indicates the XY plane.
The oTransGeom variable will be used to locate the center point of the two circles.

```
' Set a reference to the transient geometry object.
Dim oTransGeom As TransientGeometry
Set oTransGeom = ThisApplication.TransientGeometry

' Draw a circle on the sketch.
Dim OuterCircle As SketchCircle
Set OuterCircle = Sketch1.SketchCircles.AddByCenterRadius(oTransGeom.CreatePoint2d(0, 0), CenterRadiusO)
Dim InnerCircle As SketchCircle
Set InnerCircle = Sketch1.SketchCircles.AddByCenterRadius(oTransGeom.CreatePoint2d(0, 0), CenterRadiusI)
```

End Sub

Finally, we create the inner and outer circles.
You can use the Visual Basic help to assist you in completing the lines.
We locate both circle center points at 0,0.

```
' Set a reference to the transient geometry object.
Dim oTransGeom As TransientGeometry
Set oTransGeom = ThisApplication.Trans
```

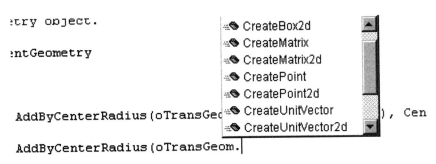

```
' Draw a circle on the sketch.
Dim OuterCircle As SketchCircle
Set OuterCircle = Sketch1.SketchCircle
Dim InnerCircle As SketchCircle
Set InnerCircle = Sketch1.SketchCircles.
```

```
is SketchCircle
= Sketch1.SketchCircles.AddByCenterRadius(oTransGeom.CreatePoint2d(0, 0), CenterRad
is SketchCircle
= Sketch1.SketchCircles.AddByCenterRadius(
              AddByCenterRadius(CenterPoint As Object, Radius As Double) As SketchCircle
```

The Help shows us that if we elect to create a sketch circle using the Add By Center Radius method, we need to define the center point's location and the radius value. OTransGeom is the variable we defined to be used to help locate the center point.

```
:try object.

:ntGeometry
                    CreateBox2d
                    CreateMatrix
                    CreateMatrix2d
                    CreatePoint
                    CreatePoint2d
AddByCenterRadius(oTransGed  CreateUnitVector      ), Cen
                    CreateUnitVector2d
AddByCenterRadius(oTransGeom.
```

Locate the CreatePoint2d in the help pop-up.

```
Radius(oTransGeom.CreatePoint2d(0, 0), CenterRadiusO)

Radius(oTransGeom.CreatePoint2d(
              CreatePoint2d([XCoord As Double], [YCoord As Double]) As
              Point2d
```

We are then prompted for what point to use. We enter 0,0 to use the origin.

We complete the line of code by defining the Center Radius as the variable CenterRadiusI.

```
'Draw a circle on the sketch
Dim OuterCircle As SketchCircle
Set OuterCircle = Sketch1.SketchCircles.AddByCenterRadius(oTransGeom.CreatePoint2d(0, 0), CenterRadiusO)
Dim InnerCircle As SketchCircle
Set InnerCircle = Sketch1.SketchCircles.AddByCenterRadius(oTransGeom.CreatePoint2d(0, 0), CenterRadiusI)
```

```
    ' Draw a circle on the sketch.
  Dim OuterCircle As SketchCircle
  Set OuterCircle = Sketch1.SketchCircles.AddByCenterRad
  Dim InnerCircle As SketchCircle
  Set InnerCircle = Sketch1.SketchCircles.AddByCenterRad


    ' Create a profile.
  Dim Profile As Profile
  Set Profile = Sketch1.Profiles.AddForSolid



End Sub
```

Next we define the profile.

```
  ' Create a solid extrusion.
  Dim Extrusion1 As ExtrudeFeature
  Set Extrusion1 = oCompDef.Features.ExtrudeFeatures.AddByDistanceExtent(Profile,
DistanceExtent, kSymmetricExtentDirection, kJoinOperation)
```

We extrude the profile.
(Profile,DistanceExtent, kSymmetricExtentDirection,kJoinOperation)
define all the variables we usually set in the Extrude dialog.

Profile refers to the Profile we defined earlier
DistanceExtent is the PipeLength Variable
kSymmetricExtentDirection indicates a mid-plane extrusion.
KJoinOperation indicates a Join.

Extrusions will probably one of the more common types of operations users will want to do, so I would like to expand a little on how extrusions work in Inventor VBA.

```
Set oExtrude = oCompDef.Features.ExtrudeFeatures.AddByDistanceExtent( _
                    oProfile, 1, kNegativeExtentDirection,
kJoinOperation)
```

In the above example, we extrude a distance of 1 unit in the negative direction.

The syntax for extrusions is outlined as follows:
AddByDistanceExtent
(Profile As Profile, Distance As Variant,
ExtentDirection As PartFeatureExtentDirectionEnum,
Operation As PartFeatureOperationEnum,
TaperAngle As Variant = 0) As ExtrudeFeature

Profile	Input Profile object used to define the shape of the extrusion. If the Operation argument is anything except kSurfaceOperation, then the input profile must have closed paths. Open paths are valid when creating surfaces.
Distance	Input Variant that defines the length of the extrusion. This can be either a numeric value or a string. A parameter for this value will be created and the supplied string or value is assigned to the parameter. If a value is input, the units are centimeters. If a string is input, the units can be specified as part of the string or it will default to the current length units of the document.
ExtentDirection	Input constant that indicates which side of the sketch plane to extrude toward. Valid input is kPositive, kNegative, or kSymmetric. kPositive defines the offset direction to be in the same direction as the normal of the sketch plane.
Operation	Input constant that indicates the type of operation to perform. Valid input is kJoinOperation, kCutOperation, kIntersectOperation, kSurfaceOperation.
TaperAngle	Optional Input Variant that defines the angle of the taper. If not supplied, the feature will be created with a taper angle of zero. This can be either a numeric value or a string. A parameter for this value will be created and the supplied string or value is assigned to the parameter. If a value is input, the units are radians. If a string is input, the units can be specified as part of the string or it will default to the current angle units of the document.

```
' Create a solid extrusion.
Dim Extrusion1 As ExtrudeFeature
Set Extrusion1 = oCompDef.Features

   ' fit the view
ThisApplication.ActiveView.Fit
```

Next, we zoom the view to fit the part.

```
End Sub
```

```
'close dialog
End
```

To close the dialog, simply type
'End'.

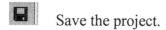 Save the project.

 To test your program, press Run in the Menu or the Run arrow.

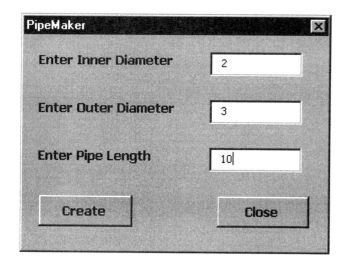

Fill in some values and press 'Create'.
Remember that our values are in centimeters by default.

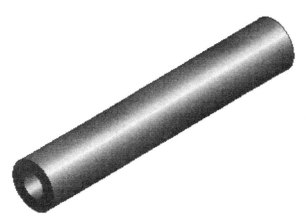

A part file is opened and our pipe is
created.

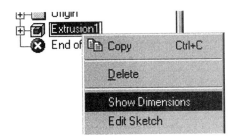

Check your part to see if it uses the dimensions you assigned.

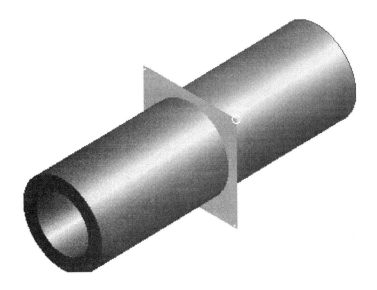

If you highlight the X-Y work plane you see that the pipe was created as a mid-plane extrusion.

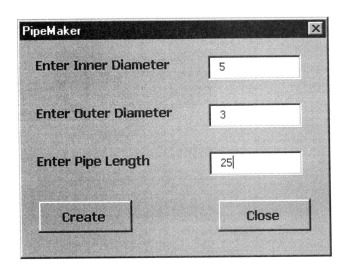

Check your error trapping by entering in a larger inner diameter than outer diameter. Then press Create.

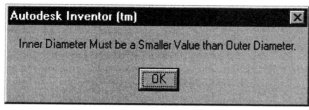

Our message box appears.

Select the Stop button.

Save the project.

Exercise 15-3:
Adding a Picture

File Name: PipeMaker.ivb
Estimated Time: 60 minutes

Create a drawing from one of the pipes you create with the dialog.

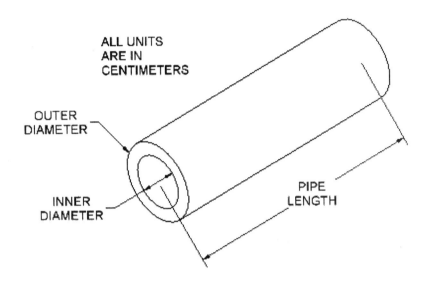

We can then use this drawing to add a picture to the dialog box.
The image will help users figure out what the pipe will look like.

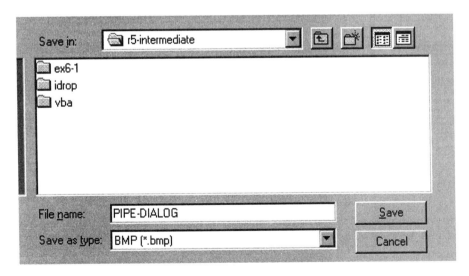

You can use the Save As option to save the drawing as a bmp or use a screen capture
program to create your image.

Activate the Visual Basic Editor.
Load the pipemaker.ivb project.

If you don't see the dialog box, you can open it.
Highlight PipeDialog under Forms.
Right click and select 'View Object'.

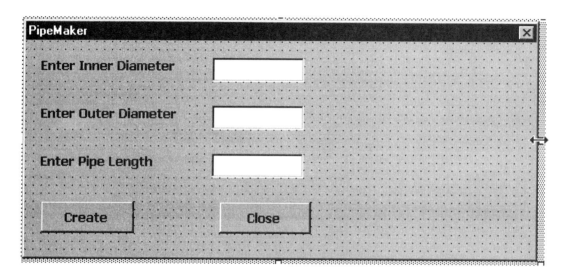

Stretch out the dialog box to make room for a graphic.

Select the Image tool from the Toolbox dialog.

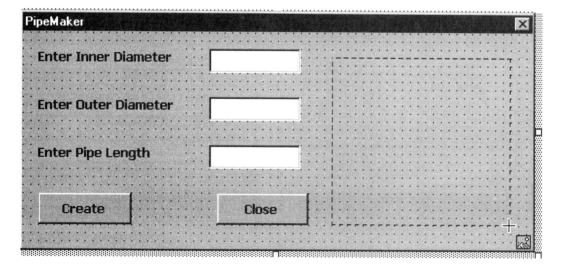

Select the two corners that will define the image window.

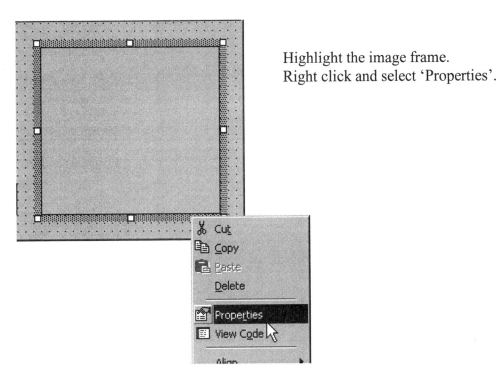

Highlight the image frame.
Right click and select 'Properties'.

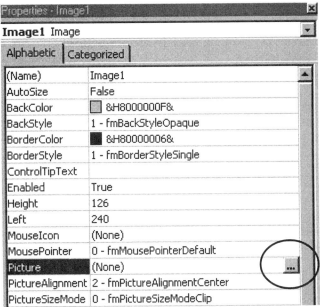

Locate Picture in the list.
Select the browse button.

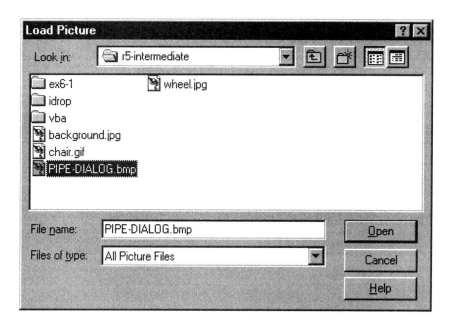

Locate the bmp file you created from the drawing.

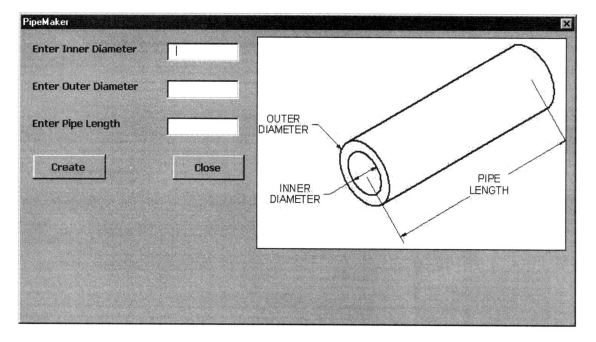

I found that jpeg files provide a better quality than a bitmap file. You may want to experiment if you decide to use graphics in your dialogs to see which file type gives the best results.

Save your project file.

Exercise 15-4:
Creating a Macro

File Name: PipeMaker.ivb
Estimated Time: 60 minutes

We can load and run a macro without having to open VBA.

Load the PipeMaker.ivb project in the Visual Basic Editor.

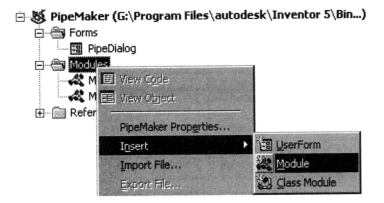

Highlight the Modules folder.
Right click and select
Insert->Module.

```
Sub CreatePipe()
    PipeDialog.Show
End Sub
```

We will call our macro CreatePipe.
All our macro does is start the dialog box we created.
The code for the dialog box will take it from there.

Type in the three lines:

```
Sub CreatePipe()
   PipeDialog.Show
End Sub
```

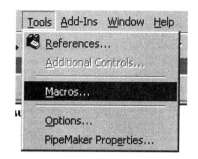

Go to Tools->Macros.

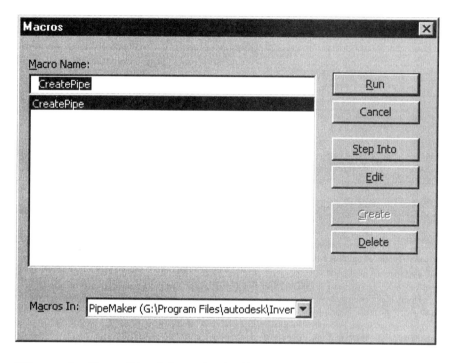

We see the CreatePipe Macro in the list.
Press 'Run' to run the macro.

Save the project file.

Close the Visual Basic Editor.

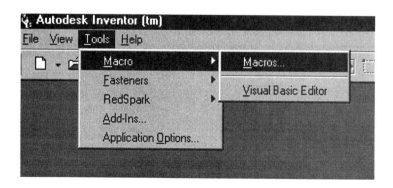

Close any open part or
assembly files.
Go to Tools->Macros->
Macros.

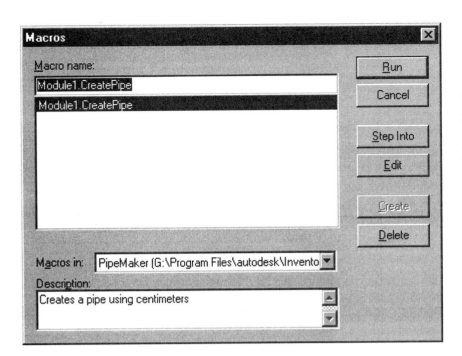

Our Macro appears in the Macro list.

Press 'Run'.

Your dialog appears and your program should work fine.

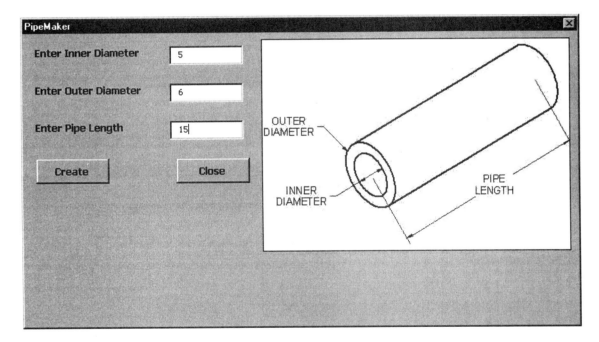

You can continue to run the macro regardless of whether or not you have other files open. Each run of the macro will create a new part file with a pipe.

Recommended Resources:

Using Visual Basic with AutoCAD by Andrew G. Roe

This book contains several projects that can be used to help you get started with Inventor. The syntax will be different for Inventor parts, but you will get some good guidance. Mr. Roe uses a similar project for making pipes in his text and you can compare what he does in AutoCAD versus how the Inventor VBA works.

Visual Basic 6 for Dummies by Wallace Wang

This book is a good choice for users who are not familiar or comfortable with programming. Most of the examples are not appropriate for CAD work, but you learn how the VBA tools work.

Learn to Program with Visual Basic 6 by John Smiley

I really enjoy the conversational tone used by the author. Again, the examples in the book are not applicable to CAD, but you get several good examples of how the code works.

VBA for Dummies by Steve Cummings

A good resource to fill in the blanks between the other books since this book is specifically about VBA, which is a limited version of Visual Basic.

Inventor also comes with several sample programs and a help manual specifically for VBA. While the on-line documentation is not as good as any of these texts, it is the only place for you to find the objects and methods specific to Inventor.

FINAL EXAM

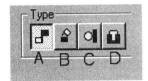

1. Identify the tangent constraint tool
2. Identify the Angle Constraint tool
3. Identify the insert constraint tool.
4. Identify the Mate Constraint tool.

5. Only model dimensions _____ to the view are available in that view.

      A. horizontal
      B. normal
      C. parallel
      D. on top

T F 6. In order to extrude a profile, it must be fully closed and non-intersecting.

T F 7. Assembly constraints can not be suppressed.

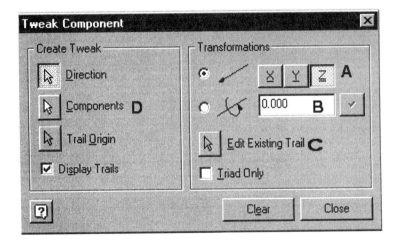

8. To select the axis the component will move along for a tweak, select here.

T F 9. The Rectangular Pattern copies a feature or features in a rectangular pattern.

T F 10. The file extension for part files is *.prt

T F 11. Constraints define the size of your sketch.

12. To quickly switch to an Isometric View:

A. Right click anywhere in the drawing window and select 'Isometric View' from the menu.
B. Select the Isometric View tool from the View toolbar.
C. Select the 3D Orbit tool, right click and select 'Isometric View.'
D. Select Isometric View from the View menu.

13. To modify a feature:

A. Right click on the feature in the browser and select 'Edit Feature'
B. Select 'Edit Feature' from the Modify menu.
C. Select the feature in the graphics window, right click and select 'Edit Feature'
D. Select 'Edit Feature from the Feature tool bar.

14. The icon shown is:

A. Leader
B. Balloon
C. Balloon All
D. Text

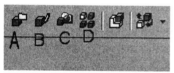

15. Identify the tool icon to create a new part within an assembly.
16. Identify the tool icon that allows the user to pattern a part in an assembly
17. Identify the tool icon that allows the user to place a part in an assembly.
18. Identify the tool icon that invokes the Standard Parts

T F 19. Hole Centers can be located on the endpoint of a line.

T F 20. Before you can place a parts list, you should add balloons to a view.

21.   The menu option 'Save Copy As':

    A.   Renames the active file and saves a copy with the previous name
    B.   Saves a copy of the file with a different name and keeps the active file open with the same name and unsaved
    C.   Saves a copy of the file with a different name and saves the active file. The user continues working on the active file.
    D.   Renames the active file and saves it

T F   22.   Inventor is a 2D modeling software.

T F   23.   You cannot add a vertex/shoulder to a balloon leader.

24.   The MATE assembly constraint has two options. They are:

    A.   MATE and FLUSH
    B.   OPPOSED and FOR
    C.   ANTI and PRO
    D.   CLOSE and FOR

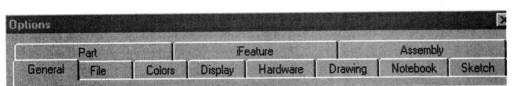

25.   The tab to select to enable 'Edit Dimension When Created'.

    A.   Sketch
    B.   Part
    C.   Drawing
    D.   General

26.   To modify an assembly constraint:

    A.   Locate the constraint in the browser, right click and select 'Edit'.
    B.   Select the 'Edit Constraint' tool from the assembly tool bar.
    C.   Select "Modify Constraint' from the Modify menu.
    D.   Locate the constraint in the graphics window and double click on it.

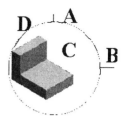

27.   Select the area to rotate the model in a horizontal direction.

28.   In order to constrain to the part's origin (center point) or any of the axes, you must:

    A.   be on a plane normal to those features
    B.   project the desired geometry
    C.   draw construction lines/points
    D.   add a geometric constraint

29.   To exit Sketch mode:

    A.   Right click and select 'Finish Sketch'
    B.   Press the 'Update' button
    C.   Enable the Features Panel Bar
    D.   All of the Above

30.   In the 3D Indicator, the red arrow is:

    A.   X axis
    B.   Y axis
    C.   Z axis
    D.   I can't tell from the picture - all the arrows are black

31.   The assembly constraint that is NOT available in Inventor is:

    A.   ANGLE
    B.   TANGENT
    C.   INSERT
    D.   COLLINEAR

32.   Revolve projects a cross section

    A.   along a path
    B.   in a single direction
    C.   around an axis
    D.   along a curved path

T F 33. After you add a dimension, you can still modify the size by enabling the grips on the object (line, circle, arc, etc) and dragging it.

T F 34. You have to select 'Finish Sketch' before you enable the Features toolbar on the panel bar.

35. The shortcut key to place a General Dimension is:

A. II
B. G
C. D
D. GD

36. To create a new sketch:

A. select a planar surface or work plane, right click and select 'New Sketch'
B. Right click and select 'New Sketch' and then select a planar surface or work plane.
C. Select 'New Sketch' from the Sketch Toolbar
D. A & B but not C

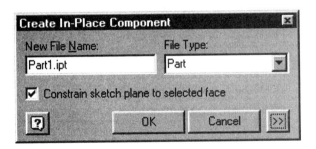

37. The button to select to define the directory to store the new part file when creating an in place component:

A. New File Name
B. File Type
C. OK
D. The More Button >>

38. You are placing an In-Place Component. You have enabled the box to constrain the new sketch to the selected face. This places a _____ constraint.

A. MATE
B. INSERT
C. FLUSH
D. Depends on the sketch created

39.   The button to select to automatically tweak the components in an assembly.

40.   To change the extrusion distance:

       A.   Modify the value in the distance edit box of the Extrude dialog box
       B.   Use the mouse to drag the extrusion into position
       C.   Right click on the extrusion and enter a value.
       D.   A & B but not C.

41.   To add text to a title block in a drawing:

       A.   Use the Text tool from the Drawing Annotation toolbar
       B.   Use the Attribute tool from the Drawing Managment toolbar
       C.   Enter the text information under File Properties
       D.   Enter the text in the Standards Dialog box

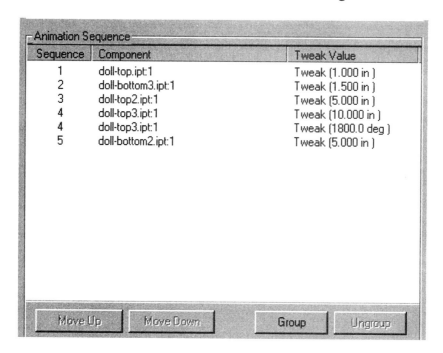

42.   There are two tweaks selected and the Group button is enabled. Why?

       A.   Doubles the tweaks together.
       B.   Causes the component to rotate and move at the same time
       C.   Determines the order in which the components move
       D.   all of the above

43. This feature tool produces a hollow part with a wall thickness the user defines.

    A. Shell
    B. Cut
    C. Extrude
    D. Sweep

T F   44. To change colors and linetypes for entities in a drawing, the user needs to define layers.

45. A grounded component is indicated by:

    A. A different color in the browser
    B. A ground symbol next to the component name
    C. A pushpin next to the component name
    D. A line through the component name

46. Select here to automatically place Trails.

T F   47. A sketch is a profile of a feature or any geometry required to create a feature.

T F   48. When building an assembly, the first component should be the main component in the assembly.

T F   49. Every part starts with a sketch.

50.   To create a Projected View:

A.   Select the view you wish to project from, right click and select 'Projected View'
B.   Select the view in the browser, right click and select 'Projected View'
C.   Select the Projected View tool from the Drawing Management toolbar and then select the view to project from.
D.   All of the above

51.   3D Models are often referred to as solids because they have _____ and _____.

A.   mass and volume
B.   3 dimensions and degrees of freedom
C.   weight and height
D.   mass and height

52.   Extrude projects a cross section....

A.   along a path
B.   in a single direction
C.   around an axis
D.   along a curved path

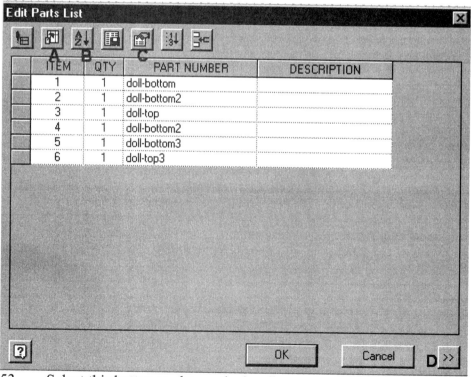

53.   Select this button to change the heading and width of columns

54.   Select here to modify the heading of a parts list

55.   Select here to change a parts list so that the item numbers go in descending order.

T F   56.   In order to create an assembly, all the parts used in the assembly must be created first.

57.   To change a line from Normal to Construction:

A.   Select the line, then right click and select 'Line Style' from the menu
B.   Select the line then select 'Construction' from the Style drop down in Command Bar
C.   You can't change a line style. You have to erase the line and start over
D.   Select 'Modify Line Style' from the Modify menu.

T F   58.   A part model is a collection of features.

59.   To create a View in a drawing

A.   Use Create View from the Drawing Management toolbar
B.   Use Create View from the Drawing Annotation toolbar
C.   Drag the part into the drawing sheet
D.   Use Insert View from the Menu

60.   To modify a parts list:

A.   Select the grip at the upper right, right click and select 'Edit Parts List'.
B.   Select the grip at the lower right, right click and select 'Edit Parts List'.
C.   Select the grip at the upper left, right click and select 'Edit Parts List'.
D.   Select the grip at the lower left, right click and select 'Edit Parts List'.

61.   This placed feature tool creates a rounded edge.

A.   Fillet
B.   Chamfer
C.   Round
D.   Circle

T F   62.   Once you create a feature it can not be modified.

T F   63.   You can extrude more than one profile at a time.

64. You select a component within the assembly browser, right click and enable 'Visibility'. This:

  A. makes the component visible
  B. makes the component see-through
  C. deletes the component from the assembly
  D. makes the assembly constraints visible

65. To edit a Parts List:

  A. Select the Parts List in the Browser, right click and select 'Edit Parts List'.
  B. Select the Parts List grip, right click and select 'Edit Parts List'.
  C. Right click in the graphics window and select 'Edit Parts List'.
  D. A& B but not C

T F 66. The Mirror Feature tool places a mirror image of a feature or features on the opposite side of an axis.

67. To draw a line, you should be in this mode:

  A. Sketch
  B. Features
  C. Solids
  D. Assembly

68. To see the assembly constraints for a component:

  A. Left click on the + next to the component name
  B. Left click on the + next to Origin
  C. Left click on the - next to the assembly name
  D. Select the Show Constraints tool on the assembly toolbar.

T F 69. If you move a component in an assembly, it will remove any assembly constraints that have been added to that component.

T F 70. Sketches can be moved by windowing around them and dragging them to the new position.

71. The first component placed in an assembly is:

  A. Grounded
  B. The most important
  C. the one that starts with the letter 'A'
  D. none of the above

T F   72.   When creating an Animation, there is no need to Reset between Plays.

T F   73.   A + next to a component name in the browser for an assembly file means the part is over constrained.

T F   74.   In order to create a hole, you must draw a circle and extrude it as a Cut.

       75.   To modify a dimension in a drawing:

     A.   Select, right click and select 'Edit'
     B.   Select, right click and select 'Modify'
     C.   Double click on the dimension you wish to modify
     D.   Select the Edit Dimension tool and then select the dimension to edit

T F   76.   Assembly files contain more than one part.

T F   77.   Once a component in an assembly is grounded, it remains grounded. The only way to remove the ground is to delete the component and start over.

       78.   The default plane to start a sketch is:

     A.   XY
     B.   YZ
     C.   XZ
     D.   None of the above

       79.   To delete an assembly constraint:

     A.   Select the Show Constraints tool, locate the constraint and delete it.
     B.   Select Delete Constraint from the Assembly Menu
     C.   Locate the Constraint in the Browser, right click and select 'Delete'.
     D.   Locate the Constraint in the graphics window and press the 'Delete' key.

       80.   To add a design element to a part, use:

     A.   Insert->Object from the Menu
     B.   Insert Design Element from the Features Toolbar
     C.   Insert Design Element from the Menu
     D.   Insert Design Element from the Sketch Toolbar

T F   81.   The three options for Extrude are Cut, Join, and Union.

T F   82.   Once a parts list is placed, you can not modify the contents.

T F   83.   Dimensions define the size of your sketch.

84.   Identify the tool shown.

    A.   Move Component
    B.   Rotate Component
    C.   Add a Tweak
    D.   Animate

85.   To add a tweak to a component in a presentation:

    A.   Select the component in the browser, right click, and select 'Tweak Components.'
    B.   Select the 'Tweak Components' tool from the Presentation toolbar.
    C.   Select Insert->Tweak Components from the Menu
    D.   All of the above

T F   86.   The file extension for drawing files is *.dwg.

87.   The number of degrees of freedom for each unconstrained part is:

    A.   2
    B.   4
    C.   6
    D.   8

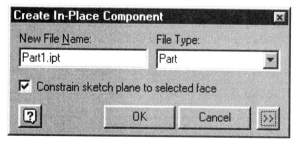

88.   The dialog box shown is brought up in this type of file:

    A.   Presentation
    B.   Drawing
    C.   Assembly
    D.   Part

T F   89.   When using the Mirror Feature tool is used, the user can select the face on the part or a work plane to mirror about.

90.   Select here to see all the tweaks added.

T F   91.   To place a parts list, you must first select a View.

T F   92.   Placed features do not require a sketch.

93.   The file extension for assembly drawings is:

A.   *.asy
B.   *.iam
C.   *.ias
D.   *.dwg

T F   94.   Inventor will extrude geometry if the line style of the geometry is construction.

95.   To start a New Part file using system defaults,

A.   Go to File-> New
B.   Select Part under the New icon in the Standard Toolbar
C.   Press the New icon in the Standard Toolbar
D.   All of the above

T F   96.   To select more than one object, hold down the SHIFT key.

97.   Identify the tool shown.

A.   Animate
B.   Rotate component
C.   Precise View Rotation
D.   Add Tweak

98.   Name the toolbar shown:

A.   Animation
B.   Scene
C.   Assembly
D.   Presentation

99.   3D Part models can be created using all the methods listed EXCEPT:

A.   Extrude
B.   Revolve
C.   Sweep
D.   Form

T F   100.   Balloons must have a circle around the number.

ANSWERS:
1) C; 2) B; 3) D; 4) A; 5) C; 6) T; 7) F; 8) A; 9) T; 10) F; 11) F; 12) A; 13) A; 14) B; 15) A; 16) D; 17) A;
18) C; 19) T; 20) F; 21) B; 22) F; 23) F; 24) A; 25) A; 26) A; 27) B; 28) B; 29) D; 30) A; 31) D; 32) C; 33) F;
34) F; 35) C; 36) D; 37) D; 38) C; 39) D; 40) D; 41) C; 42) B; 43) A; 44) F; 45) C; 46) C; 47) T; 48) T;
49) T; 50) D; 51) A; 52) B; 53) D; 54) C; 55) B; 56) F; 57) B; 58) T; 59) A; 60) A; 61) A; 62) F; 63) T;
64) A; 65) D; 66) F; 67) A; 68) A; 69) F; 70) T; 71) A; 72) F; 73) F; 74) F; 75) C; 76) T; 77) F; 78) A; 79) C;
80) B; 81) F; 82) F; 83) T; 84) C; 85) D; 86) F; 87) C; 89) T; 90) D; 91) T; 92) T; 93) B;94) F; 95) D); 96) F;
97) A; 98) D;99) D; 100) F

INDEX

About the Author

Elise Moss has worked for the past twenty years as a mechanical designer in Silicon Valley, primarily creating sheet metal designs. She has written articles for Autodesk's Toplines magazine, AUGI's PaperSpace, DigitalCAD.com and Tenlinks.com. She is President of Moss Designs, a Registered Autodesk Developer, creating custom applications and designs for corporate clients. She is also President of Silicon Valley AutoCAD Power Users, the largest AutoCAD user's group in the United States. She has taught CAD classes at DeAnza College, Silicon Valley College, and for Autodesk resellers. Autodesk has named her as a Faculty of Distinction for the curriculum she has developed for Autodesk products. She holds a baccalaureate degree from San Jose State.

She is married with two sons. Her older son, Benjamin, is currently studying electrical engineering at UC Santa Cruz. Her younger son, Daniel, is studying architecture at local community colleges and is a Lance Corporal in the United States Marines. Her husband, Ari, has a distinguished career in software development.

Elise is a third generation engineer. Her father, Robert Moss, is a metallurgical engineer in the aerospace industry. Her grandfather, Solomon Kupperman, was a civil engineer for the City of Chicago.

She can be contacted via email at elise_moss@mossdesigns.com.

More information about the author and her work can be found on her website at www.mossdesigns.com.

Other books by Elise Moss

Autodesk Inventor R5 Fundamentals: Conquering the Rubicon
AutoCAD 2000i Mechanical Drafting for Beginners
Architectural Desktop R3.3: Laying a Sound Foundation